Substitute Teacher Handb🍎🍏k

Proven Professional
Management Skills &
Teaching Strategies

UtahState
UNIVERSITY

© Substitute Teaching Institute
Utah State University
6516 Old Main Hill
Logan, UT 84322-6516
(435) 797-3182
(800) 922-4693
SubEd@cc.usu.edu
http://subed.usu.edu
ISBN# 1-890563-15-3

FIFTH EDITION
K-12

What It's All About

Preface

Congratulations! You've decided to become a substitute teacher. Substitute teaching is an important educational component in our schools. It is a rare teacher who never needs a substitute for either personal or professional reasons. Principals, teachers, parents, and students value a good substitute teacher. Research has shown that a student spends over one full year with a substitute teacher by the time s/he graduates from high school. Skilled substitute teachers can have a significant, positive impact on the quality of education while the permanent teacher is away.

Regardless of whether or not you are a certified teacher, you can still become an expert in substitute teaching. Successful teachers are those who have either consciously, or subconsciously, developed the skills that make them effective in the classroom. In other words, by learning certain skills, techniques, and methods, you can be a successful teacher. With these skills in your repertoire, you will be in such demand that you will be scheduling your substitute teaching assignments weeks in advance, students will see you in the hall and ask when you are coming to their class, and parents will be calling the district requesting they hire you full-time.

For information on Substitute Skills visit:

http:// subed.usu.edu

Research conducted by the Substitute Teaching Institute has identified the following:

■ *The number one request by permanent teachers and district personnel is that substitute teachers be prepared and professional.*

■ *The number one request by substitute teachers is that they learn skills to successfully manage classroom/behavior situations.*

■ *The number one request by students is that substitutes present stimulating lessons and exciting fill-in activities.*

■ *The number one trait of a successful substitute teacher is the use of a SubPack or resource kit.*

The contents of this book present these as well as other skills and strategies. Considerable time has been devoted to researching, documenting, and field-testing the ideas presented. In order to narrow the content to specific "do's" and "don'ts" of strategies and techniques to ensure successful substitute teaching, most of the theory behind these skills and strategies has been intentionally left out. The implementation of these skills and strategies will be one of the keys to your success as a substitute teacher.

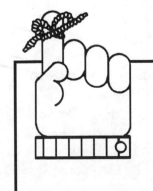

Remember

The information in this handbook is not intended to replace the rules and regulations of the district. Use only those suggestions and activities from this handbook that do not conflict with the district's policies and established practices.

Using This Book

This handbook is designed to give you, the substitute teacher, techniques, skills, and material to be more effective as you teach.

Useful Icons

The icons (pictures) throughout the book are used to give visual recognition to tips, activities, and chapters. These icons will enable you to quickly locate each section and better understand what you are reading.

One Professional to Another

This icon presents key points in the section you are reading. By reviewing each box, you can quickly identify topics covered in the chapter.

Substitute Teacher Handbook
- Being Professional
- Classroom Management
- Teaching Strategies
- Fill-In Activities
- Legal Issues

Points to Ponder

This icon indicates key points to ponder or additional background information for the section you are reading.

Remember

The remember icon points out important items or ideas you need to remember or take into consideration.

SubPack

The most common trait of successful substitute teachers is their possession of a "bag of tricks" that they bring to each assignment. During your study of this handbook, put together your own pack, bag, or resource kit to use in your classes. Suggested contents for a *SubPack* are listed on page 70.

Handbook Overview

Preface

The preface is an introduction to this book, its purpose, and contents. Hopefully, this section will answer questions you have about using the handbook.

Chapter 1: Being a Professional

Permanent teachers and district personnel unanimously request that substitute teachers be professional. Chapter one outlines aspects of being a professional substitute teacher, beginning well before the bell rings.

- At Home
- Prior to Entering the Classroom
- In the Classroom Before School
- Throughout the Day
- At the End of the Day

Chapter 2: Classroom Management

No learning takes place in classrooms that are out-of-control. Chapter two deals with managing the classroom learning environment. It contains ideas for starting the day, setting the tone, behavior management skills, and suggestions for managing challenging classroom scenarios.

Chapter 3: Other Stuff You Should Know

The other stuff you should know about includes:

- Safe Schools and Emergency Procedures

- First Aid

- Legal Aspects of the Job

- Disabilities and Special Education

- Gifted and Talented

- Multiculturism

- Alternative Learning

- Evacuation and Other Out-of-Classroom Activities

The information in this chapter should only be used to supplement local district policies and procedures.

Chapter 4: Teaching Strategies, Skills, and Suggestions

Chapter four contains suggestions for the contents of your *SubPack*, methods for presenting the permanent teacher's lesson plans, and ideas for low cost/no cost rewards and motivators.

- Brainstorming

- Concept Mapping

- K-W-L

- Questions for Higher Level Thinking

- Cooperative Learning

- Using Audio Visual Materials Effectively

Chapter 5: Fill-In Activities

This chapter will give you many lesson and activity ideas for your *SubPack*. These "fill-in" activities can provide hours of meaningful learning. A detailed *Reference Guide for Activities* listing individual activities is found in chapter five on pages 122-123. According to the type of activity, this chapter has been divided into three sections:

Five-Minute Fillers

Isn't it time to go yet?

Whole-class critical thinking activities for those extra five minutes that occur throughout the day.

Early Finishers

Independent activities for students who finish assignments early.

Can you come back tomorrow?

Short Activities

Teacher-directed activities and lessons. This section is organized by subject and includes lessons that can be taught in an hour or less.

  • Art

 • Critical Thinking

 • Foreign Language

 • Geography

 • Government/History

 • Language Arts

 • Math

 • Music

 • Science

 • Speech/Drama

Overview Icon outlines the subject, grade level, materials needed, advance preparation required, and objective for each activity or lesson.

Notes For The Teacher:

These are found at the end of each *Short Activity* to point out classroom management techniques and background information specific to that lesson.

Contributing Authors

Geoffrey G. Smith

Mr. Smith is the director of the Substitute Teaching Institute at Utah State University (STI/USU), the principal investigator for STEP-IN (Substitute Teacher Educational Program Initiative), and has been the principal investigator of research for many substitute teacher projects. He is the publisher of the *Substitute Teacher Handbooks, SubJournal* and the *SubExchange* newsletter. He holds an MBA degree, a Master in Educational Economics, and has been involved with teacher-professional development for a number of years.

Max L. Longhurst

Mr. Longhurst is the elementary education specialist at STI/USU. He develops materials for substitute teachers, and writes, field-tests, and conducts seminars and training sessions for educators. Having been in the classroom both as a permanent teacher and a substitute, his experience provides practical applications for teaching and learning strategies.

Glenn Latham

Dr. Latham was a professor emeritus of special education at USU and served as a principal investigator at the Mountain Plains Regional Resource Center, which provides technical assistance for working with hard-to-teach and hard-to-manage students. Dr. Latham also served as a consultant and advisor to numerous schools and school systems, both nationally and internationally. His publications include over 200 technical papers and journal articles as well as the book, *The Power of Positive Parenting: A Wonderful Way to Raise Children*.

Cynthia Murdock

Ms. Murdock has served as the curriculum development director at STI/USU. Her teacher-leader ability, along with experience as a substitute and permanent teacher, provided a plethora of ideas and materials for substitute teachers. She has written and edited the *SubExchange* newsletter, several *Substitute Teacher Handbooks*, and has also been a teacher-professional development instructor.

Barbara Goldenhersh

Dr. Goldenhersh serves as an assistant professor of education at Harris-Stowe State College in St. Louis, Missouri. Along with teaching, she consults and presents nationally on various topics including being an effective substitute teacher and school law. Books authored by Dr. Goldenhersh include *The Guest Teacher: A Fresh Approach to Substitute Teaching* and *Read It With Bookmarks*.

A special thanks to: Carrie Owen, Barbara Haines, Blaine Sorenson, and Andrae Ferguson.

Table of Contents

The Professional Substitute Teacher

Chapter 1

Introduction

Through thousands of surveys, questionnaires, and interviews, we have learned that permanent teachers, school administrators, and district personnel unanimously praise and value substitute teachers who are professional in dress, attitude, and presentation.

Being a professional substitute teacher is an all-day job. It involves many aspects of attitude and conduct. In this chapter, these aspects have been organized into the following five time frames:

1. At Home

2. Prior to Entering the Classroom

3. In the Classroom Before School

4. Throughout the Day

5. At the End of the Day

For additional information regarding the Professional Substitute Teacher, visit:

http://subed.usu.edu

The Professional Substitute Teacher

At Home

There are a number of things you can do at home before you ever get that early morning call to substitute teach.

- Prepare a set of note cards, one for each school where you may be called to teach. On each card, list the name of the school, principal, and secretary, school phone numbers, start time, address, driving directions, and the approximate time it will take to travel from your house to this location.

- Place a notebook and pencil by the phone you will be using to answer early morning calls. You may even want to jot down a couple of pertinent questions to ask when the call comes, such as, *"What is the name and grade level of the teacher I will be substituting for?"*

- Assemble a *SubPack* filled with teaching supplies and activity ideas for the grade levels you teach. (For more information about *SubPacks*, see page 70.)

- Designate a section of your closet for substitute teaching clothes. Assemble entire outfits, including shoes and socks, which are ironed and ready to be put on at a moment's notice. Be sure to select comfortable shoes, since as an effective substitute you will be on your feet all day. Have several different outfits ready so that you are prepared to dress appropriately for different grade levels and subject assignments.

- Research has shown that teachers who dress professionally command more respect in the classroom than those who dress casually or inappropriately. Gain the respect you deserve by the way you dress.

Appropriate Attire Guidelines for Men and Women

Women: Avoid high heels, short skirts, and low-cut tops. Select comfortable outfits in which you can bend down, stoop over, and write on chalkboards with ease.

Men: Consider wearing a tie with a button-down shirt. You can always take off the tie, undo the neck button, and roll up your sleeves if you find yourself "over-dressed" for the assignment.

As a general rule, jeans, t-shirts, sandals, and other casual clothing are not considered professional or appropriate for the classroom setting. You should always dress at least as professionally as your permanent teacher counterpart.

When the call comes, answer the phone yourself. A groggy spouse or roommate does not always make a professional impression, and you will be wasting the caller's time while they are waiting for you to wake up and get to the phone.

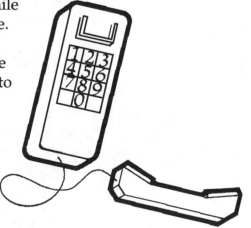

After you hang up the phone, take a look at your note card for the school, determine how long it will take you to get there, and plan the rest of the morning accordingly. Remember that you want to be at the school at least 20 minutes prior to either the beginning of class or when students arrive. Get ready and don't forget to grab your *SubPack* as you head out the door.

Prior to Entering the Classroom

Arrive at the school enthusiastic about the day, while serious about your role. If possible, arrive at least 20 minutes prior to the beginning of class. Report to the principal or office to let them know you have arrived, and ask pertinent questions:

Will I be responsible for playground, lunch, or bus duty?

Do any of the students have medical problems I should be aware of?

If the need arises, how do I refer a student to the office?

How do I report students who are tardy or absent?

Obtain any keys that might be necessary.

Find the locations of restrooms, the teacher's lounge, the cafeteria, the auditorium, the media center, and the nearest drinking fountain before school begins.

Meet neighboring teachers.

In the Classroom Before School

Enter the classroom with confidence and your *SubPack*. Put your name on the board, then familiarize yourself with the room. Locate and review the classroom rules and evacuation map.

Read through the lesson plans left by the permanent teacher and identify books, handouts, and papers that will be needed throughout the day. Study the classroom seating chart. If you can't find a seating chart, get ready to make your own (see page 17).

When the bell rings, stand in the doorway and greet students as they enter the classroom. Be professional, friendly, and enthusiastic about the day. This first impression will take you a long way.

Throughout the Day

Do your best to follow the lesson plans and carry out the assigned duties left by the permanent teacher. Over 75 percent of permanent teachers report that they spend at least 45 minutes preparing lesson plans and materials for substitute teachers. Having invested both time and energy into these plans, permanent teachers feel very strongly about having them carried out.

On the other hand, you may enter a classroom where you are unable to locate the lesson plans or necessary materials. In such a case, act quickly, calmly, and confidently. By utilizing materials and ideas in your *SubPack*, you can still have a productive day.

Whatever situation or challenge you are faced with, always strive to be positive and respectful. Permanent teachers care about the students in their class. They know each student's strengths and weaknesses, and will want to see these handled appropriately. They hope the substitute teacher will appreciate the good in their students and bring out the best in them.

Permanent teachers urge substitute teachers to be aware of how small things, like using a normal voice, giving praise, and having an upbeat attitude, can affect students. Students resent teachers who talk down to them, make promises or threats they don't intend to keep, and are not fair in administering rewards and consequences. Treating students as individuals is important. Don't blame the whole class or punish the group for the misdeeds of a few. (See chapter two for suggestions on classroom management.)

When a substitute teacher uses good judgment, avoids criticism, and adapts to circumstances in a positive way, the substitute becomes a professional role model for both the students in the class and other teachers.

At the End of the Day

Being a professional is just as important at the end of the day as it is at the beginning. What you do just before the final bell will be the impression students take home with them. How you leave the classroom will be the first impression the permanent teacher has of you when they return.

Before the Students Leave

There are several things you should do during the last few minutes of class before the students leave:

- If the teacher has classroom sets (calculators, scissors, books, etc.), be sure to have them all returned before the students leave the room. It is much easier to locate a missing calculator in a class of 30 than trying to find it somewhere in the whole school.

- Challenge students to recall, and list on the board, projects and topics they have studied that day. *(Now they will have a positive answer when parents ask what they did in school, instead of the traditional, 'Nothing,' we had a Sub.")*

- Remind students of homework. Writing homework assignments on the board throughout the day will help both you and the students remember.

- Have students straighten and clean-up the area around their desk.

After the Students Have Left

After the students have gone, take a few minutes to complete your professional duties as a substitute teacher. Fill out a "Substitute Teacher Report" for the permanent teacher (see sample forms on the following pages). Write a detailed summary of what was accomplished throughout the day, along with any problems that arose and notes about things that went well, or students that were particularly helpful.

If, for any reason, you were unable to carry out the plans left by the permanent teacher, be sure to explain why you were unable to carry them out and what you did instead. Leave your name, phone number, and an invitation for the permanent teacher to contact you if they have any questions, or to request you as their substitute again in the future.

Leave the teacher's desk and assignments turned in by students neatly organized. Close windows, turn off lights and equipment, and double check to make sure the room is in good order before you lock the door and head for the office. At the office, return keys, turn in any money collected, express appreciation for assistance provided, and check to see if you will be needed again the next day.

In Conclusion

Teachers have high expectations of others who come into their classroom. By implementing the ideas in this chapter, you can become a professional that meets and exceeds these expectations. Always remember that you are a valued and important part of the educational system. Never diminish your role as a substitute teacher. Teachers appreciate having a person come into their classroom who is caring and capable. By being prepared, poised, and professional, you will greatly reduce the stress on the teacher, students, and yourself. The checklist on pages 9 and 10 will help you stay on the right track throughout the day. Additional hints and suggestions are found at the end of chapter four, on pages 101-103.

Substitute Teacher Report

Substitute: _____   Date: _____

Phone Number: _____   Grade: _____

Substituted for: _____   School: _____

Notes regarding lesson plans:

I also taught:

Notes regarding behavior:

Terrific helpers:

Students who were absent:

Messages for the permanent teacher:

Please let me know of any areas you feel I can improve to be a better substitute for you.

Substitute Teacher Report

Substitute: _____   Date: _____

Phone Number: _____   Class: _____

Substituted for: _____   School: _____

Period	Notes about lessons (see back)	Notes about students (see back)
1		
2		
3		
4		
5		
6		
7		
8		

Messages for the permanent teacher:

Please let me know any areas you feel I can improve, to be a better substitute for you.

☑ Professional Substitute Teacher Checklist

At Home

_____ Compile a set of note cards containing pertinent information about the schools where you may be assigned.

_____ Keep a notebook and pen by the phone you use to answer early morning calls.

_____ Assemble a *SubPack*. Keep it well stocked and ready.

_____ Organize several appropriate substitute teacher outfits in a section of your closet.

_____ Leave early enough to arrive at school at least 20 minutes prior to the beginning of school.

Prior to Entering the Classroom

_____ Report to the principal or the office.

_____ Ask about student passes, playground rules, bus duty, and lunch procedures.

_____ Ask if there will be any special duties associated with the permanent teacher's assignment.

_____ Find out how to refer a student to the office.

_____ Review the school's discipline policy.

_____ Ask if any children have medical problems.

_____ Obtain necessary keys.

_____ Ask how to report students who are tardy or absent.

_____ Find the locations of restrooms, the teachers' lounge, and other important places in the school.

_____ Introduce yourself to the teachers on both sides of your classroom.

In the Classroom Before School

_____ Enter the classroom with confidence and your *SubPack*.

_____ Put your name on the board.

_____ Review the classroom rules.

_____ Locate and review the school evacuation map.

_____ Read through the lesson plans left by the permanent teacher.

_____ Locate books, papers, and materials which will be needed throughout the day.

_____ Study the seating chart and if you can't find one, get ready to make your own.

_____ When the bell rings, stand in the doorway and greet students as they enter the classroom.

Throughout the Day

_____ Greet students at the door and get them involved in learning activities quickly.

_____ Carry out the lesson plans and assigned duties to the best of your ability.

_____ Improvise using the materials in your *SubPack* to fill extra time, enhance activities, or supplement sketchy lesson plans as needed.

_____ Be fair and carry out the rewards and consequences you establish.

_____ Be positive and respectful in your interactions with students and school personnel.

At the End of the Day

_____ Make sure all classroom sets are accounted for.

_____ Challenge students to recall projects and topics they have studied that day.

_____ Remind students of homework.

_____ Have students straighten and clean the area around their desks.

_____ Complete a "Substitute Teacher Report" for the permanent teacher.

_____ Neatly organize papers turned in by students.

_____ Close windows, turn off lights and equipment, and make sure the room is in good order before you lock the door.

_____ Turn in keys and any money collected at the office.

_____ Thank individuals who provided assistance during the day.

_____ Check to see if you will be needed again the next day.

Classroom Management

Chapter 2

Effective Classroom and Behavior Management

* Dr. Latham was the principal investigator for the Mountain Plains Regional Resource Center at Utah State University.

This chapter explains five behavior management skills and various strategies to help you effectively manage student behavior and the classroom environment. The skills presented have been developed by Dr. Glenn Latham* and, when implemented correctly, have been statistically proven to prevent/eliminate 94 percent of inappropriate student behavior.

As you come to understand and implement these skills and strategies, your ability to effectively manage the classroom environment (use of time, organization of events, etc.) and direct student behavior will increase. Unfortunately, there isn't one "true" recipe that guarantees appropriate student behavior or a successful day in the classroom, but these guiding principles and skills have been proven successful in making the most of any situation.

To adapt more skills as a Professional Substitute Teacher, visit:

http://subed.usu.edu

Behavior Management

A Brief Note About Principles of Human Behavior

Behavior is largely a product of its immediate environment.

Behavior is largely a product of its immediate environment.

If students misbehave, act out, are easily distracted, and so on, it is very likely that this is in response to something in the immediate classroom environment. To a large degree, your actions as a teacher determine this environment.

Behavior is strengthened or weakened by its consequences.

The persistent behavior of students who are disruptive or non-attentive can invariably be explained by the classroom consequences of this behavior.

Behavior ultimately responds better to positive than to negative consequences.

By genuinely reinforcing appropriate behavior through positive consequences, many undesirable behaviors will become extinct and appropriate behavior among all students will increase.

Whether a behavior has been punished or reinforced is known only by the course of that behavior in the future.

The only way you can tell if a response to a behavior is punishing or reinforcing is to watch what happens to the behavior after the response. What is a punishment to one student may reinforce and perpetuate a behavior in another.

Five Skills for Effective Behavior Management
- Teaching expectations
- Getting and keeping students on-task
- Maintaining positive teacher-to-pupil interactions and risk-free student response opportunities
- Responding noncoercively
- Avoiding being trapped

Five Skills for Effective Behavior Management

The following skills for managing student behavior are based on the basic principles of human behavior. Understanding and effectively implementing these skills will help prevent unnecessary classroom management problems, as well as prepare you to manage any challenging situations which may occur.

Skill #1   The ability to teach expectations.

Skill #2   The ability to get and keep students on-task.

Skill #3   The ability to maintain a high rate of positive teacher-to-pupil interactions and risk-free student response opportunities.

Skill #4   The ability to respond noncoercively.

Skill #5   The ability to avoid being trapped.

Skill #1: The ability to teach expectations.

Teaching expectations involves communicating to students the behaviors that are expected in the classroom. Types of expectations include:

1. Classroom expectations (rules)
2. Instructional expectations
3. Procedural expectations

Expectations should provide boundaries and establish standards for student success.

As a substitute teacher, your first objective should be to model the expectations of the permanent teacher. Locate the classroom rules posted in the classroom and try to determine the procedures and strategies used by the permanent teacher to get the attention of the class. This can be accomplished by reviewing the lesson plans and talking to students. If there are no rules or procedures in evidence, be prepared to implement your own.

Classroom expectations should be concise, specific, instructive, operational, and must convey an expectation of student behavior. Phrases such as *"be cooperative," "respect others,"* and *"be polite and helpful"* are too general and take too much time to explain. Effective expectations such as *"Follow directions the first time they are given,"* are direct, provide specific standards, and are appropriate for any grade level. The number of expectations should correlate with the age and ability of the students; in general, it is recommended they be limited to five or less.

Rules: General standards of behavior that are expected throughout the day (i.e., use appropriate language at all times).

Instructions: Information about what students are supposed to do (i.e., complete the crossword puzzle).

Procedures: The manner and methods students use to follow instructions and comply with rules (i.e., read silently).

Once general classroom behavior expectations have been taught, they should be posted somewhere in the room. Hopefully, the permanent teacher has already done this. If not, you can post them on the board or on a poster-size sheet of paper you carry in your *SubPack*. In primary grades using pictures, in addition to words, is a good way to convey your expectations.

Each assignment and activity throughout the day will have its own set of instructional and procedural expectations. *Instructional expectations* and *procedural expectations* need to be communicated to students in order for students to successfully complete their assignments.

As you develop and explain instructional and procedural expectations, realize that students need three things in order to successfully meet the expectations you establish:

1. They need to know exactly what it is they are supposed to do. Example: Finish your math assignment.

2. They need to know how they are expected to do it. Example: Work with your partner and raise your hand if you need help.

3. They need to have the necessary tools to accomplish the expected task. Examples: Paper, pencil, calculator, etc.

Explaining instructional and procedural expectations in the form of a step-by-step process often makes it easier for students to remember the expectations and complete the corresponding task appropriately.

Examples of Instructional Expectations:

- Pass your worksheet to the front of the row.
- Number your paper from 1 to 10.
- Write a 500 word essay.
- Read the story.

Examples of Procedural Expectations:

- Work silently.
- Keep all your materials on the desk.
- Walk in a single file line.
- Talk with group members using a quiet voice.

Sample Classroom Expectations (Rules)

- Follow directions the first time they are given.
- Raise your hand for permission to speak.
- Keep hands, feet, and objects to yourself.
- Always walk in the classroom and halls.
- Complete assignments in the allotted time.
- Perform your tasks during group activities.
- Do your best work.
- Use appropriate language.

Step-By-Step Strategy

One reoccurring teaching situation where it is especially important to designate specific expectations is when students are making the transition from one activity to another. Students often waste time between activities because seemingly simple instructions such as, *"Get ready for math,"* are, in reality, quite ambiguous. Students need to know the following five specific things to make a quick transition from one activity to the next:

1. How to close their engagement in the current activity.

2. What to do with the materials they are using.

3. What new materials they will need.

4. What to do with these new materials.

5. How much time they have to make the transition.

Example: *"Stop reading and quietly put your reading book away. Get out your math book and paper. Open the book to page 112. You have one minute to do this. Please begin."*

Just telling students what your expectations are is often not enough. Expectations should be explained, restated by the students, demonstrated, and role-played until you are sure the students understand what is expected of them. Questioning students can help determine if this has been accomplished. Having students respond as an entire group and act out behaviors, such as raising their hand, is also a good idea because it requires every student in the class to understand and acknowledge the expectation.

Have Students Restate Expectations

Having students restate expectations is one way to ensure that they understand/acknowledge the expectations.

Teacher: (Calling on an attentive student) *"Robbie, thank you for paying attention. What do I expect you to do when you want to answer a question or say something?"*

Robbie: *"You want me to raise my hand."*

Teacher: *"That's right, Robbie. I expect you to raise your hand."*

The few minutes it takes to communicate expectations for each activity are well worth the stress and inappropriate behavior that will be prevented. Once you have established your expectations, stick with them! Students will remember what you have said and expect you to follow through. Firmness, fairness, and consistency are the keys to classroom management. Praising students when expectations are met will reinforce and perpetuate appropriate student behavior.

Skill #2: The ability to get and keep students on-task.

Students cannot learn if they are not actively engaged in learning activities. To be actively engaged in an assigned activity is commonly referred to as being "on-task." When students are on-task, they will learn more and create fewer classroom management problems. Getting and keeping students on-task can usually be accomplished using two simple strategies:

1. Begin instruction/activities immediately.

2. Manage by walking around.

Begin Instruction/Activities Immediately

The shorter the time between the beginning of class and when students are actively involved in a productive activity the better. Begin the day by introducing yourself and immediately engaging students in a structured activity. Some permanent teachers may leave instructions for a "self-starter" activity which students routinely complete at the beginning of class. If such an activity is not outlined in the lesson plans, implement an activity of your own. Many effective substitute teachers start the day by having students make name tags, help construct a seating chart, write in a student journal, engage in silent reading, or participate in one of the *Five-Minute Filler* activities found in chapter five.

Introductory activities serve two purposes in the classroom. First, they get students actively engaged in a learning activity, thereby decreasing the opportunity for inappropriate behavior. Second, they provide a means for you as the substitute teacher to assess the personality of the class. This assessment can help you as you begin implementing the lesson plans left by the permanent teacher.

Name Tags

Name tags can be worn or kept on students' desks throughout the day. They can be made using commercial stick-on name tags, adhesive file folder labels, or strips of masking tape. Name tags are a tremendous help when facilitating class discussions and managing student behavior.

Begin Class Immediately

"Hello. My name is ... and I am your teacher today. Please spend the next five minutes completing the activity I have outlined on the board."

Starting the Day

- Greet students at the door.
- Introduce yourself as the teacher.
- Get students doing something.
- Have Name Tags or a Seating Chart.
- Establish a plan for the day.

Seating Chart

A seating chart is a valuable tool you can use throughout the day to take roll and assist you in calling students by name. However, sometimes you may not be able to locate a seating chart or the seating chart left by the permanent teacher may not be current. If this is the case, it is easy for you to quickly make a seating chart using small Post-it Notes® and a file folder from your *SubPack*. Distribute one Post-it Note® to each student and have them write their name on it. After students have done this, arrange the names on the file folder in the same configuration as the desks in the classroom (see example below). The few minutes it takes to establish an accurate seating chart at the beginning of class is well worth the benefits it will provide.

After an introductory activity, try to minimize the time spent on procedural matters such as taking roll and lunch count. Dragging these activities out simply provides time for students to get bored and start behaving inappropriately. After taking roll and attending to any other beginning-of-class matters, outline for students your plan and schedule of activities for the day. Now is the time to quickly review expectations, explain consequences of student behavior, and

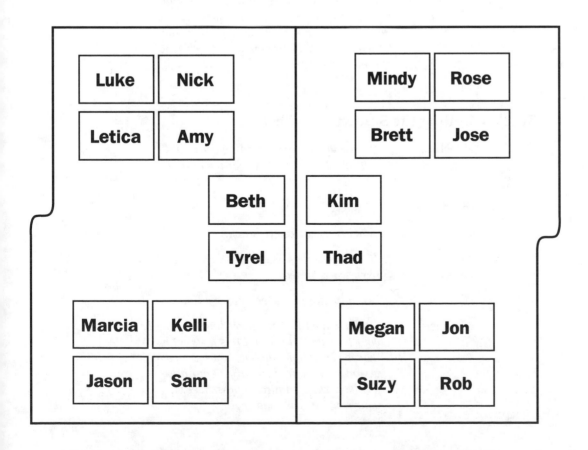

introduce any incentives or special activities you will be using. Share any information left by the permanent teacher regarding what they should accomplish during the day, then get students involved in the next learning activity as quickly as possible.

The sooner you get students on-task, the easier it is to keep them actively engaged in constructive activities. Do not allow yourself to get drawn off-task by student protests and long, useless discussions. If students complain, respond with empathy, understanding, and firmness, but don't compromise your expectations or waste instructional time being overly sympathetic.

Don't let students draw you off-task.

Students Getting the Teacher Off-Task

Teacher:	*"Please take out your reading books and read silently at your desk for the next 20 minutes."*
Students:	*"Reading is boring."*
	"We never read before lunch."
	"Our teacher lets us sit anywhere in the room when we read."
	"Twenty minutes is too long of a time."
Teacher:	*"You know when I was your age, I thought reading was boring too. Sometimes I used to just sit at my desk, hold my book open, and pretend to read. Have any of you ever done anything like that?"*

Respond to protests with empathy, firmness, and fairness.

Teacher Getting the Students On-Task

Teacher:	*"Please take out your reading books and read silently at your desk for the next 20 minutes."*
Students:	*"Reading is boring."*
	"We never read before lunch."
	"Our teacher lets us sit anywhere in the room when we read."
	"Twenty minutes is too long of a time."
Teacher:	*"I understand that silent reading may not be your favorite activity and this may not be the way Mrs. Jones does it, however, today we are going to read silently, at our desks, for the next 20 minutes. Please take out your reading books and begin."*

Manage by Walking Around

The easiest and most effective strategy for keeping students on-task is for the teacher to walk around the classroom in a random pattern. By moving about the room, you can observe the progress of students, acknowledge and reinforce positive behavior, and manage off-task behavior with proximity (nearness to the student). There is a direct relationship between how close a teacher is to students and how well students behave. Proximity is important! So wear comfortable shoes and plan to be on your feet all day monitoring, assisting, providing positive reinforcement, and using proximity to keep students on-task.

Other On-Task Strategies

In some circumstances, additional strategies are needed to get and keep students on-task. Sometimes an event outside the classroom, such as an assembly, fire drill, pep rally, or rousing game of soccer at recess, will make it difficult to get and keep students on-task. On other occasions, the entire class may be off-task or out of control for no apparent reason at all. Often the permanent teacher may have strategies and techniques such as silent signals or prompt/response drills, which can be implemented to get the attention of, or refocus, the class. If such techniques have been outlined in the lesson plans or explained by a student, don't hesitate to implement them. If you are left to manage the situation on your own, implement appropriate, positive, and proactive strategies.

Refocusing the Class: Captivate and Redirect

◄ Strategy

Often the best way to deal with major disruptions such as assemblies and fire drills is to minimize the event by capturing and redirecting students' attention. For example, complete an activity that requires mental concentration such as a *Five-Minute Filler* or *Critical Thinking Activity* from this book. Involving students in a fun and mentally challenging learning activity will help them settle back down to the routine of the day.

Getting Their Attention Strategies: Whisper, Write and Erase, and Lights Out

Occasionally, the entire class may be off-task, in the middle of an assignment, or just finishing an activity, when you need to get their attention in order to get everyone back on-task, give further instructions, or conclude the activity. The first thing you should do is try the strategy usually used by the permanent teacher such as a silent signal or prompt/response. If this is unsuccessful, or you don't know what the permanent teacher usually does, the following are three strategies that will get the attention of the entire class.

Strategy ▶

Whisper

Your first instinct in a situation where the entire class is noisy and off-task may be to raise your voice above the noise level of the room and demand attention. However, this can incur some unwelcome side effects, such as the students hearing you speak loudly and assuming it is OK for them to raise their voices as well. A productive strategy is to whisper. Move to the front of the room and begin giving instructions very quietly. As students hear you, they will need to become quiet in order to understand what you are saying. Soon students who are still talking and interacting will instinctively begin to feel uncomfortable and become silent also. When you have the attention of the entire class, you can then give instructions or directions as needed.

Strategy ▶

Write and Erase

If the class is between activities and talking among themselves, one way to get their attention and give further instructions is to begin writing and erasing the student instructions on the board one word at a time. For example, if you wanted them to get their Social Studies book out of their desk you would write the word "Get" on the chalkboard then erase it, then you would write the word "your" and erase it, then write the word "Social" and erase it, etc. Students will soon become so involved in trying to figure out what you are writing (and what words they missed) that you will very quickly have the undivided attention of the entire class.

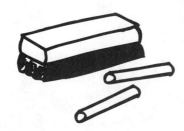

Lights Out

This strategy should only be used when you need the attention of the entire class and when you will not be unnecessarily interrupting students who are on-task (i.e., students are busy working on group projects and you need everyone's attention to quickly give instructions for concluding the activity before lunch). Quickly turn the classroom lights off then on again. Be prepared to begin speaking in the moment of surprised silence, when you have everyone's undivided attention. If you wait too long to start talking, the class will begin talking about the lights going out and the event itself will become a real distraction.

Skill #3: **The ability to maintain a high rate of positive teacher-to-pupil interactions and risk-free student response opportunities.**

Positive Teacher-to-Pupil Interactions

Student behaviors are reinforced as they are recognized through teacher-to-pupil interactions. On average, educators allow 98 percent of all appropriate behavior to go unrecognized and are two to three times more likely to recognize inappropriate behavior. It has been shown that strengthening desirable behavior through positive reinforcement, rather than trying to weaken undesirable behavior using averse or negative processes, will do more to make a classroom conducive to learning than any other single skill.

In general, positive verbal praise, a smile, a nod, and other appropriate gestures are among the very best ways to interact in a positive manner with students. Negative and corrective interactions should be outnumbered by positive interactions. A ratio of one negative to eight positive interactions is recommended. For ideas of positive things you can say to students, see the list of *101 Ways to Say Good Job* on page 95.

To become more positive in challenging situations, you must identify and practice positive interaction skills. One way to do this is to determine situations in which you are most inclined to be negative, using a form such as the one on page 22.

On the left side of the paper, describe a problem or inappropriate behavior that is most likely to elicit a negative response from you. On the right side of the paper, write a positive, proactive response(s) that could be used instead. Remember that you are learning a new skill and need to practice several times in order to become proficient.

Anticipated Problem	Positive, Proactive Response
I tend to scold or criticize students when they get noisy or out of control.	*I'll reinforce a behaving student then look for an opportunity, 30 seconds to a minute later, to verbally reinforce the disruptive student for being on task* *I'll reteach my expectations followed, 30 seconds to a minute later, by verbal praise for being on-task.*

At times, situations will arise that will be so annoying and unnerving that every positive interaction you have ever practiced will completely escape your recollection. When you can't think of an appropriate way to respond and are overwhelmed with the urge to react in a negative manner, **don't do anything**! Unless what you are about to say or do has a high probability for making things better, it is better to do nothing at all.

Strategy ▶ Positive Interaction Strategy: The Designated Problem Student

On occasion, a teacher may leave a note about a student to "watch out for," or a neighboring teacher may warn you about a "trouble maker." In such situations, you can often gain the compliance of the student and prevent potential problems by being proactive and positive. When the students arrive, determine who the identified student is and request that he or she be a "helper" for the day. Ask him or her to help you and provide special jobs that keep him/her positively occupied. Be positive in your interactions and thank them for their assistance. Provide the attention usually gained through negative behavior for acting as a helper. This strategy often diffuses the problem before it ever becomes one and creates a "ringleader" for positive behavior.

Strategy ▶ Positive Interaction Strategy: The "You vs. Them" Class

Sometimes you may get the feeling that the whole class, or at least several of the students, have secretly planned to make the day as difficult as possible for you, the substitute teacher. Most "You vs. Them" scenarios turn out to be a lose-lose situation for everyone involved. Take the initiative early in the day to do a "teacher and student interactive activity." You might try an activity from the

Five-Minute Filler section of this book, such as a Mystery Box, a Silly Story, or Number Phrase. Interact with the students, let them see that you have a sense of humor and get to know you better. Chances are, once you break the ice and establish rapport with students, the remainder of the day will go more smoothly. Making the classroom a battleground for control will usually make things worse.

Risk-Free Student Response Opportunities

Student response opportunities and active participation in the learning process play an important role in student achievement. As an added benefit, when students are engaged in appropriate responses to learning activities they have neither the inclination, nor the time, to be engaged in inappropriate behavior.

One aspect of providing risk-free student response opportunities is to provide these opportunities in the first place. Lecture little and question much. Let students answer questions that illustrate or explain the point you are trying to get across.

A second aspect of risk-free student response is to provide all students with opportunities and invitations to respond and inquire. There are always students with their hands raised continually, anxious to say just about anything. On the other hand, there are also those students who sit in class like a lump, never asking a question or making a comment. As a teacher, it is easy to get in the habit of calling on students who are attentive, interested, and willing to volunteer information. A simple way to insure that all students have a chance to respond, while at the same time maintaining the students' attention, is to place the names of all the students in a container and draw them out randomly. After a student has responded, put his/her name back in the container, otherwise they will lose interest and stop paying attention because they think they won't be called on again.

The third component of risk-free student response is to maintain a learning environment where students are not afraid to respond, an environment that is "risk-free" of failure and criticism. This can be accomplished by:

1. Asking the student to repeat what has been said.

2. Prompting the student in the direction of a correct response.

3. Asking students who you think know the answer.

4. Directing students' attention to a correct response.

Failure is a negative, ineffective, and poor teacher. In order to establish and maintain a risk-free classroom environment, do everything possible to help students have successful experiences. As you provide opportunities for students to give correct responses, you are also setting up opportunities to positively acknowledge these successes.

Strategy ▶

Handling Wrong Answers: Echo the Correct Response

Suppose you asked a student a question expecting a correct response but for whatever reason the student didn't give the right answer. In such situations, don't dwell on the failure of the student or the incorrectness of the answer. Instead, direct the question and the student's attention to another student who you are quite sure knows the answer. Once the question has been answered correctly, come back to the original student and ask the question again, allowing them to echo the correct response, and thus creating a successful experience for the student.

Teacher:	*"Jenny, how do you spell the word 'symphony'?"*
Jenny:	*"S - Y - M - F - O - N - Y"*
Teacher:	*"Very good, Jenny. You are very close. Is there any one else that thinks they know how you spell symphony? Josh, why don't you give it a try.*
Josh:	*"S - Y - M - P - H - O - N - Y"*
Teacher:	*"That is correct, good job Josh. Jenny, will you please spell symphony again?"*
Jenny:	*"S - Y - M - P - H - O - N - Y"*
Teacher:	*"Very good! That is exactly right."*

Occasionally, students will respond inaccurately, inappropriately, or even foolishly on purpose. Do not allow yourself to be drawn off target and into their control. Even though the student response was inappropriate, it is probably inconsequential. Overlook it and move forward with the instructional activity. Redirect the question to another student who is likely to respond correctly and appropriately, provide positive reinforcement for the correct response, then continue with the discussion. Responding to the inappropriate comment will most likely reinforce the behavior and prompt other students to engage in such responses.

Skill #4: The ability to respond noncoercively.

Any time a student behaves inappropriately you will probably find it annoying. However, the type of behavior, rather than the annoyance level, should be your guide for implementing an appropriate teacher response strategy. Inappropriate student behaviors can be classified as either consequential or inconsequential. Consequential behaviors are those which have a significant negative effect on the learning environment and interfere with the rights of other students to learn. Inconsequential behaviors are those which the classroom environment would be better off without, but their negative impact on student learning is minimal. Inconsequential behaviors, such as tapping a pencil on the desk, can become consequential if they escalate or persist over a period of time.

Ignore the Inconsequential

Ignore inconsequential behavior.

Most inappropriate student behavior, regardless of how annoying it is, is inconsequential. This means that it is not life threatening, it isn't going to destroy the building or its contents, nor does it indicate that a student is on the road to rack and ruin. A substitute teacher responding to inconsequential student behavior is providing reinforcement, and the frequency of these behaviors will likely increase. A better approach is to ignore inconsequential behavior and respond positively to appropriate behavior with a smile, verbal praise, or other appropriate gestures.

Example of Ignoring Inconsequential Behavior

When asking a question of the class, a student responds without raising his/her hand for permission to speak or speaks out-of-turn when a student response is not called for.

Step 1: Do not respond to the disruptive student. Look positively at those who are raising their hand and call on one of them saying, *"Thank you for raising your hand,"* then allow them to answer the question.

Step 2: If the student continues to speak without raising their hand when you ask the next question, continue to reinforce the students who are behaving appropriately and move closer to the student who is not cooperating.

Do not acknowledge the student who is speaking out of turn. If you give in and let that student answer, you will be reinforcing the inappropriate behavior. Generally after Steps 1 and 2, a noncompliant student will cooperate and the inappropriate behavior will have stopped. It is important to quickly recognize and reinforce the appropriate behavior of students as they stop behaving inappropriately and comply with expectations.

Respond noncoercively to consequential behavior.

Respond Noncoercively to Consequential Behavior

While most student behavior is inconsequential, there are inappropriate student behaviors that are of consequence and need to be addressed. Such behaviors would include those in which a student persists in disruptive behavior and is increasingly destroying the learning environment, or when students are physically or verbally abusive to one another. Coercion is a common inappropriate response to such behavior.

Coercion involves interactions with students that attempt to achieve compliance through the use of threats or force. The intent is to compel students to behave out of a fear of what will happen to them if they don't. Coercion makes a student want to escape or avoid their coercer, it does nothing to address the problem. At best, it will instill a sense of fear in students which prevents them from acting out. While on the surface the problem seems to have gone away, in reality you've threatened the student's self-confidence and destroyed the atmosphere of risk-free student response opportunities you are trying to create.

A better way to handle such situations is to stop, then redirect student behavior. This should be done as privately and quietly as possible. The following are six steps for stopping and redirecting inappropriate student behavior:

1. Say something positive.

2. Briefly describe the problem behavior.

3. Describe the desired alternative behavior.

4. Give a reason why the new behavior is more desirable.

5. Practice the desired behavior.

6. Provide positive feedback.

An example of how this would be done in the classroom setting:

1. Say something positive.	*"Beth, I enjoy having you in class. You have a lot of very creative ideas."*
2. Describe the problem behavior.	*"Just now when I asked you to stop tapping on your desk with your pencil and read silently, you continued to tap your pencil."*
3. Describe the desired behavior.	*"When I ask you to do something, you need to look at me, say OK or nod, and follow my instructions immediately."*
4. Reason the new behavior is desirable.	*"If you will stop tapping your pencil, the classroom will be quieter and everyone, including you, will be able to finish the reading assignment more quickly."*
5. Practice the desired behavior.	*"Beth, what are the three things you should do when I give you instructions?"* (Beth says, *"Look at you, say OK, and do it."*) If Beth does not respond, prompt her. If she responds inappropriately, repeat the question without displaying anger. Then say, *"Let's practice. I'll ask you to put your pencil down on the desk, and you show me the correct way to follow these instructions."*
6. Provide positive feedback.	*"Beth, you did a great job saying OK and putting down your pencil, but you forgot to look at me. Let's try it again, and this time remember to do all three steps."* (Beth responds correctly the second time.) The teacher says, *"Great! This time you looked at me, said OK, and put down your pencil. Good job!"*

Though this process may seem cumbersome and complicated, it actually takes less than two minutes and will become quite natural when practiced consistently. At this point, you might be thinking, "Well that's all right for young students, but not for the kids I work with." It may interest you to know that this strategy was developed at Boy's Town in Omaha, Nebraska, and is used daily with boys and girls of all ages, all the way through high school. This strategy demonstrates the best that research has to offer for stopping inappropriate behavior.

OTHER NONCOERCIVE STRATEGIES

The following are examples of other noncoercive response strategies that can be used to respond to inappropriate student behaviors that are of consequence. Remember, the main objective of all response strategies is to "stop" inappropriate behavior by getting the full attention of the student, then "redirect" student actions to an appropriate activity.

Strategy ▶

Reevaluate the Situation

One of the first steps you should take when a student or group of students is behaving inappropriately is to reevaluate the situation. If you have a group of students that won't quit talking, step back and see if you can determine why they are talking. Perhaps they do not understand the assignment and are trying to figure it out together. Maybe something has happened at lunch that needs to be addressed. If you find that this is the case, you may need to deal with the disruptive event, reteach the objective, or perhaps even restructure the assignment to be completed as a class or in small groups.

Strategy ▶

Reinforce Appropriate Behavior

Recognition and praise reinforce students who are behaving appropriately. Phrases such as, *"Thank you for raising your hand, Andy,"* and *"I appreciate that Jose, Su-Ling, and Monica followed my directions so quickly,"* or tangible rewards, such as points and tickets, provide motivation and incentives to behave appropriately. Overlooking inconsequential off-task behaviors and giving attention to students who are meeting expectations will create a positive classroom atmosphere where all students have a reason to behave appropriately.

Strategy ▶

Proximity

Proximity is an easy-to-use strategy for dealing with many inappropriate behaviors. If a student or group of students is off-task or disrupting the class, move closer to the student or group in incremental steps. As you *move toward the problem*, often the behavior will change, and students will comply with expectations without you even saying a word.

Restate Expectations

◀ Strategy

Sometimes students are off-task or behave inappropriately because they do not fully understand your expectations or the related consequences. Often restating the expected behavior, motivators, and consequences, followed by a check for student understanding is all it takes to get a class back on-task.

Example: *"It is important for everyone to behave appropriately as you work on this assignment. Please listen as I restate the expectations for this activity. The expectations are: put your feet on the floor, turn your bodies facing forward, and work silently. If you have a question or need help, please raise your hand and I will come to your desk. Students who meet these expectations will receive a ticket (or other motivator). Leroy, please repeat for the class the behavior that is expected during this activity."*

◀ Strategy

State the Facts

In some situations, stating the facts will motivate students to behave appropriately. For example, if you suspect students have switched seats, make a statement to the effect that it is better for everyone involved if you know the students' correct names as listed on the seating chart. Explain that this information would be vital in the case of an emergency and will also help to ensure that the wrong student doesn't get blamed for inappropriate behavior when you write your report to the permanent teacher at the end of the day.

◀ Strategy

Acknowledge and Restate/I Understand

Some students may vocally express negative opinions, inappropriate views, and frustrations. Verbally acknowledging a student's comment validates them as a person and will often diffuse an emotionally charged situation. Phrases such as, *"I understand,"* or *"I can tell that you,"* and *"It is obvious that,"* can be used to acknowledge what the student said without getting emotionally involved yourself. Transition words such as "however" and "nevertheless" will bring the dialogue back to restating the expected behavior.

Example: *"I can tell that you are not very interested in this topic, nevertheless the assignment is to construct a timeline for the industrial revolution and you are expected to have it completed by the end of class."*

Strategy ▶

Remove, Identify, and Redirect

In some instances, it is best to remove the student from the situation before addressing the behavior. Since it is necessary for you to maintain supervision over all of the students in the class, removal of the student should take him/her out of earshot, but allow you to maintain visual contact with the rest of the class. Calmly ask the student to go to the front or back of the room, or into the doorway. Direct the class to resume their work, then approach the student. Stay calm and in control of the situation. Identify the rule that was broken or explain that their behavior was unacceptable. State the consequences and go on to explain the consequences if the behavior continues. Express your confidence in the student's ability to behave appropriately, have the student restate what is expected of him/her, and then return to his/her desk and begin working.

Strategy ▶

Consequences

Another aspect of responding noncoercively to inappropriate behavior is the implementation of consequences. Many times you will teach in classrooms where the permanent teacher has already established consequences for behavior. Using these established consequences helps maintain continuity of the learning environment for students and makes it so that you don't have to develop consequences of your own. In situations where you do have to devise and implement consequences, keep the following in mind:

"I Understand"

There are two words that can stop most protests from any student and let you take control of the situation. These words are, "I understand."

If a student says, "But that's not fair!" you can say, "I understand, however, these are the expectations for today."

If a student says, "I hate you!" you can say, "I understand, however, I am the teacher today and you are expected to follow my directions."

If a student says, "This assignment is stupid," you can say, "I understand, nevertheless, you will need to have it completed for class tomorrow."

- When possible, consequences should be a natural outcome or directly related to the behavior. For example, if a student is off-task and doesn't finish his/her assignment, the consequence could be that s/he is required to work on the assignment while the rest of the class participates in a fun activity.

- Consequences and their implementation should not provide undue attention to misbehaving students.

- What is a negative consequence to one student may be a reinforcing consequence to another. If the consequence doesn't change the behavior in time, change the consequence.

- Consequences should be administered quickly and quietly without getting emotionally involved.

- All consequences should be reasonable, appropriate, and in accordance with district or school guidelines and policies.

Consequences should always be made known to students before they are administered. In other words, consequences should not be sprung on students out of nowhere after the behavior has already taken place. Students need to know in advance what they can expect as a result of their behavior, both positive and negative, so they can make informed choices about how to behave. Consequences should be communicated to students as predetermined outcomes of behavior rather than threats. It is a good idea to discuss consequences in conjunction with explaining expectations for the classroom or particular activity.

Effective Discussion of Expectations and Consequences

Teacher: *"During today's science activity, you will be using water and working with syringes at your desk. I expect you to use the syringes, water, and other materials appropriately as outlined in the activity. Anyone who uses these materials inappropriately will be asked to leave their group and observe the remainder of the activity in a seat away from the lab area."*

Teacher: *"Jordan, what is it that I expect during this activity?"*

Jordan: *"To use the syringes, water, and other materials appropriately as outlined in the activity."*

Teacher:	*"Shelley, what are the benefits of using these materials appropriately?"*
Shelley:	*"I can remain with my group and complete the activity."*
Teacher:	*"That is right. What will be the consequences if someone uses the materials inappropriately, Tyrel?"*
Tyrel:	*"They will be asked to leave their group and watch the rest of the activity from a seat away from the lab area."*

Correct Individuals

When necessary, you should correct individuals and implement consequences at the individual student level rather than punishing the whole group. Punishing the entire class for the misbehavior of one student usually results in two negative outcomes. First, the student receives a lot of attention as s/he is singled out and recognized as the cause for the class consequences. Second, any trust you had established with the remaining students is lost due to your unfair actions. By correcting and applying consequences to an individual, that student receives direction and is not over recognized for his/her negative behavior.

CHALLENGING SCENARIOS

The following are four challenging situations you might encounter. Suggestions on how to respond to them in a noncoercive, calm, and proactive manner are included.

Responding Noncoercively to a Refusal to do Work

In some classrooms, you may have a student or students who refuse to complete assignments or participate in activities. Your first response should be recognition of students who are on-task and positive encouragement for the noncompliant student. If after you encourage the student to complete the assignment, s/he makes a statement such as, *"You can't make me,"* an appropriate strategy would be to acknowledge and restate. Disarm the student by acknowledging that s/he is correct, then restate your expectations and consequences if they are not met.

Example: *"You're right, I can't make you complete this assignment. I can, however, expect you to have it completed before recess. If it is not finished by then, you will stay in and work on it. I also expect you to remain quiet and not disrupt the other students who are choosing to complete the assignment at this time."*

It is important to note that many times a refusal to do work is an indication that students don't know how to complete the assignment. They would rather appear bad than stupid. If this is the case, you may need to reteach the concept or provide extra assistance to the student. Emphasize what the student can do or has already accomplished and recognize student effort.

Responding Noncoercively to Inappropriate Language/Derogatory Remarks

At times, students may use profanity or make a derogatory remark about you, another student, or the permanent teacher. In such situations, it is important that you try not to take the remarks personally, respond to the behavior in a professional manner, and don't let your emotions override your behavior management skills.

The classroom expectations and consequences established at the beginning of the day have provisions for dealing with this challenging situation — Implement them! You might say something like, "*Susan, you chose to break the classroom rule regarding using appropriate language. What is the consequence?*" The student should then state the consequence and it should be carried out. Do not ask the student why s/he said what s/he said (you really don't want to know), just acknowledge that the student *chose* to break a rule or behave inappropriately and implement an appropriate consequence. Dismiss the incident as quickly as possible and resume class work.

Responding Noncoercively to a Fight

Should you see two students yelling at each other, or poised for a fist fight, respond quickly and decisively, do not hesitate to get help from another teacher if needed.

Verbal jousting can usually be extinguished by a firm command as you move toward the problem saying, "*I need both of you to take a quiet seat,*" or "*Stop this right now and take a quiet seat against the wall.*" Your calm, authoritative voice combined with an instructive statement will most often yield compliance to your directive.

If students are engaged physically, you must quickly, and with authority, tell them to step back away from each other. Placing yourself between the students may stop the engagement, but can be dangerous for you. Do not get angry, excited, or show a lot of emotion, this will compound the situation. When given firm and instructive directions, students will usually respond and comply as requested.

Responding Noncoercively to Threats

Threats are difficult to handle, the best strategy and response will vary with each situation. However, should a student threaten you or another student, the most important thing you must do is to stay calm and emotionally detached so you can evaluate and manage the situation professionally.

Threat Strategy 1: Acknowledge and Redirect

A threat is often the result of an emotional response. Ignoring the student will probably evoke more threats, and perhaps even aggression. Responding with threats of your own may accelerate the confrontation. The sooner the threat is acknowledged and the situation diffused, the better. Once the student has calmed down you can then direct his/her actions to something constructive. If you feel the student needs to discuss the situation, it is often wise to wait until after class, later in the day, or refer the student to a school counselor so that emotional distance and perspective on the situation can be achieved.

Example: *"I understand that you are very angry right now. However, I need you to sit down and begin completing page 112 in your math book. We will discuss this situation after lunch."*

Threat Strategy 2: Get Help!

If you feel that you or any of the students are in danger of physical harm, stay calm and immediately send a student or call the office to elicit the help of a permanent teacher or principal. After help has arrived and the situation is under control, document the occurrence. Record what happened prior to the threat, what you said and did, what the student said and did, as well as the involvement or actions of anyone else in the situation.

Skill #5: The ability to avoid being trapped.

There are seven traps in which educators, including substitute teachers, often get themselves caught. Once "trapped," teachers lose some of their power to be effective educators. Recognizing and avoiding these traps will help provide students with a better learning environment and avoid a lot of classroom management stress.

Trap #1: The Criticism Trap

Students require attention. Whether they get attention for being "good" or "bad," they will get attention. The criticism trap refers to a situation where the more students are criticized for their inappropriate behavior, the more likely they are to behave inappropriately, in order to continue getting attention from the teacher.

▶ **Criticism / Negative Interactions**

"That's not what I told you to do."

"You've done the whole assignment wrong."

"I've never taught in a class this noisy before."

"I don't want to say this again. Go to work!"

"Didn't you read the instructions?"

Traps to Avoid
- The Criticism Trap
- The Common Sense Trap
- The Questioning Trap
- The Sarcasm Trap
- The Despair and Pleading Trap
- The Threat Trap
- The Physical and Verbal Force Trap

How to Avoid the Criticism Trap

By recognizing and providing reinforcement for appropriate behavior, the need for students to act out in order to get attention is virtually eliminated. As a general rule, teachers should never have more than one negative or critical interaction with a student for every four or five positive interactions.

▶ **Positive Interactions**

"Thank you for following directions."

"You have the first five problems right."

"I'm glad you remembered to put your name on the top of the page."

"I can tell you were listening because of your correct answers."

"You have accomplished a lot this morning."

Trap #2: The Common Sense Trap

The common sense trap is also known as the reasoning or logic trap. It is a situation where common sense, reasoning, and logic are used to try and persuade a student to change their behavior. The reason this strategy is ineffective is that the student neigher learns anything new, nor are they offered a single reasonable incentive to change the behavior.

▶ Getting Caught in the Common Sense Trap

"Nicki, let's go over this again. As I explained earlier, you should have your assignment completed by the end of class. Look at how much you have left to do. You keep telling me that you'll get done in time, but unless you go to work you never will. It's up to you to get it done. If you don't complete your assignments, you're going to have a lot of homework."

How to Avoid the Common Sense Trap

Avoiding the common sense trap involves creating a positive environment where there are incentives to change and where positive consequences reinforce that change.

▶ Avoiding the Common Sense Trap

"Nicki, you have done the first four problems right. However, I can see that you still have a lot of this assignment left to complete. In order to participate in the end of the day activity, you will need to hurry and finish your work. I'll be back in a few minutes to see how you are doing."

Trap #3: The Questioning Trap

For the most part, questioning students about inappropriate behavior is useless and counterproductive. There are three reasons for not questioning a student about their behavior. First, you really don't want an answer, you want to change the behavior. A student can answer your question and still not comply with the way you want him/her to behave. Second, one question usually leads to more pointless questions that accomplish nothing and waste educational time. Third, as you question a student about an inappropriate behavior, you are actually calling attention to and reinforcing the behavior you want to eliminate. This attention may strengthen the behavior and increase the probability that it will occur again.

▶ Answers to Questions that Don't Change Behaviors

Teacher: *"Why did you hit Doug?"*

Student: *"I hit him because he is ugly and I was trying to fix his face. You see my long-term goal in life is to be a plastic surgeon and make ugly people beautiful. Since I haven't yet learned the precise surgical skills needed to do this, I am doing the best I can for a boy my age."*

In this (admittedly absurd) illustration, the student answered the question but it didn't accomplish anything. The teacher gained no new information to help in changing the problem behavior and has probably been incited to ask further useless, infuriating questions.

▶ **One Pointless Question Leads to Another**

Teacher:	*"Why aren't you working on your assignment?"*
Student:	*"Because I don't want to."*
Teacher:	*"Why don't you want to?"*
Student:	*"It's stupid."*
Teacher:	*"What's stupid about it?"*
Etc.	

How to Avoid the Questioning Trap

As tempting as it may be, don't ask students questions about their inappropriate behavior unless you really need the information to redirect the behavior. A better approach is to restate the expected behavior, have the student demonstrate an understanding of the expectation, then positively reinforce the expected behavior as was discussed in Skill #4, *Dealing Noncoercively with Inappropriate Behavior*.

Trap #4: The Sarcasm Trap

Probably nothing lowers a student's respect for a teacher more than does the use of sarcasm. Belittling students with ridicule destroys a positive classroom environment and may prompt them to lash out with inappropriate remarks of their own. The use of sarcasm suggests that you, as the teacher, do not know any better way of interacting and sets the stage for similar negative interactions between students themselves.

▶ **Getting Caught in the Sarcasm Trap**

Teacher:	*"My, my aren't you a smart class. It looks like by age 12 you have all finally learned to find your own seats and sit down after the bell, and to think it only took you half of the morning to do it. I don't know if there is another class in the entire school as smart or quick as you guys."*

How to Avoid the Sarcasm Trap

Avoiding the sarcasm trap is easy; do not use sarcasm! Better ways of communicating with students are discussed throughout this chapter.

▶ **Communicating Without Sarcasm**

"One of the expectations of this class is to be seated and ready to go to work when the bell rings. I appreciate those of you who were quietly seated when the bell rang today."

Trap #5: The Despair and Pleading Trap

The despair and pleading trap involves making desperate pleas to students and asking them to "have a heart" and behave appropriately. Teachers often become their own worst enemies when they communicate to students that they feel inadequate and incapable of managing the classroom and need help.

There will be days when nothing you do seems to work. As tempting as it may be to confide your feelings of inadequacy and frustration to the students and plead for their help in solving the problem, it will rarely accomplish the desired outcome. More often than not students will interpret your pleas as an indication that you have no idea what you are doing and the inappropriate behavior will accelerate rather than diminish.

▶ **What the Despair and Pleading Trap Sounds Like**

Teacher: (With a distraught expression and hopeless voice) *"Come on, can't you guys do me a favor and just be quiet for the rest of class? I've tried everything I know to get you to behave and nothing has worked. What do you think I should do? How can I get you to be quiet?"*

Student: *"Don't ask me, you're the teacher!"*

How to Avoid the Despair and Pleading Trap

The best defense against the despair and pleading trap is a good offense. Come to the classroom prepared with several classroom management strategies. For some classes, positive verbal reinforcement will be enough to gain compliance. In others, you may need to introduce tangible reinforcers such as point systems, end of the day drawings, or special awards (see page 97 for ideas). When you find that one strategy isn't working with an individual or class, don't be afraid to try something else.

▶ **An Option to the Despair and Pleading Trap**

Teacher: *"Between now and the end of class, I am going to be awarding points to groups who follow my instructions and are on-task. At the end of class, the group with the most points will get to choose a reward."*

Trap #6: The Threat Trap

Threats are just one step beyond despair and pleading on the scale of helplessness. The majority of threats are either inappropriate or unenforceable. They are typically hollow expressions of frustration which tell students that the teacher is at wit's end, out of control, and in over his or her head. Unreasonable and out-of-control threats may sound intimidating, but if students choose to call your bluff you will lose control of the situation because you can't carry out the consequence you've established. You should never threaten consequences that are unenforceable or unreasonable.

▶ **Getting Caught in the Threat Trap**

Teacher: *"If you don't sit down and be quiet right this minute, I'm going to call your parents and have them come and sit by you for the rest of class!"*

How to Avoid the Threat Trap

The best way to avoid frustrating situations that may evoke threats is to formulate and state both expectations and appropriate consequences in advance. Then reinforce appropriate student behavior and administer established consequences as needed.

Teacher: *"During this group activity, you are expected to remain in your seat and work quietly with other group members. Should you choose not to do this, you will not be allowed to participate with your group in the review game at the end of the activity."* Wait several minutes for students to comply. *"Group number three is doing an excellent job of staying in their seats and working quietly."*

Trap #7: The Physical and Verbal Force Trap

The use of physical and verbal force, except in instances where life or property is at risk, is absolutely inappropriate. Certainly, it is far less appropriate than the behavior that it is intended to stop. Physical force in the classroom as a behavior management tool is not only unproductive and inappropriate, in many states it is also illegal.

▶ **Example of Physical Force**

Teacher: *"I told you to take your seat."* Teacher pushes student into his/her desk. *"Now stay there until class is over."*

Avoiding the Physical and Verbal Force Trap

Concentrate on restating the expectation in a proactive way, then have the student restate and demonstrate the expectation. Keep your cool, count to ten, walk to the other side of the room, do whatever it takes to keep from resorting to force.

The Seven Traps Conclusion

The use of any trap-related management strategies is evidence of an unprofessional, frantic, desperate, even drastic attempt at managing student behavior. While trap-related strategies may result in initial student compliance, over time they are certain to backfire and result in the steady deterioration of the school and classroom environment.

Behavior Management Summary

By gaining an understanding of basic human behavior and utilizing the skills discussed in this chapter, you will be better prepared to more effectively manage the behavior of students in the classroom. Reviewing this chapter often will assist you as you continue to develop and expand your repertoire of classroom and behavior management skills.

Five Skills for Effective Behavior Management

1. The ability to teach expectations.

2. The ability to get and keep students on-task.

3. The ability to maintain a high rate of positive teacher-to-pupil interactions and risk-free student response opportunities.

4. The ability to respond noncoercively to inappropriate behavior that is consequential.

5. The ability to avoid being trapped.

   - The Criticism Trap

   - The Common Sense Trap

   - The Questioning Trap

   - The Sarcasm Trap

   - The Despair and Pleading Trap

   - The Threat Trap

   - The Physical and Verbal Force Trap

Classroom and Behavior Management involves using techniques and implementing strategies that foster appropriate student behavior in the classroom.

Other Stuff You Should Know

Chapter 3

Introduction

This chapter is a compilation of important topics that, as a substitute teacher, you should know about, including:

- Safe Schools
- First Aid and Safety
- Legal Aspects of the Job
- Child Abuse Reporting
- Sexual Harassment
- Disabilities and Special Education
- Gifted and Talented Students
- Multiculturism
- Alternative Learning
- Evacuation and Other Out-of-Classroom Activities

The information presented here is only an overview of general guidelines. As you review this information, you may think of additional questions relating to these or other topics. Do not be afraid to ask fellow teachers, school administrators, or district personnel about anything you would like to know. You should take the initiative to learn about specific district policies and state laws.

For additional tips on preparing yourself and becoming a Professional Substitute Teacher, visit:

http://subed.usu.edu

Safe Schools

Most school districts have established a *Safe Schools Policy* to foster a safe environment for students, staff, community, neighbors, and visitors where learning can take place without unnecessary disruptions.

Although each district will have its own version/edition of a Safe Schools Policy, some general guidelines usually apply.

School administrators should have a school-wide behavior management program in place at the beginning of the year, including:

Administrators, staff, teachers, and substitute teachers all have the responsibility and liability of ensuring that the Safe Schools Policy is enforced.

- A variety of positive reinforcements
- A variety of consequences for inappropriate behavior
- A plan for serious misbehavior
- High visibility of teachers, staff, and administration
- Early intervention programs
- Special training programs
- Parent involvement
- Written policies on expulsion and suspension
- Accommodations for special needs students

Help make your school a safe place to work, learn, and play!

Students have requirements and restrictions that foster safe schools, including:

- Knowing and complying with the school's rules of conduct
- Complying with all federal, state, and local laws
- Showing respect for other people
- Obeying people in authority at the school

Your district's Safe Schools Policy may be included with your substitute teaching manual. If not, be sure to request a copy from your district office and review it thoroughly.

First Aid

Most classroom and playground accidents should be handled with common sense. Students who are injured should be sent to the office where a school nurse or secretary can administer first aid. Don't fall into the *"band-aid"* or *"ice"* trap, where students are continually asking to go to the office for ice or band-aids for fake injuries. In the event of a severe injury, **do not** move the student. Remain with the student, send another student or teacher for help, and try to keep the other children calm.

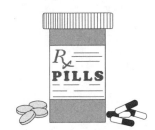

You should never give medication to a student, not even aspirin. If a student requires medication, it should be administered through the school nurse, secretary, or other designated medical personnel.

Learn how to handle situations involving blood and other bodily fluids. Listed below are the OSHA Universal Precautions for dealing with these situations. Contact the school district to find out their specific policies and procedures which should be followed.

OSHA Universal Precautions for Handling Exposure to Blood/Bodily Fluids

1. *All blood/bodily fluids should be considered infectious regardless of the perceived status of the individual.*

2. *Avoid contact with blood/bodily fluids if possible. Immediately notify the school nurse, administrator, or his/her designated first aid person.*

3. *Allow the individual to clean the injury if possible.*

4. *If it is not possible for the individual to clean the injury, disposable gloves should be worn. Gloves are to be discarded in a designated lined bag or container.*

5. *Clothing that has been exposed should be placed in a plastic bag and sent home with the individual.*

6. *Upon removal of gloves, hands should be washed thoroughly with warm water and soap.*

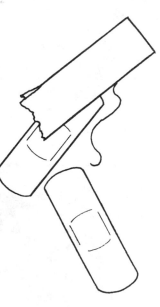

7. *Surfaces contaminated with blood/bodily fluids should be cleaned thoroughly with disinfectant. The cleaning should be completed by the custodian, administrator, or his/her designated individual responsible for clean-up.*

As a general rule: **Do not touch a student who is bleeding even if you use gloves.** For example, if a student has a bloody nose or cut knee, hand him/her the box of tissues or paper towel, and instruct him/her to hold it on the wound, then send him/her to the office or infirmary for further care. Students who are bleeding should not be allowed to participate in class activities until the bleeding has stopped and the wound has been cleaned and completely covered.

First aid

First Aid

- Handle accidents with common sense.
- Only the school nurse or other designated personnel should administer first aid including dispensing medication.
- Do not move a severely injured student.
- Learn school district policy for handling situations involving blood/bodily fluids.
- Always remain with the class and send a student or another teacher to get help when needed.

Advice from School Nurses for Substitute Teachers

Berks County Intermediate Unit
Reading, PA

1. Do not dispense medication (prescription or over-the-counter) to any students. Send them to the office or school clinic where they will have a record of the written permission to give the student the medication, the prescribed amount, and a system for recording the times and dosage administered.

2. Refer all students with injuries (even minor ones) to the office so the normal school procedures can be followed. In an emergency, you may need to escort the student to the office. Or, in a less serious situation, have another student accompany the injured child.

3. Carry to school each day a pair of disposable gloves that are waterproof and made of either latex or vinyl, in the event of an emergency that requires you to come in direct contact with a student's injury.

4. Always wear protective gloves when you come in contact with blood, bodily fluids, and torn skin, or when handling materials soiled with the same.

5. If you come in contact with bodily fluids from a student, throw your gloves away in a lined garbage can. Better yet, first seal the soiled gloves in a small plastic bag before depositing them in the trash. Wash your hands for 10 seconds with soap and warm water after you remove the gloves.

6. Encourage students to wash their hands before meals and when using the restrooms to reduce exposure to germs.

7. Do not allow students who are bleeding to participate in class until the bleeding has stopped and the wound has been cleaned and completely covered.

8. Check with the school office when there is a student injury. Some schools may require that you complete an accident report form. If so, leave a copy for the permanent teacher, and keep one for your records.

9. Prevention is the most important antidote for medical emergencies. Always stay with the students. Contact another adult if you need to leave the students at any time. If you have recess duty, walk around the playground being proactive about potentially dangerous behavior. Remember, you are the adult in charge.

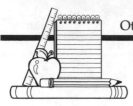

⚖ Legal Aspects of the Job ⚖

An overall consideration when substitute teaching is your legal responsibility in the classroom and school. The following are some legal responsibilities you should be aware of. An understanding of these responsibilities will require some questioning on your part as to specific school/district policies.

- **Supervision Of Students** — The substitute teacher who has physical control of a classroom has a duty to keep these children safe and orderly. In many states, a teacher acts *in loco parentis* — in the place of a parent — and is allowed to use his/her judgment in a manner similar to a parent. The standard is the reasonable use of professional judgment for the safety and orderly education of students.

- **Due Care And Caution** — A teacher is required to exercise due care and caution for the safety of the students in his/her charge. Essentially, this means acting reasonably and with safety in mind, being able to explain circumstances and your actions, as well as following school safety policies and procedures.

- **Release Of Children** — Due to possible restraints on who may have custody of a child, children should not be allowed to leave the building during the school day without express consent from the office.

- **Administering Medication** — Medication should only be administered by the school nurse or other appropriate health personnel, not the classroom or substitute teacher. If you know of medication requirements of a student, the health professional should be notified.

- **Confidentiality** — It is unprofessional and against the law in many states to disclose confidential information about your students. Generally, a substitute teacher should avoid comments about individual students that convey private information: grades, medical conditions, learning or discipline problems, etc.

- **Anecdotal Records** — Maintaining notes on particular incidents in the classroom can protect you in problematic situations. If you feel that your actions might be questioned, note the date and time, the individuals involved, the choices for action considered, and the actions taken.

- **Discipline Policies** — A substitute teacher should know the state's position on corporal punishment and the school's policy over various aspects of discipline. Some states require a school to have a policy, and often these policies indicate a specific person such as the principal as disciplinarian. If in doubt, referring students to the building principal is sound advice. When sending a student to the principal due to discipline matters, the substitute teacher maintains the duties of supervision and due care for both the individual child and the remainder of the class. Proper action may be detailed in the school policy or may require your independent sound judgment. Possible actions include having another child accompany the child, sending a child to bring someone from the office to intervene, or having another teacher watch your class while you take the child to the office.

- **Dangerous Situations** — A substitute teacher is responsible for making sure the learning environment is safe. This includes things such as the arrangement of desks so as not to block exits and proper supervision during the use of potentially dangerous classroom equipment. A teacher must also consider the potential for problems in certain kinds of classes. Planned activities in a physical education, science, shop, or home economics class may be uncomfortable for the substitute teacher. In such cases, the substitute teacher may choose to do an alternate activity which they feel they can conduct safely.

 **Never** Leave Your Students Unsupervised.

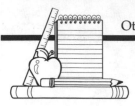
Child Abuse Reporting

Purpose

The purpose of child abuse reporting legislation is to protect the **best interests of children**, offer protective services to prevent harm to children, stabilize the home environment, preserve family life whenever possible, and encourage cooperation among the states in dealing with the problem of child abuse.

Any person, official, or institution required to report a case of suspected child abuse, sexual abuse, or neglect and fails to do so is guilty of a class B misdemeanor.

Duty to Notify

Any school employee (including a substitute teacher) who knows or reasonably believes that a child has been neglected, or physically or sexually abused, should **immediately notify** the building principal, the nearest peace officer, law enforcement agency, or office of the State Division of Human Services.

It is not the responsibility of school employees to prove that the child has been abused or neglected, or determine if the child is in need of protection. Investigations are the responsibility of the Division of Human Services. Investigations by education personnel prior to submitting a report should not go beyond what is necessary to support a reasonable belief that a reportable problem exists.

IT'S THE LAW!

Persons making reports or participating in an investigation of alleged child abuse or neglect in good faith are immune from any civil or criminal liability that might otherwise arise from those actions.

Everything you Need to Know About Sexual Harassment*

What is sexual harassment?

Definition: Unwelcome sexual advances, requests for sexual favors, and other verbal or physical conduct of a sexual nature when:

1. submission to such conduct is made, either <u>explicitly</u> or <u>implicitly</u>, a term or condition of a person's employment or a student's academic success

2. submission to or rejection of such conduct by an individual is used as the basis for employment or academic decisions affecting such individuals

3. such conduct unreasonably interferes with an individual's work or academic performance or creates an intimidating, hostile, or offensive working, or learning, environment

What is a "yardstick" for determining what constitutes sexual harassment?

Sexual harassment is behavior that:

Sexual Harassment is illegal. Don't do it- Don't tolerate it!

1. is unwanted or unwelcome

2. is sexual in nature or gender-based

3. is severe, pervasive and/or repeated

4. has an adverse impact on the workplace or academic environment

5. often occurs in the context of a relationship where one person has more formal power than the other (supervisor/employee, faculty/student, etc.)

To whom can I talk about sexual harassment concerns?

1. Your local principal, superintendent, or personnel/ human resources office

2. Your City or State office of Anti-Discrimination

3. Your State office of Equal Employment Opportunity Commission (EEOC)

4. The Office of Civil Rights, U.S. Department of Education

Well, It's A Start

What are some examples of verbal, non-verbal, and physical sexual harassment?

The following are behaviors which <u>could</u> be viewed as sexual harassment <u>when they are unwelcome</u>:

Verbal
- whistling or making cat calls at someone
- making sexual comments about a person's clothing or body
- telling sexual jokes or stories
- referring to an adult woman or man as a hunk, doll, babe, or honey
- spreading rumors about a person's personal sex life
- repeatedly "asking out" a person who is not interested

Non-verbal
- paying unwanted attention to someone (staring, following)
- making facial expressions (winking, throwing kisses, licking)
- making lewd gestures
- giving gifts of a sexual nature

Physical
- hanging around, standing close, or brushing up against a person
- touching a person's clothing, hair, or body
- touching oneself in a sexual manner around another person
- hugging, kissing, patting, stroking, massaging

What should I do if I feel I am being sexually harassed?

Sexual harassment can be directed at or perpetrated by you, administrators, faculty members, staff members, or students.

1. Talk to your harasser if possible. Tell her/him that you find the behavior offensive.

2. Continue going to work/classes.

3. Document all sexual harassment incidents. Record the time, date, place, and people involved.

4. Consider talking to others to see if they have experienced sexual harassment.

5. Put your objection in writing, sending a copy by registered mail to the harasser and keeping a copy in your file. Say:

   A. On "this date" you did "this."

   B. It made me feel "this."

   C. I want "this" to happen next (i.e., I want "this" to stop).

6. Report the harassment to the building administrator and district personnel/human resource director.

Disabilities and Special Education

Inclusion: Placing children with mild, moderate, or severe disabilities in regular education classrooms.

Five affective, or attitudinal benefits:

1. The nondisabled student learns to be more responsive to others

2. New and valued relationships develop

3. Nondisabled students learn something about their own lives and situations

4. Children learn about values and principles

5. Children gain an appreciation of diversity in general

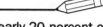

If the child is able to participate in school activities, academic lessons, lunchroom activities, recess, games, etc., s/he MUST be included.

Public Law 94-142

Passed in 1975, **"The Education for All Handicapped Children Act"** has been amended and is now called "**IDEA**" or the "Individuals with Disabilities Education Act." It provides that all handicapped children between the ages of 3 and 21 are entitled to **free public education**. Presently, the terms **disability** and **disabled** are used <u>in place of</u> handicap and handicapped.

The law defines individuals with disabilities to include those who are *mentally retarded, hard of hearing, deaf, speech-impaired, visually handicapped, seriously emotionally disturbed, or orthopedically impaired; have multiple handicaps; or have other health impairments or learning disabilities* and therefore need special educational services.

IDEA also provides that ALL students with disabilities have the right to be served in the **least restrictive environment**—this means that they must be educated and treated in a manner similar to their nondisabled peers. This usually consists of **mainstreaming** which is placing children with disabilities in the regular classroom.

Who decides which children are disabled and how they will be educated? Federal Law requires that a team consisting of the student, his/her parent(s), teachers, principal, and other professionals develop an **IEP** (individual education plan) detailing the goals and objectives of the educational services to be provided. The IEP lists all special and regular activities that the student will participate in.

Nearly 20 percent of all children 3-17 have one or more developmental, learning, or behavioral disorders. This means 1 in 5 have a social or learning problem that requires special attention!

Federal Law states that NO ONE has access to a student's IEP without the parent's permission. It is always a good idea to check with the permanent teacher and/or administrator, preferably before taking over a classroom, to determine how best to deliver educational services.

Students with disabilities in one area may be capable or even exceptional in others. By eliminating or modifying barriers to participation, students with disabilities may enjoy regular classroom activities and assignments.

Guidelines for adapting games and activities for students with disabilities

1. Often, children with disabilities already know their capabilities and limits – simply encourage them and be ready to assist if needed.

2. Focus on children's abilities – not disabilities.

3. It is okay to modify the game/rules to meet the needs of the <u>entire</u> group.

4. Keep the game/activity as complete and original as possible.

5. Be sensitive, especially with new students/disabilities – start slowly and develop gradually.

Ideas for adapting games/activities

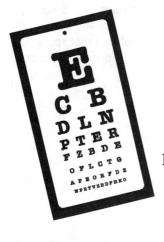

- Reduce the size of the playing area.

- Adjust the boundaries, change the number of players, lower the net.

- Use walls, fences, or designated "helpers" to aid in keeping the ball in-bounds.

- Find bigger/lighter equipment.

- Incorporate plastic bats, rubber racquets, jumbo gloves, enlarged hoops, expanded goals, etc.

- Substitute beach balls, nerf balls, whiffle balls, bladder balls, styrofoam balls, balloons, etc.

- Slow it down.

- Throw underhand, roll the ball, bounce the ball, hold the ball still, use a batting tee, etc.

- Allow an "extra" bounce, count before throwing, use "left" (or right) hand, no hands, etc.

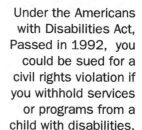

Under the Americans with Disabilities Act, Passed in 1992, you could be sued for a civil rights violation if you withhold services or programs from a child with disabilities.

Guidelines for adapting assignments and activities for students with disabilities

1. Generally, the permanent teacher and/or resource person will already have policies in place. Find out what they are and use them.

2. Focus on the children's abilities – not disabilities.

3. It is okay to modify the assignment for certain students and not others.

4. Keep assignments as similar to the rest of the class as possible.

5. Be sensitive, especially with new students/disabilities – start slowly, develop gradually.

Ideas for adapting activities/assignments

- Reduce the number of pages or questions.

- Reduce to half the page or problem, every other page or problem, the first page or problem, the last page or problem, only pages or problems with pictures, pick your own pages or problems.

- Reduce the difficulty of activities/assignments (barriers due to physical or emotional disabilities).

- Read out loud, write on board, use overheads, move desk for better hearing, seeing, and monitoring, speak more slowly, speak louder, repeat, rephrase, redirect instructions and questions.

- Increase confidence, compassion, and cooperation.

- Use lots of examples, use "warm-ups," model, review, practice, practice, practice; I do one and you do one, I do part and you do part, provide patterns or steps to follow.

- Be patient and smile.

Advice from Special Educators for Substitute Teachers

Berks County Intermediate Unit
Reading, PA

In some cases, you may be assigned to teach in a special education "resource room" where all of the students have been identified as having special needs. In other cases, you may be teaching in a regular classroom where there are particular students with identified special needs. Whichever is the case, here are some thoughts on how to facilitate the learning of these students.

1. Respect is the key attitude for success with all students.

2. These students may have a variety of learning challenges. Do not think first of their special needs, but think of them first as learners.

3. All children respond to sincere encouragement, but don't overdo it. Be sensitive to the fact that learning is more difficult for these students than for many others.

4. Depending on the grade level you are teaching, these students may have experienced years of school failure. Be aware of this as you respond to their needs and work to help them find success.

5. Depending on the student's learning challenge, you may find you need to repeat yourself more often. Be patient. Check for student understanding after giving directions.

6. If there are problems, do not single out a child in front of the class, but deal with him/her privately.

7. Many children with special needs have Individualized Education Plans (IEPs). Consult these plans when available, as they provide structure for the students' learning. The teacher should have daily plans drawn from these IEPs.

8. You often may be privy to confidential information about students with special needs. It is critical that all information you obtain about students during your teaching day remain confidential. Depending on the grade level, students may feel self-conscious that you know they have learning challenges, this can set up a defensiveness on their part.

9. During your teaching day, you may need to locate yourself in close proximity to these children to offer assistance and help them stay focused. A gentle reminder will oftentimes suffice for them.

10. An instructional assistant or aide may be in the classroom. Such a person can be of tremendous help because they have a history with the students and are aware of routines, personalities, and other important background information.

11. Do not hesitate to ask for assistance from the principal or another teacher if you have concerns or questions during the day.

12. Carefully note the daily schedules for students with special needs. They often have support personnel (language or hearing specialists) who come into the classroom. At other times, they may leave the classroom to attend regular or special classes.

13. There may be specialized teaching equipment or machines in special education classrooms. Check with the instructional assistant, the principal, or another teacher before using these items.

14. Sometimes students are allowed to use certain learning aids to assist them with their work. Hopefully, the regular teacher will leave information instructing you as to which students may use the aids, and under what circumstances.

15. In some special education classes, behavior reports go home daily to parents that record the behavior of the child throughout the day. Become as familiar as possible with the system, or ask the assistant to focus on or give the feedback for the particular student(s) for the day.

16. In class discussions, if a student responds with an incorrect answer, provide clues or a follow-up question to help him/her think of the correct answer. Look for ways to praise students for their thinking and behavior as well as correct answers.

17. Present short and varied instructional tasks planned with students' success in mind.

18. Have on hand an ability-appropriate book to read, audio tapes, flash cards of facts, games, puzzles, mental math exercises, or other activities for substituting in these classes.

Gifted and Talented Students

Gifted and talented students usually have above average ability, a high level of task commitment, and highly developed creativity. Many children will excel in one of these areas. Truly gifted children will excel in all three.

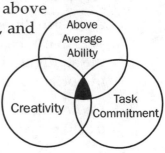

(Renzulli model)

You may have a gifted student if she or he...

_____ has a vocabulary noticeably above her or his peers

_____ is a voracious reader – usually more advanced content

_____ has a well-developed sense of humor – gets jokes peers don't understand

_____ is intrinsically motivated – works hard with or without teacher approval

_____ has a personal standard of quality – independent of others' work

_____ thinks at a higher/independent level – often appears to "day dream"

_____ is able to go beyond basic lesson concepts – expand, elaborate, and synthesize

Often, gifted and talented students seem to be round pegs in square holes. They do not necessarily fit the mold of an "ideal student." They may become bored with class or deeply involved with something unrelated to the lesson. Their friendships and alliances include a need for intellectual peers (often older students or adults) and chronological peers (kids their same age). Moreover, their attention span does not always coincide with the standard time allotted for classroom lessons and activities.

Some Do's and Don'ts When Working with Gifted and Talented Students

Do

✓ Enrichment and extension activities

✓ Puzzles and games

✓ Alternative projects (collages and posters are good)

✓ Comparisons, similes, and analogies

Don't

✗ Make them do things they've already mastered

✗ Give them busy-work if/ when they finish early

✗ Force them to always work with slower students

✗ Have them memorize, recite, and copy

Multiculturalism

The United States is home to a diverse population. No other nation enjoys the rich and varied cultural heritages found within our borders. Since this diversity is reflected in our schools, it only makes sense that our instructional methods should benefit from and be sensitive to the special abilities and needs of people from different groups.

Making your classroom multicultural friendly

General definitions of Terms

Ethnic Diversity:
Similarities and differences of groups of people classified according to common traits, values, and heritage. Examples may include food, clothing, music, and rituals.

Racial Diversity:
Similarities and differences of groups of individuals with certain physical or genetic features. These features may include skin color, body type, and facial features.

Cultural Diversity:
Similarities and differences of groups and/or individuals that align themselves with others based on common racial and/or ethnic characteristics or affiliations. Typical associations often include language, customs, and beliefs.

- Discuss various groups' heritage, values, and practices/rituals.

- Use local role models from various groups as guest speakers and advisors.

- Plan activities that use materials/objects that reflect various customs and cultures.

- Honor each student's unique background/heritage and how it enhances society's characteristics.

- Encourage discussion of current topics and how they relate to various groups within our society.

- Present stories and/or artifacts from different groups as a basis for various activities.

- Write stories, sing songs, draw pictures, or play games depicting various cultural influences.

- Showcase different groups' contributions and/or participation involving historical events, literary works, art, music, medicine, sports, and industry.

Showing respect for your students' heritage and beliefs— as well as your own— will encourage your class to be more accepting of you and others and will create a positive and cooperative learning environment.

Alternative Learning

We are all different. We look differently and we act differently. We also learn differently. Unfortunately, we tend to teach students as if they were all the same. We all know of people that can't bounce a ball, but can do math story problems in their heads—or the person with two left feet that can sing like a bird. No one can do everything, but most of us do excel in one or more areas. It is in these areas that we learn best. By using a variety of teaching methods and activities that incorporate these abilities, we can increase students' ability to stay on-task, pay attention, and enjoy learning.

Here are some main categories of skills and abilities with just a few examples of each:

Verbal/Linguistic
Reading/writing
Vocabulary
Speech

Logical/Mathematical
Calculation
Formulas
Codes

Visual/Spatial
Imagination
Patterns/designs
Sculpture/painting

Body/Kinesthetic
Dance
Drama
Sports/games

Interpersonal
Group work
Empathy
Cooperation

Intrapersonal
Self-reflection
Thinking strategies
Reasoning skills

Musical
Rhythms
Sounds/tones
Singing/playing

The following are ideas for new ways to teach "old" materials that might appeal to your students' particular abilities and interests:

Math

- Compose a song to help remember a formula
- "Illustrate" the problem on the board
- Solve the problem as a group

Language

- Act out the story
- Write key words using a code
- Listen with eyes closed

History

- Reenact a battle
- Write a commercial for that time period
- Do a mock interview of an historical person

Physical Education

- Research and play an historic game
- Keep score using Roman numerals or fractions
- Skip or hop instead of running

Running out of ideas?

Ask your students how they can turn a writing assignment into a math assignment, or how they can incorporate art into a soccer game. You'll be surprised at the results and your students will enjoy the challenge.

Evacuation and Other Out-of-Classroom Activities

In addition to regular classroom management, there are several special situations which you need to be aware of and prepared for. These situations include emergency and evacuation procedures, assemblies, playground and lunch duty, field trips, inclement weather days, and escorting students to the bus. As you review the following suggestions, keep in mind that you are the teacher, and as such, assume full responsibility for all of the students in your care.

Emergency and Evacuation Procedures

- Ask the district office for information about emergency action plans and protocol. Find out what to do in the event of fire, flood, earthquake, bomb threat, etc.

- Since every building and classroom is different, it is important to know where the nearest exit is and have a class list available to grab when you evacuate the building.

- If you hear the fire alarm or a message over the intercom, instruct the students to quickly and quietly leave the room in single file toward the designated exit door.

- Some classrooms now have an "emergency backpack" hanging by the door. If you see such a backpack, take it with you when you evacuate.

- After evacuating the building, use the class list to account for all of the students in your class.

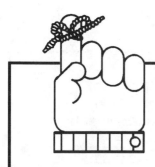

Most Important: Evacuate the students in your classroom and have a class list with you as you leave the building.

Assemblies/Pep Rallies

At first thought, an assembly seems like a pleasant break in the school-day routine. However, it can turn into a nightmare for a substitute teacher who does not have a plan for managing students during this activity. Here are some suggestions to help you survive the event with nerves still intact:

1. Find out the time and location of the assembly and whether or not the students will need to bring chairs from the classroom. In a middle or high school, you should also check to see how the regular class schedule will be altered to accommodate the assembly.

2. Talk to neighboring permanent teachers. Many schools have specific procedures for going to and returning from an assembly, as well as assigned seating for each class.

3. If such procedures exist, familiarize yourself with them and do your best to follow them.

4. If there are no established procedures, devise your own (walk in a single file line down the hall to the assembly, sit together as a class, return in a single file line, etc.).

5. Determine the specific behavior you expect during the assembly, with consequences and rewards dependent upon how these expectations are met. Beware of punishing the whole class for the misdeeds of a few. This can create a hostile environment with the students acting out against each other as well as you.

6. Teach or review with the students the procedures, expected behavior, and consequences or rewards associated with the activity.

Field Trips

A field trip is a method of providing students with first-hand learning opportunities. Field trips are often used to introduce or conclude a specific topic of study. As a substitute teacher called on the day of a field trip, you have many duties in order to successfully carry out the planned learning experience.

- Parental permission to participate in the field trip must be secured prior to the trip. Be certain that such permission, usually a signed release/consent form, has been obtained for each of the students in the class.

- Find out the school policy for any students who do not have documented parental permission to participate in the field trip. If a student without permission is required to remain at school, it is often arranged for them to attend another teacher's class.

- Student behavior is an important part of any educational experience. Prior to the trip reiterate with the students some do's and don'ts of expected behavior.

Do	Don't
* be courteous	* ask personal or irrelevant questions
* stay with the group	
* listen attentively	* lag behind
* follow safety regulations	* interrupt
	* take samples or touch, unless given specific permission to do so

- Since you will most likely be unfamiliar with the students, create name tags to be worn on students' shirts or coats. If you are visiting a location where there may be many school groups, use a distinctive shape or color for your students' name tags.

- Students should be assigned a travel partner and chaperones should be given a specific group of students with a list of their names. You may want to consider giving each chaperone's group a different color name tag.

- Safety precautions must be considered at all times. Take a first aid kit along.

SAFETY

- Count the number of students before leaving the classroom and often throughout the excursion, especially when loading and unloading buses or moving from one area to another.

- Students should have been informed of special things to look for and what they will likely see and hear on the trip. Familiarize yourself with the learning agenda, if possible, and use this information to facilitate student learning on the trip.

- Means of note-taking may have been planned for upper grade students. This may include using clipboards, taking notebooks, or completing specific note-taking sheets prepared for the trip. Do your best to carry out the plans left by the permanent teacher.

- Follow the planned time frame and sequence for the visit. Set aside time for note-taking, questions and answers, or sketching, as needed.

- Processing the trip is essential for true learning to take place. On the return trip or back at school, have students share what particular experiences interested them. You may also want to follow up with a summative writing assignment.

- Remember, you are responsible for the supervision and conduct of your students at all times, including on the bus and at the field-trip destination.

Playground and Lunch Duty

Being on playground or lunch duty involves more than just physically being in the vicinity of the students. Your job is to supervise their actions and activities to ensure a safe environment and experience. Take proactive measures to deter potential problem situations. Intervene before situations get out of control. Should a serious problem arise, don't hesitate to elicit help from another teacher or school administrator, or send a student to get this help. Never leave a group of students unsupervised.

Inclement Weather Days

In the event of inclement weather, schools often have different procedures for students during lunch and recess. Often teachers are expected to return to the classroom with students after lunch or keep them in the classroom during recess. Be sure to find out what is required of you so that your students are adequately supervised. Have several activity ideas in your *SubPack* to keep students constructively occupied in the classroom.

Escorting Students to the Bus

In some schools, you may be expected to escort students from the classroom to the bus. Find out exactly what is expected. Do you walk the entire class out and at what time? Do you need to stay in the bus loading area until the buses have left? What about students who don't ride a bus? Every school is different, and sometimes even classes within the same school have different bus policies. Do your best to find out what you need to do from the office, neighboring teachers, or students before the end of the day.

Teaching Strategies, Skills, and Suggestions

Chapter 4

Introduction

Have you ever had difficulty teaching the lessons left by the permanent teacher, tried to line up a class of 30 active second graders, or realized that you are spending a small fortune on good behavior rewards and thought to yourself, "there must be a better way?" There is! *Teaching Strategies, Skills, and Suggestions* is filled with tips and suggestions from the files of permanent and substitute teachers. It includes:

- Suggestions for the contents of your *SubPack*

- Strategies for presenting the permanent teacher's lesson plans:

    - Brainstorming

    - Concept Mapping

    - K-W-L

    - Cooperative Learning

    - Questioning

    - Effective Implementation of Audio Visual Materials

- Ideas for low cost/no cost rewards and motivators and many other helpful hints from experienced teachers who have been there, done that, and have some great advice to offer.

For additional information regarding Teaching Strategies, visit:

http:// subed.usu.edu

Suggested Contents For Your SubPack

Classroom Supplies

- ❏ Crayons
- ❏ Rubber bands
- ❏ Markers and/or colored pencils
- ❏ Labeled ball-point pens (red, blue, black)
- ❏ Pencils and small pencil sharpener
- ❏ Transparent and masking tape
- ❏ Scissors
- ❏ Glue sticks
- ❏ Paper clips, staples, a small stapler
- ❏ Post-it Notes® (various sizes and colors)
- ❏ Ruler
- ❏ File folders
- ❏ Calculator
- ❏ Lined and blank paper
- ❏ Name tag materials (address labels or masking tape will work)

Rewards/Motivators

- ❏ Mystery Box
- ❏ Tickets
- ❏ Certificates
- ❏ Stickers
- ❏ Stamp and Ink Pad
- ❏ Privilege Cards (get a drink, first in line, etc.)

Personal/Professional

- ❏ Clipboard
- ❏ Substitute Teacher Report
- ❏ District information (maps, addresses, phone numbers, policies, starting times, etc.)
- ❏ Coffee mug or water bottle
- ❏ Whistle (useful for P.E. and playground duty)
- ❏ Small package of tissues
- ❏ Snack (granola bar, pretzels, etc.)
- ❏ Individualized Hall Pass
- ❏ Small bag or coin purse for keys, driver's license, money (enough for lunch), and other essential items. Do not bring a purse or planner with a lot of money, checks, and credit cards (there may not be a secure place to keep it).
- ❏ Band-aids
- ❏ Small sewing kit with safety pins
- ❏ Disposable gloves and small plastic bags

Activity Materials

- ❏ The *Substitute Teacher Handbook*
- ❏ Tangrams
- ❏ Bookmarks
- ❏ "Prop" (puppet, stuffed animal, etc.)
- ❏ Picture and activity books
- ❏ A number cube or dice for games
- ❏ Estimation jar
- ❏ Newspaper
- ❏ Timer or stopwatch

SubPack

A *SubPack* is like an emergency preparedness kit for the classroom. It should contain a variety of useful and necessary classroom supplies and materials. The contents of a *SubPack* can be organized into four categories: Personal and Professional Items, Classroom Supplies, Rewards and Motivators, and Activity Materials. The specific contents of your *SubPack* will be personalized to fit your teaching style and the grade levels you most often teach.

SubPack Container

When selecting a container for your *SubPack*, choose one that is easy to carry, large enough to hold all of your supplies, has a secure lid or closure device, and looks professional.

SubPack Contents

Most of the suggested *SubPack* contents listed on page 70 are self-explanatory. The following is a brief explanation of some of the not-so-obvious items:

Clipboard: Carrying a clipboard will provide quick access to a seating chart, the roll, and anecdotal records, as well as convey a sense of authority.

Disposable Gloves & Plastic Bags: Whenever you encounter blood or bodily fluid you should wear disposable gloves to help safeguard against many of today's medical concerns. A plastic bag can be used in an emergency when you must dispose of items exposed to blood or bodily fluids.

Estimation Jar: Estimation jars are great motivators for students to behave appropriately and complete assignments efficiently so they can earn guessing tickets (see page 98).

Mystery Box: Place a common item such as a toothbrush or piece of chalk in a small box. Allow students to lift, shake, smell, and otherwise observe the box throughout the day. At the end of the day, have students guess what is in the box and award a small prize to the student who identifies the contents correctly.

Newspaper: A newspaper can be used as the basis for a story starter, spelling review, current events discussion, and a host of other activities (see page 209).

Props: A puppet, magic trick, or even a set of juggling props can capture student interest. Props provide great motivation to complete assignments in order to participate in, learn more about, or see additional prop-related activities.

Tangrams: Tangrams are geometric shapes that can be used as filler activities, as well as, instructional material to teach shapes and geometry (see page 128).

Tickets: Tickets are a great way to reward students for appropriate behavior. Students can use tickets to enter an end of the day drawing or redeem them for special privileges and prizes (see page 99).

A clipboard is one of the most important items in your SubPack.

Brainstorming

Brainstorming is an essential part of teaching creativity and problem-solving processes that form the basis for active learning. With younger children, it makes sense to compare a brainstorm to a rainstorm.

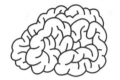

Can you feel and count the individual drops of rain in a rainstorm when the rain begins to fall? (Yes)

As the storm gets bigger and bigger, can you count the drops of rain? (No)

A brainstorm is like that too, only we are going to use our creative minds to think of many, varied, and unusual ideas; so many that we will hardly be able to write them down quickly enough.

There are four simple rules that help make the brainstorming process a peaceful and orderly one. Teach these **"DOVE"** rules to the students:

D Don't judge others' ideas—evaluation comes later.
O Original and offbeat ideas are encouraged.
V Volume of ideas—as many as possible in time limit.
E Everyone participates.

It is very common for students to run out of ideas in a short amount of time. This is called "hitting the wall." Help students keep thinking, because the most interesting, and unusual ideas, often come after the immediate and obvious ones have been expressed. You may have a student read their list in order to help others start thinking of new ideas. Remind students that it is okay to "piggyback" on someone else's ideas. Often a really unique idea from one person can spark another good idea from someone else.

It is important in brainstorming to limit the time. A shorter time limit is better than one that is too long. One to three minutes is usually about right, occasionally up to five minutes might be needed. It is better to start with a short time and extend the activity than to have the students lose interest.

Brainstorming can be very useful when teaching students about creativity. Brainstorming new and crazy uses for an object teaches students to be flexible in their thinking. The following examples work well:

• Brainstorm uses for a pencil.
• Brainstorm uses for a set of keys.
• Brainstorm all of the things that would be in the perfect classroom.

Brainstorming at the beginning of a lesson is a good way to introduce the lesson and assess what students know about the topic, as well as being a method of channeling their thinking in a specific direction.

Depending on the topic of the lesson, brainstorm attributes or facts that relate to the lesson:

- Brainstorm things that are red (or read).
  . . . things in your home that are man-made, things that are natural.
  . . . things in the classroom that are geometric shapes.
  . . . things that live in the ocean, names of birds or flowers, insects, folktales, etc.

Brainstorming is also very effective as one of the steps in problem-solving and solution-finding situations:

- What problems might you have if you came home from school and were locked out of the house?
- What might happen if an earthquake destroyed your city?
- What are a variety of ways that you can prepare for a test?
- What are some things you can say to friends who want you to smoke, drink alcohol, or take drugs?

Brainstorming can also be used to help children evaluate an idea. For example, brainstorm all of the possible consequences:

- What if a light bulb that lasted 20 years was invented?
- What if the sun didn't shine for a year?
- What if students were required to wear school uniforms?
- What if school buses were allowed to have advertising on them?
- What if you ran for school president and won?
- What if your mother let you eat all of the junk food you wanted?

After many ideas have been generated, use those ideas to advance the objectives of the lesson. For example, if you brainstormed the consequences of eating all of the junk food you wanted, a lesson on nutrition might follow.

Evaluation of brainstormed ideas should not happen during the brainstorming process. If someone says *"Boy, that won't work"* or *"That's a stupid idea,"* then ideas are squelched and some students will stop participating. If evaluation is a step you want to use, it comes later after all ideas have been freely given.

Concept Mapping

Like brainstorming, concept mapping can be used to introduce a topic. It can also be used to evaluate what students have learned at the conclusion of a lesson.

As an introductory exercise, concept mapping provides you with information regarding what the students already know. You won't waste time covering the material they are already familiar with and can concentrate your efforts on presenting new information.

As a follow-up activity, concept mapping illustrates the learning that has taken place. It is fascinating to compare pre-lesson concept maps with post-lesson concept maps. Both you and the students will be amazed at how much they have learned.

Example of a Concept Map:

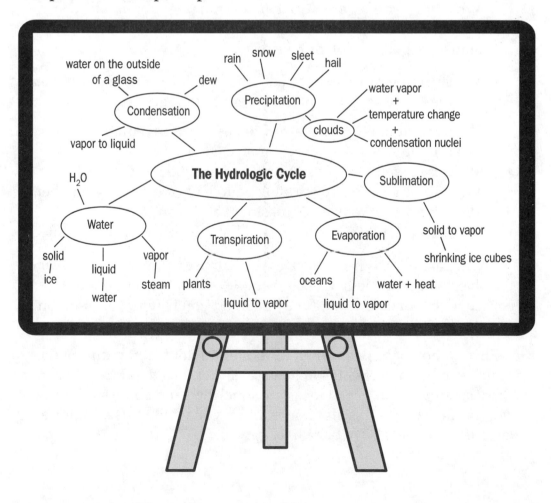

Concept mapping usually involves placing a word or idea in the middle of the board or on a piece of paper. Students then share what they know or associate with this concept. The information volunteered by the students is recorded with lines drawn to show how different concepts are related to one another. Concept maps can either be developed by the entire class, in small groups, or on an individual basis.

Concept mapping is also an effective method of reviewing information. It requires students to synthesize information they have read, heard, or observed and restate it in a concise manner using key words and terms which they understand. Once students have identified what they know in a concept map, another effective exercise is to have them incorporate examples and applications of the information into their map.

Both brainstorming and concept mapping can be used with any topic at any grade level. In either exercise, it is imperative that you, as the teacher, cultivate a risk-free classroom environment where students are not afraid to share their thoughts and ideas.

K-W-L

A major challenge of substitute teaching, particularly in the upper grades, is trying to teach a subject you know absolutely nothing about. One method of providing a meaningful learning experience in such a situation is the utilization of a K-W-L Chart. K-W-L stands for:

- "What do I **K**now?"

- "What do I **W**ant to know?"

- "What have I **L**earned?"

A K-W-L chart provides an outline for having students teach you. As you are being taught, the students will be teaching each other, and clarifying concepts in their own minds.

A lesson using K-W-L would begin by the teacher listing the letters K, W, and L across the top of the board. Under the appropriate letter would be written, "What do I know?" "What do I want to know?" and "What have I learned?" (see page 77). Generated by the students, the teacher lists facts which they know about the subject in the first column. In the second column, the teacher lists things students want to know or understand. A brief look at a student textbook will help to list "want to know" topics and ideas which students will be capable of addressing. Students are then asked to help answer and explain the items listed in the "W" column. Encouraging students to refer to their textbooks and other resources to answer your questions will help ensure that correct principles are being taught and explained.

South America

At the end of the time period or lesson, the students and the teacher complete the final column, listing what they have learned during the class, with students checking to make sure the "learned" information is correct.

An example of a K-W-L Chart that could be used for learning about volcanoes:

K What do I **Know**?	W What do I **Want** to know?	L What have I **Learned**?
1. Lava comes out of volcanoes. 2. There are volcanoes in Hawaii. 3. Volcanoes erupt. 4. The lava from volcanoes is hot. 5. Volcanoes can be dangerous.	1. What is lava? 2. Where does lava come from? 3. Where are most of the volcanoes in the world? 4. Why do volcanoes erupt? 5. etc.	1. Lava is melted rock. 2. When lava is still under ground, it is called magma. 3. etc.

An adaptation of this teaching method is to have students complete individual K-W-L charts (see page 78). This works well with assignments such as reading science chapters or watching videos. Before the activity, students write down what they know and what they want to/think they will learn during the activity. At the end of the activity, they complete the third column. A class discussion of the information students list in the third column will help clarify any confusing points and provide a review of the material covered.

K-W-L

K
What do I **Know**?

1.
2.
3.
4.
5.
6.
7.
8.
9.
10.

W
What do I **Want** to Know?

1.
2.
3.
4.
5.
6.
7.
8.
9.
10.

L
What have I **Learned**?

1.
2.
3.
4.
5.
6.
7.
8.
9.
10.

Cooperative Learning

Many teaching strategies and activities call for students to work together in small groups. This is often referred to as "cooperative learning." In cooperative learning, the teacher acts as a facilitator rather than a presenter. Students learn as they interact with and teach each other.

Outlined below are instructions for a simplified version of cooperative learning developed by Dr. Carolyn Andrews-Beck called "Bargain Basement Group Work."

1. Group students. Have students count off or form groups based on the seating arrangement. Do not let students self-select groups. Keep the groups small, usually between two and five students per group.

2. State the objective and instructions for the group work, then have students do the following:

    A. Circle—Arrange themselves in a small compact group so that they can all see everyone else's face.

    B. Introductions—Have students state their name to be sure everyone in the group knows each other.

    C. State the assigned task—The job is . . . .

        We will know we are done when . . . .

3. Set a time limit for the activity.

4. Have students begin working together toward accomplishing the objective outlined in step number two.

Assigning roles to students is also helpful in facilitating learning. By giving each member of the group a specific assignment, you guarantee their involvement. Students who are actively involved are more likely to learn.

Notes For The Teacher:

Successful implementation of the Cooperative Learning teaching strategy will be challenging if the permanent teacher has not already used it in the regular teaching routine.

Common Role Assignments

Director, Captain, Leader, or Manager: The group leader responsible for keeping the group members on-task and working towards the objective.

Recorder: Records information for the group's activities, fills out worksheets, or prepares written material from information provided by the group.

Materials Manager: Responsible for obtaining and returning equipment, materials, and supplies necessary for the activity.

Procedure Director: Reads instructions, explains procedures, makes sure the activity is being carried out correctly.

Clean-up Leader: Supervises the clean-up of the group's area at the end of the activity or project.

Setting Up a Cooperative Learning Activity in the Classroom

Group Students	Teacher: Starting with Cherice and going up and down the rows please count off one through five. Cherice: One Next Student: Two Next Student: Three, Etc. Teacher: I would like all of the "ones" to bring a pencil and paper and form a circle by the door. I would like all of the "twos" to bring a pencil and paper and form a circle by the bulletin board in the back of the room. I would like all of the "threes". . . . Please move to your assigned location and form a circle now.
State the Objective and Instructions for the Group	Teacher: In your groups you are going to make up a two minute skit about one of the reasons we have listed on the board why young people shouldn't start smoking. After you have made up the skit and had a chance to practice it, each group will present their skit for the rest of the class. Who can tell me what the assignment is? Noah? Noah: Use one of the reasons for not smoking on the board to make up a skit for the class. Teacher: How will you know when your group is done? Trish? Trish: After we have practiced our skit and are ready to present it to the class.
Set a Time Limit	Teacher: You will have 15 minutes to make up and practice your skit before we begin the class presentations.
Establish Roles and Have Students Begin Working	Teacher: Identify the person in your group who is wearing the most blue. This person will be the skit director, they are responsible for selecting a reason from the board and making sure everyone has a part in the skit. The person sitting to the right of the director will be the time monitor who makes sure your skit isn't more than 2 minutes long and that your group is ready to present in 15 minutes. Everyone else will help develop the skit and be actors. Are there any questions? . . . . O.K., you may begin.

Questioning

Good questions lead to good thinking—and good thinking leads to learning.

Good questions should:

- Be developed logically and sequentially
- Be adapted to students' abilities
- Cause students to think - not merely recite
- Encourage students to ask questions

Good questions will:

- Help keep students on-task and focused
- Help determine skill and knowledge levels
- Promote higher level thinking
- Encourage broader student participation

A Basic Rule . . . Ask, Pause, Call
Too often, good questions fail to be valuable because:

A. Teachers don't allow enough time for the questions to be answered. Teachers frequently ask a question and then go ahead and answer it themselves - students quickly learn that they do not have to think or respond.

B. Teachers fail to direct their questions to specific students. They give a question to the entire class which often makes it scary or "uncool" for any one student to volunteer to answer.

Using the (Ask, Pause, Call) method will increase the effectiveness of your questions.

ASK   A well thought out question to the class

PAUSE   Long enough for students to think about a response

CALL   On a specific student to respond to the question

Pauses Cause Them to Think

The 1ˢᵗ pause gives the entire class time to formulate an answer

The 2ⁿᵈ pause provides the student time to verbalize a response

The 3ʳᵈ pause encourages the student and/or class to really "get into" the question

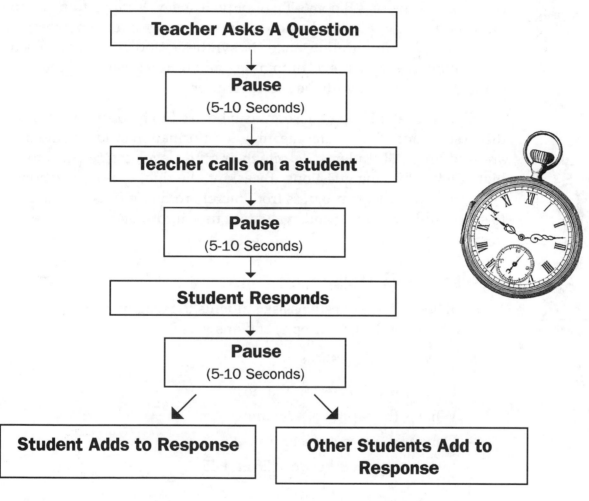

| Teacher Asks A Question |

↓

| **Pause** (5-10 Seconds) |

↓

| Teacher calls on a student |

↓

| **Pause** (5-10 Seconds) |

↓

| **Student Responds** |

↓

| **Pause** (5-10 Seconds) |

↙ ↘

| **Student Adds to Response** | **Other Students Add to Response** |

Do

✓ Be positive. Focus on what they DO know.

✓ Wait until the class is listening before asking a question.

✓ Ask questions in a clear direct manner.

✓ Expect an answer.

Don't

✗ Try to rush an answer (or simply answer it yourself).

✗ Use discouraging language (wrong, no-way, missed, etc.).

✗ Call on the same students (give others a chance).

✗ Automatically repeat questions (teach them to listen the *first* time).

Questions to Promote Higher Level Thinking

Effective questions keep students thinking and involved in the learning process. Dr. Benjamin Bloom divided thinking into six levels commonly known as Bloom's Taxonomy. The levels range from simple knowledge to complex evaluation in the following order: knowledge, comprehension, application, analysis, synthesis, and evaluation. Each level involves a higher level of thinking and thus a greater degree of student involvement with the subject matter.

Higher level thinking questions can be used to help stimulate class discussions and give greater meaning to information or ideas students are studying. All students, despite their grade level, can respond to higher level thinking questions. By asking the right type of questions, you can help students progress from merely recalling facts and figures, to successfully applying and evaluating new information in a variety of situations.

Knowledge Level Questions

Knowledge level questions ask students to recognize, recall, and state facts, terms, basic concepts, and answers.

Sample Knowledge Level Questions

- Name the characters in the story.
- What is the capitol of Wyoming?
- Define the word *condensation*.
- List the numbers between 23 and 45.

Comprehension Level Questions

Comprehension is the ability to understand concepts at a basic level. The student knows the meaning of the information, but does not relate or apply it to other situations.

Sample Comprehension Level Questions

- List three examples of plants.
- Describe the setting of the story.
- Classify the characters in the story as good guys or bad guys.
- Compare a cup of milk with a cup of water.

Application Level Questions

Application is the ability to use learned knowledge in particular and concrete situations. The student can apply rules, principles, and concepts in new and appropriate contexts.

Sample Application Level Questions

- Why is the sun important to life on Earth?
- Using what you have learned, how would you solve the following problem?
- How would schools be different if there was no electricity?
- How much money would you have if you saved a dollar a day for seven years?

Analysis Level Questions

Analysis is the ability to breakdown a concept into its component parts.

Sample Analysis Level Questions

- Why did the boy in the story give away his gold coin?
- Diagram the parts of a flower.
- Explain the differences between a raindrop and a snowflake?
- Which characters in the movie were necessary for the plot?

Synthesis Level Questions

Synthesis is the ability to put together elements or parts to form a whole. The student arranges and combines pieces to form a pattern, structure, or idea that was not clearly evident before.

Sample Synthesis Level Questions

- How could you change the characters' personalities to make them more likable?
- Design a new invention for . . .
- Organize the books you have read this year into three categories.
- Prepare a shopping list for Thanksgiving dinner.

Evaluation Level Questions

Evaluation is the ability to judge the value of materials, methods, or ideas. This level of thinking requires the highest level of intellectual functioning. It requires students to not only understand the material but to also make a judgment based on this understanding.

Sample Evaluation Level Questions

- Should students be allowed to bring cell phones to school?
- Would you recommend this book/movie to a friend? Why?
- How would the discovery of life on another planet affect the U.S. Space Program?
- Does the protection of endangered species justify the loss of job opportunities?

Verbs Often Used to Promote Higher Level Thinking

Level of Thinking	Typical Verbs Used	Examples of Teacher Questions
Knowledge	define draw repeat record label identify name list	*Name* the author of the book.
Comprehension	classify compare contrast translate explain summarize give examples	*Compare* the weather today with the weather yesterday.
Application	apply calculate complete demonstrate illustrate practice solve use predict show	*Complete* the sentence using a vocabulary word from the lesson.
Analysis	analyze classify discuss divide explain infer inspect	*Explain* why it is important to have classroom rules.
Synthesis	arrange combine construct create design develop generalize organize plan predict categorize rearrange	*Predict* what would happen if a law was passed which made commercials on TV illegal.
Evaluation	assess critique estimate evaluate judge rank rate recommend test value justify	What requirements for hiring a new teacher would you *recommend* to the principal?

Effective Implementation of Audio Visual Materials

Many times the lesson plans left by a permanent teacher will include the presentation of audio visual materials such as videos or filmstrips. While audio visual presentations do not thoroughly captivate students as they once did, they can still be an effective means of presenting content material. The key to encouraging learning during the presentation is to involve students as active, rather than passive, viewers. Listed below are five strategies for involving students and conducting effective audio visual presentations.

Keep the Lights On

A darkened classroom is an invitation for problems. As it dulls your mental alertness, it will embolden students to try and get away with things they would never attempt in broad daylight. A well-lit classroom is consistent with the traditional learning environment and makes it possible for students to take notes or complete assignments concurrent with the presentation.

Stand in the Back

Another critical aspect of audio visual presentations is what you as the teacher are doing. The students' job is to watch the presentation, your job is to monitor student behavior and learning during the presentation. Sitting behind the teacher's desk correcting papers or reading a book is not an effective means of doing this. Consider standing at the back of the room. Because you are already on your feet, you can easily move to problem areas in the classroom and, with proximity, stop problems before they start. By positioning yourself behind the students, they cannot see if you are paying attention directly to them; therefore, they must assume that you are and behave accordingly.

K-W-L

Use individual K-W-L charts such as the one found on page 78. Before the presentation, have students complete the first two columns indicating what they already know about the topic and what they think they will learn. As the video or filmstrip is presented, students write down information they are learning in the third column. After the presentation, have students share what they listed in the third column to create a comprehensive class list of the information that was presented.

Concept Mapping

Assign students to take notes during the presentation in the form of concept maps. Start by listing the topic of the video or filmstrip in the center of the page. As the presentation progresses, they should jot down key words and bits of information they are learning (see the sample concept map on page 74). At the end of the presentation, have students turn in their concept maps for teacher review or give a short quiz on the information during which students are allowed to refer to the concept maps they have constructed.

Question Exchange

Either during or after the presentation, have students write three questions which meet the following two criteria:

1. the answer to the question must have been given during the presentation,

2. the student writing the question must know the answer.

At the conclusion of the presentation, students exchange questions and try to answer them.

How Should I Do That?

When substituting, you are expected to cover the material outlined in the permanent teacher's lesson plan. However, sometimes lesson plan instructions are general and very nonspecific with regard to lesson presentation. Here are several techniques for presenting lesson plans that will cover the material in a positive and creative way.

Lesson Plan: *Have students read chapter 18 and answer questions.*

1. Pre-test and Post-test: Ask students to guess what will be covered before they start reading. Share ideas aloud and write down five facts or ideas as predictions. Afterward, conduct a post-test by checking the accuracy of their predictions.

2. Togetherness: Read the assignment out loud with students to find the answers. By making the assignment a class activity, you promote classroom cooperation.

3. Group Effort: Divide the class into groups and ask each group to report on part of the reading. This method is best used with material that does not require continuity to be meaningful.

4. Quiz Board: Give the assignment and tell the students that you will stop 15 minutes before the end of the class and establish a quiz board. Appoint three to five students or select volunteers to be members of the board. Ask them to come to the front of the room. The rest of the students pose questions to these students about the day's reading. After a certain number of questions have been answered, a new board may be selected. This technique works well for review. An added advantage is that you need not know the subject well in order to handle it.

Lesson Plan: *Have the class write a composition about X Y Z.*

1. Sentence Starters: To make any topic more meaningful, encourage students to relate to it personally. One way is to write sentence starters that use the students' natural speech pattern, such as, "I wish," "I like," "I'm glad I'm allowed to," "I think."

2. Whole Class: If the students are assigned to write a story, suggest that they first decide on a cast of characters, a setting, a time, etc., as a class. By doing the groundwork together, the students will be "into" the story before they lift a pencil.

3. Brainstorm: If the assignment is an essay, consider using a brainstorming technique. Ask students to say whatever comes to

mind about the topic and write their ideas on the board in some quick, abbreviated form. When everyone has had a chance to study the list, students can begin to write using whatever brainstorming ideas they wish.

4. <u>Free Association</u>: Whatever the topic, propose that the students write free association word lists about it. Tell them to start with the given word, such as "freedom," "pets," or "winter," and then add up to ten other words that immediately come to mind about the key word. Now the students can write their own compositions.

5. <u>Clarify Values</u>: Before students start to write, initiate a values clarification exercise that will help students relate an abstract subject to their own lives. For example, if the topic is "conservation of electricity," have the students start by listing five electrical gadgets or appliances they use, that they could do without. Record their answers on the board. From this specific exercise, the students can move on to the broader issue.

Lesson Plan: *The class has a test tomorrow. Have them study and review.*

1. <u>Games</u>: Try a game format for drill material, such as spelling, number facts, state capitals, and vocabulary. Use familiar games like tic-tac-toe, Jeopardy, Baseball, etc.

2. <u>Model Tests</u>: Have pairs or small groups of students make up model tests. Assign one group true and false questions, another multiple choice questions, etc. Spend the last part of the class going over the questions. Ask each group to read their test, while the rest of the class gives the answers.

3. <u>Students as Teachers</u>: Have the students teach each other:

    A. Give five minutes in which students are to write five to ten things they know about the material covered without opening their books or using their notes.

    B. Ask students to compare their list with the student next to them. In pairs, have them add additional items during the next ten minutes.

    C. Have the students remain in pairs and open their books and notes. Add to their lists using their notes and text during the next ten minutes.

D. Allow each student pair to join an adjacent pair and ask the groups of four to compare their lists and add additional information during the next ten minutes. Encourage students to discuss and clarify their knowledge.

E. In a full class discussion, have students consider all known knowledge. Allow students to ask questions of one another and have knowledgeable students clarify misunderstandings.

Lesson Plan: *Discuss topics A B C with class.*

1. <u>Students take Lead</u>: Have a student lead the discussion, or call on two or three students.

2. <u>Speak their Minds</u>: Have the class spill out all sorts of ideas related to the discussion topic. Do not judge the ideas - anything goes! Just encourage the students to speak their minds. After about five minutes, start the discussion again, this time arranging their ideas in a more orderly fashion.

3. <u>Debate</u>: If the topic is controversial, divide the class into sections, each representing a special-interest group. During the discussion, each group will give its point of view on the subject.

Lesson Plan: *Show the film or filmstrip, then discuss.*

1. <u>Pre-test and Post-test</u>: To heighten student interest in the audio visual materials, use the pre-test and post-test technique. Introduce the activity with a comment such as, "If you were making a movie about crocodiles, earthquakes, or China, what would you include?" As they watch, have students check their lists against the film. How does the film compare to the students' expectations?

2. <u>Questions</u>: As students watch, have them write down three questions that are answered in the film or video, then discuss the questions with the class after the presentation.

For additional audio visual suggestions, see page 88.

Verbal Guidance

Throughout the day a teacher will need to convey instructions, warnings, directions, reprimands, and encouragement to students. Of the many ways to convey these messages, the most common is by speaking directly to the student or students. To be most effective, verbal guidance should be brief, firm, and positive.

SAY:	DO NOT SAY:
Talk in a quiet voice.	Don't shout.
Use both hands when you climb.	You will fall if you don't watch out.
Climb down the ladder.	Don't jump.
Keep the puzzle on the table.	Don't dump the puzzle pieces on the floor.
Turn the pages carefully.	Don't tear the book.
Be sure the ladder is safe.	Be careful, you might fall.
Sit on your chair.	Don't rock in your chair.
Time to go inside.	Are you ready to go inside?

You will find it necessary to acquire techniques in keeping with your personality. However, the following general rules should be observed.

DO

1. Speak in a calm, kind voice.

2. Speak directly to the student, do not call across the room.

3. Speak in short, meaningful sentences which the student can understand.

4. Try to express your request in a positive way.

5. Keep your voice and facial expressions pleasant.

DO NOT

1. Make fun of the student.

2. Give students a choice if they cannot have one.

3. Compare one student with another, *"Look at how many questions Susan has completed."*

Adapted from: "Guidance of the Young Child," by Louise M. Langford.

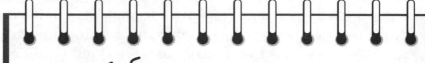

Advice from Students

- Trust us.
- Be fair to everyone.
- Punish only the troublemakers.
- Make learning fun.
- Give us our assignment and let us go to work.
- Allow study time in class.
- Show concern and be willing to help with assignments.
- If I raise my hand, don't ignore me.
- You can be both strict and nice.
- Don't yell.
- Be straightforward with us.
- Be organized.
- Speak quietly and be patient.
- Give us something to work toward.
- Leave your personal life at home.
- Think positively of every student.
- Speak clearly.
- Be reasonable in your expectations.
- Have a sense of humor.
- Follow through with promises and consequences.

101 Ways to Say "Good Job!"

Everyone knows a little praise goes a long way in the classroom. Whether it is spoken or written at the top of a student's paper, praise reinforces good behavior and encourages quality work. But the same traditional phrases used over and over can sound rehearsed and become ineffective. Here are 101 variations of ways to give praise, show interest, and offer encouragement:

1. You've got it made.
2. Super!
3. That's right!
4. That's good!
5. You are very good at that.
6. Good work!
7. Exactly right!
8. You've just about got it.
9. You are doing a good job!
10. That's it!
11. Now you've figured it out.
12. Great!
13. I knew you could do it.
14. Congratulations!
15. Not bad.
16. Keep working on it; you're improving.
17. Now you have it.
18. You are learning fast.
19. Good for you!
20. Couldn't have done it better myself.
21. Beautiful!
22. One more time and you'll have it.
23. That's the right way to do it.
24. You did it that time!
25. You're getting better and better.
26. You're on the right track now.
27. Nice going.
28. You haven't missed a thing.
29. Wow!
30. That's the way.
31. Keep up the good work.
32. Terrific!
33. Nothing can stop you now.
34. That's the way to do it.
35. Sensational!
36. You've got your brain in gear today.
37. That's better.
38. Excellent!
39. That was first class work.
40. That's the best ever.
41. You've just about mastered that.
42. Perfect!
43. That's better than ever.
44. Much better!
45. Wonderful!
46. You must have been practicing.
47. You did that very well.
48. Fine!
49. Nice going.
50. Outstanding!
51. Fantastic!
52. Tremendous!
53. Now that's what I call a fine job.
54. That's great.
55. You're really improving.
56. Superb!
57. Good remembering!
58. You've got that down pat.
59. You certainly did well today.
60. Keep it up!
61. Congratulations, you got it right!
62. You did a lot of work today.
63. That's it!
64. Marvelous!
65. I like that.
66. Cool!
67. Way to go.
68. You've got the hang of it!
69. You're doing fine.
70. Good thinking.
71. You are learning a lot.
72. Good going.
73. I've never seen anyone do it better.
74. That's a real work of art.
75. Keep on trying!
76. Good for you!
77. Good job!
78. You remembered!
79. That's really nice.
80. Thanks!
81. What neat work.
82. That's "A" work.
83. That's clever.
84. Very interesting.
85. You make it look easy.
86. Excellent effort.
87. Awesome!
88. That's a good point.
89. Superior work.
90. Nice going.
91. I knew you could do it.
92. That looks like it is going to be a great paper.
93. That's coming along nicely.
94. That's an interesting way of looking at it.
95. Out of sight.
96. It looks like you've put a lot of work into this.
97. Right on!
98. Congratulations, you only missed . . .
99. Super-Duper!
100. It's a classic.
101. I'm impressed!

The Line Up!

30 ways to get elementary kids in a row

Line up if you can tell me...

1. a safety rule for home or school: don't play with matches ...
2. the name of a state: Missouri, Kansas, Colorado, New Mexico ...
3. the name of a country: Scotland, Canada, India, Italy ...
4. your favorite subject in school ...
5. your favorite place to visit: the woods, the ocean, the park, the gym ...
6. a book title, author, character, illustrator ...
7. a kind of fruit: banana, plum, grapes ...
8. a kind of vegetable: lettuce, beans, corn ...
9. a type of tree: oak, maple, weeping willow, elm, lilac ...
10. a type of flower: rose, tulip, daisy, iris, marigold ...
11. a hobby or collection: gardening, stamps, stickers, dolls, biking, shells ...
12. an animal in the zoo: an ostrich, panda, monkey, rattlesnake...
13. an animal on a farm: rooster, goat, pig, cow, hen, duck ...
14. your address, phone number, birthday ...
15. one thing you learned in school this week ...

Line up if you have...

16. a tooth missing, two teeth, three, four ...
17. blue as your favorite color, purple, orange ...
18. a T-shirt on, short sleeves, long sleeves ...
19. a ribbon in your hair, a watch on your left arm ...
20. a "Z" in your name, a "B," an "F," a "Q" ...
21. a birthday in January, February, March ...
22. sneakers on, boots, sandals ...
23. two people in your family, three, four ...
24. a pet dog, cat, bird, fish, turtle, horse ...
25. striped socks on, pink socks, brown socks ...
26. helped parents mow the lawn, wash the car, clean the kitchen ...
27. blue eyes, brown eyes, hazel, black ...
28. been to a hospital for tonsils, broken bones, to visit a friend ...
29. written a poem, story, song, play ...
30. stood on your head, played tag, skipped rope, raced ...

Low Cost/No Cost
Rewards and Motivators

In the ideal classroom, all students would be intrinsically motivated to behave appropriately and work hard on every assignment. However, this is not usually the case. Many substitute teachers experience success in motivating classes by providing rewards throughout the day. The following are ideas for low and no-cost rewards and motivators.

- **Certificates** Photocopy blank certificates (see pages 99-100) to be filled out and given to exceptional students, groups, or the entire class at the end of the day or as prizes for classroom activities.

- **Pencils and Paper Clips** Colorful variations of these school supply basics are well received at any grade level as contest prizes. They can often be purchased very inexpensively at discount and dollar stores.

- **Stickers** These can be given intermittently throughout the day to students who are on task or placed on completed assignments to denote outstanding work.

- **Tickets** Throughout the day, students can be given tickets for being on-task, cooperating, and following directions. These good behavior tickets are then turned in for a drawing to win a special prize prior to going home (see page 99).

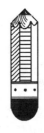

- **Candy** Always a favorite, but be cautious when using it. Some students may have health conditions which do not allow them to enjoy this reward. In addition, many state health codes require that candy be commercially manufactured and individually wrapped. If you do give out candy in the classroom, be sure that the wrappers are disposed of properly.

- **Extra Recess Time** Being allowed five extra minutes of recess can provide tremendous motivation for many students. Be sure to check with the principal or neighboring teacher beforehand to make sure that this reward will not interfere with the schedule of anyone else in the school.

- **Privilege Cards** Individual students can be rewarded for good work or appropriate behavior with special privileges. You can make privilege cards that entitle students to things such as being first in line, getting a drink, being the teacher's assistant for an activity, choosing the end of the day activity, etc. (see page 100). When the student redeems the privilege, collect the card and put it back in your *SubPack* for your next assignment.

- **Fun Activity** The promise of a fun activity later in the day can motivate students for hours. The activity might be a *Five Minute Filler* or *Short Activity* from this book, or any other activity you think they would enjoy. Remember, being "fun" is usually anything that is different from the routine of an ordinary day.

- **Story Time** One successful substitute teacher uses the promise of a story at the end of the day to motivate classes. She brings to school an old pop-up book about a dinosaur. At the beginning of the day, the word "DINOSAUR" is written on the board. A letter is erased each time the students are off-task or behaving inappropriately. At the end of the day if there is any of the word "DINOSAUR" still left on the board, they get to hear the story. Second-hand book stores are a good place to look for inexpensive books that your students will not have seen before.*

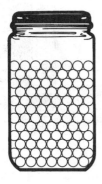

- **Estimation Jar** Fill a jar with pennies, marbles, beans, or rubber bands. Recognize students who are on task, setting a good example, or working hard, by giving them a slip of paper to write their name and guess the number of items on. The more times they are recognized for good behavior throughout the day the more chances they will have to "guess." At the end of the day, reveal the total number of items in the jar and award a prize to the student whose guess was the closest.

- **Talk Time** Middle school students really like moving to another seat and being allowed to sit and talk with friends during the last five minutes of class. To ensure an orderly classroom, you may need to insist that students select their new seat and then not be allowed to get up until class is over. Elementary students also enjoy this activity while waiting to go to lunch or at the end of the day.

Notes For The Teacher:

Establish rewards and motivators not as "bribes to be good" but as "goals" that students can work toward and achieve through good behavior and diligent effort.

Submitted by Marilyn Machosky of Sylvania, Ohio

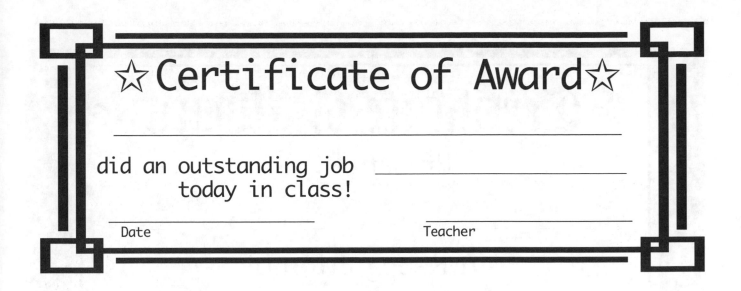

☆ Certificate of Award ☆

_____

did an outstanding job
today in class!   _____

_____   _____
Date   Teacher

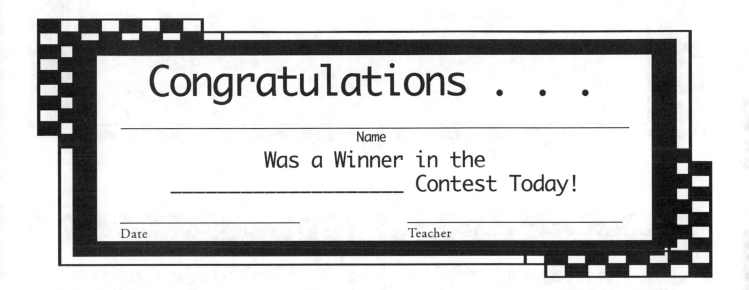

Congratulations . . .

_____
Name

Was a Winner in the
_____ Contest Today!

_____   _____
Date   Teacher

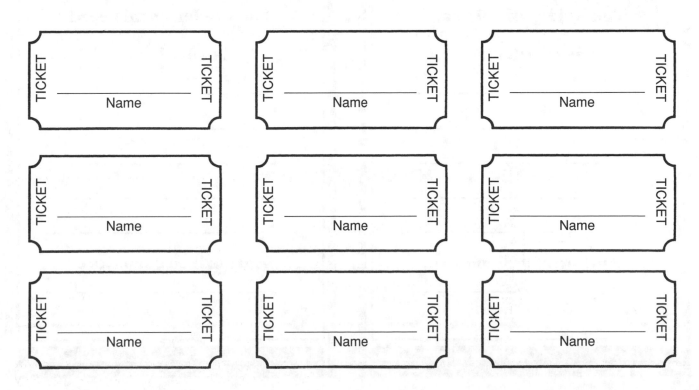

TICKET   TICKET
_____
Name

TICKET   TICKET
_____
Name

TICKET   TICKET
_____
Name

TICKET   TICKET
_____
Name

TICKET   TICKET
_____
Name

TICKET   TICKET
_____
Name

TICKET   TICKET
_____
Name

TICKET   TICKET
_____
Name

TICKET   TICKET
_____
Name

✫ Certificate of Award ✫

Presented to

_____

In Recognition of

_____

Date _____   Teacher _____

✫ Privilege Card ✫

The holder of this card
is entitled to

_____

_____

_____

_____

_____

Authorized Signature

_____

✫ Privilege Card ✫

The holder of this card
is entitled to

_____

_____

_____

_____

_____

Authorized Signature

_____

Substitute Hints and Suggestions

1. Know the teacher next door. Introduce yourself so you can call on someone to answer questions about schedules or material for the class throughout the day.

2. When students need to go to the restroom or the library, send only one student at a time. When the first one returns, a second one may go.

3. If there is not a seating chart left by the teacher, quickly make one. It is much easier to maintain discipline when you can call students by name.

4. If a student doesn't respond when you call him/her by name, you may suspect the students have switched seats. Tell them it is better if you have their correct names so the wrong student doesn't get in trouble and written about to the permanent teacher.

5. Do not let students start any name calling or being rude to other students. It is much easier to stop a verbal disagreement than pushing or fighting.

6. Try to be in the hall between classes. It is a good idea to stand in the doorway so you can keep one eye on the hallway traffic and one eye on students coming in the classroom. If the students see a teacher, they are less likely to behave inappropriately.

7. Have a couple of extra pens or pencils with you for students who have "forgotten" and would rather go to their lockers and walk the halls than be in class.

8. If you give a student a pen or pencil and would like it back, be sure to ask the student for his lunch card, or something of value that s/he will be sure to remember they want back. Many students just forget that it isn't their pen.

9. Try to identify the names of one or two trustworthy students who will tell you the truth and help out in class.

10. Never let a class go early for lunch or the next class unless the teacher for whom you are substituting or the teacher next door says it is okay. Some schools have very strict rules about the number of students in the cafeteria/hallways at a time.

11. Never let a student have a pen without an ink cartridge. It might be used as a spit ball thrower.

12. Establish your rules and expectations very clearly at the beginning of the day.

13. Do not let students use a phone in the classroom. Have them use the phone in the office.

14. Do not discuss the teacher's class with other people, especially out of school. You are a professional and shouldn't discuss individual students or problems.

15. If you need to talk to someone about a problem, talk to the principal.

16. Be neat in your appearance.

17. Follow the lesson plans the teacher has left. Incorporate your own ideas if there is extra time.

18. Correct the students' work for the day if possible.

19. Even though a few students can upset your plans, try to find out the names of students who have been good or helpful and let the teacher know about them also.

20. Most students will acquiesce to your leadership, but there will be some who will question your plans or authority. It is better not to argue. Instead say, *"I know this may not be the way Mr. Smith does it, but this is the plan for today."*

21. If you are not sure how the teacher wants an assignment done, ask another teacher or develop your own plan. Then be sure to leave a note for the permanent teacher explaining what you assigned.

22. Be assertive so students don't feel they can manipulate your decisions and authority. Use statements such as:

> I need you to start reading now.
>
> I want everyone to pass their papers forward.
>
> I don't need...
>
> I don't want...

23. Don't let students manipulate you by protesting or saying, *"We never do that!"* Calmly tell them, *"I understand, but today we will read aloud instead of silently."*

24. Walk around the room. Don't just sit by the desk, especially during independent work, or a test. Students will be less likely to talk or cheat when you are close by them.

25. Don't let students wear hats during a test. Sometimes they have been known to write answers in the brim.

26. Don't try to catch a student by grabbing an arm or clothes. They could fall and you could twist his/her arm, or rip his/her clothes.

27. Don't let any student possess a knife or any other weapon. Report suspected violators to the principal's office or send a reliable student to the office.

28. Do not touch the blood of a bleeding child. Use a napkin, towel, or a cloth to cover the cut. Whenever possible, have the student treat the injury until the proper individuals have been notified.

29. If a teacher has classroom sets that are used by the students, be sure to have them all returned before the entire class leaves. It is easier to locate one book or calculator in a class of 30 than trying to find it in the whole school. Hopefully, the calculators or books are numbered and have been assigned in a given order so you know who has the missing book.

30. Don't make statements lightly — "Students remember!"

Thank you for coming today!

Getting a . . .

Many substitute teachers are working toward the goal of getting a permanent teaching assignment and classroom of their own. If you are such a substitute, below are some suggestions that might help.

- **Be Proactive**

  Meet with principals and district personnel early in the year to let them know that you are excited about working in the district and hope, at some point, to be offered a permanent teaching position. Let your intentions be known.

- **Be Available**

  Districts are looking for people on whom they can depend. Once you have signed up to substitute, try to be available to teach whenever you are needed. Your willingness to fill in at the "last minute" will make a lasting, favorable impression on those who will be making personnel decisions later in the year.

- **Be Professional**

  You are a teacher in the school district. You should act, dress, and speak appropriately. Arrive early and stay late. Volunteer to help with after school activities. If your intentions to become a permanent teacher are known, you will be evaluated for this position in everything you do and say throughout the school year.

- **Avoid Criticism**

  Anything negative you say about a school, principal, or teacher will eventually come back to haunt you. Stay positive and compliment those around you whenever possible. If you can't say anything nice, don't say anything at all.

. . . Permanent Job!

- **Be Confident**

  Walk tall, teach with confidence, but don't be overbearing.

- **Evaluations**

  When appropriate, ask for positive evaluation forms or letters of support/recognition to be filed at the district office. Many times only negative evaluations are filled out and sent in.

  In some districts, up to 25 percent of the new hires come from the substitute pool.

- **Learn From Experience**

  Don't assume that one bad experience or evaluation will take you out of the running. Learn from the experience, ask for advice from other teachers or principals.

- **Grow Professionally**

  Attend workshops sponsored by the district. Some districts even invite substitute teachers to attend professional development workshops scheduled for permanent teachers. You may also consider subscribing to current education journals or magazines. This illustrates that you are serious about a career in education and want to stay current with what is happening in the profession. Check with media center personnel for subscription information.

- **Get To Know The District**

  One of the most commonly used phrases in prospective teacher interviews is, *"Are you familiar with . . ."* By illustrating your knowledge of special programs, textbooks, or the mission statement of a district, you show that you are interested and up-to-date with what is going on in the district. Applicants who are familiar with district programs and practices have a better chance at getting a job.

Fill-In
Activities

Chapter 5

Can you come
back
tomorrow?

Fill-In Activities

Introduction

As a substitute, it can be difficult to see the big picture and how a particular assignment or activity fits into the teacher's overall plan, but the teacher expects students to complete the work and it is your job to see that it gets done. The fill-in activities and lessons you bring should be used only when the assigned work is completed, or the plans are unable to be carried out.

There will be situations when the permanent teacher, for some reason, cannot leave lessons plans, when the plans left are impossible to decipher, or activities are too short for the time available. These situations leave you with the challenge of filling class time with manageable and worthwhile activities. Every substitute should have some "tried and true" activities that work in a variety of situations. Such activities can be found in this book and kept in your *SubPack*. They will keep the students occupied and learning at the same time.

The activities and lessons in this chapter are not intended to replace the lesson plans of the permanent teacher, but rather to supplement them in three specific ways. *Five-Minute Fillers*, *Early Finishers*, and *Short Activities* are three types of fill-in activities. *Five-Minute Fillers* are whole class, teacher directed activities for those few extra minutes which often occur throughout the school day. *Early Finisher Activities* are for when individual students finish assignments early and need something constructive to do. *Short Activities* include lesson plans and activities that can be completed in 20 to 40 minutes.

Visit The Professional Substitute Teacher Website and test your knowledge at:

http://subed.usu.edu

In the beginning of this chapter you will be introduced to each type of activity. Following the introduction, the chapter is organized according to content area where you will select activities to meet your needs as a substitute teacher. Note that most activities can be adapted as needed for use as *Five-Minute Fillers*, *Early Finishers*, or *Short Activities*.

Suggestions for Implementing Activities and Lessons

- Many of the activities and lessons in this book indicate an approximate time needed to complete the activity. However, these are guidelines only. These lessons can be adapted for grade levels other than those suggested and the time needed to complete each activity will vary with the age and ability of the students.

- Contents are arranged by topic, however, many lessons are appropriate for several different subjects. By familiarizing yourself with all of the lessons, you will be able to make the best use of everything this book has to offer.

- The worksheets and activities in this chapter are designed to stimulate thinking, provide practice in deduction, as well as to enhance the standard core curriculum. Try to convey them as an opportunity to learn something new, rather than as an evaluation of what students already know.

- Consider letting students work in groups to complete assignments, or work independently then in groups for the last five minutes. This removes some of the extreme pressure students feel to get the "right" answer.

- When using worksheets, prepare the students with a discussion or brainstorming activity before handing them out. If their minds are in gear and they are already thinking about the topic, they will learn more as they process the information on the page.

- If you don't have the time or resources to photocopy student worksheets, consider completing them orally. Read the questions aloud and then allow students to respond. The material can be adapted to fit any time frame using this presentation style.

- Be specific in your instructions. If the assignment should be done without talking, say, "Work Silently," if it needs to be completed in 15 minutes let the students know.

- Allow enough time to check answers or share results at the end of an activity or assignment. If this is not possible, at least leave an answer key with the permanent teacher for students to check their work the next day.

- Answers for students to check their own work can be provided in a number of ways. The teacher can read them aloud at the end of the activity. An answer key can be taped to a desk or wall for students to consult, or answer keys can be photocopied and distributed when students finish the assignment.

- Always evaluate student work before returning it to them. Even just a couple of words at the top of the page recognizes student effort and validates the worth of the assignment.

- If you gave the assignment, it's your responsibility to correct and evaluate the students' work.

- Summarizing the activity helps to ensure that learning has taken place. One simple way to do this is to have students, or groups, take turns stating one new thing they learned from the activity.

- If handouts are used from your *SubPack*, ask if you may use the photocopy machine in the office to replenish your supply.

© Substitute Teaching Institute/Utah State University

Of Special Note

In many of the lesson plans that follow, the last procedure is *"hand in work for teacher evaluation."* It is important that you, the teacher for that lesson, note some type of evaluation on the students' papers. Often it will work out so you can evaluate and return papers to students before they go home. Other times it may take a few minutes after school to make a note on the papers and leave them for the permanent teacher to distribute. In either case it is important that *you,* the teacher who assigned the work, be the one to evaluate it. This validates the students' work and helps them feel like the assignment had a purpose. If you simply leave the papers for the permanent teacher they will probably be either handed back without an evaluation or perhaps even thrown away. In either case, the students will come to believe that assignments they do with a substitute teacher are not really important because no one took the time to look at their work and comment about it. A stamp, a sticker, or a few positive words at the top of the page is all it takes to make students feel good about their efforts.

Evaluating student work validates student effort.

101 Ways to Get to the Zoo

by Devan Williams

Very creative ideas!
Nice Work!

1. Walk

2. Take the subway

3. Ride your bike

4. On a motorcycle

5. Skate board

6. Ride a horse

7. Dog sled

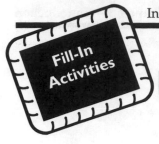
Fill-In Activities

Five-Minute Fillers

This type of filler activity is designed to use critical thinking in order to keep an entire class attentive and involved during those last five minutes before lunch, to get everyone re-focused after recess, or at any other odd moments that occur throughout the day. Students can complete *Five-Minute Filler* activities independently, in groups, or as a whole class. These fillers can also be developed to introduce, enhance, or compliment the lesson for the day. The next two pages are examples of *Five-Minute Filler* activities. You will find numerous activities that can be used as *Five-Minute Fillers* throughout the rest of this chapter.

Quick Fillers

Grades 2-12

These lists may be created orally or verbally. You may have the students brainstorm as a class, or have them create individual lists.

1. How many different languages can you name?

2. Scramble five vocabulary words from today's lesson, trade with someone, and unscramble them.

3. Make a list of the 10 largest animals you can think of.

4. List as many breakfast cereals as you can.

5. Write down all of the different places you find sand.

6. List as many U.S. presidents as you can.

7. List as many states and their capitals as you can.

8. Name as many holidays as you can think of.

9. Write down all of the different flavors of ice-cream you can.

10. Name as many countries of the world as you can.

11. List all of the forms of transportation you can think of.

12. Name as many teachers at the school as you can.

13. Name the different sections of a newspaper.

14. Name all of the states that have the letter "E" in them.

15. Name all of the different types of musical instruments you can.

Number Phrases

Copy one or more of the abbreviated phrases below on the board, then challenge students to guess the phrase. (see answers below)

A.   26 - L. of the A.

B.   7 - W. of the W.

C.   54 - C. in a D. (with the J.)

D.   88 - P. K.

E.   18 - H. on a G. C.

F.   90 - D. in a R. A.

G.   4 - Q. in a G.

H.   24 - H. in a D.

I.   11 - P. on a F. T.

J.   29 - D. in F. in a L. Y.

K.   76 - T. L. the B. P.

L.   20,000 - L. U. T. S.

M.   7 - D. of the W.

N.   12 - E. in a D.

O.   3 - B. M. (S. H. T. R.!)

ANSWERS:

A.   26 letters of the alphabet

B.   7 wonders of the world

C.   54 cards in a deck (with the Joker)

D.   88 piano keys

E.   18 holes on a golf course

F.   90 degrees in a right angle

G.   4 quarts in a gallon

H.   24 hours in a day

I.   11 players on a football team

J.   29 days in February in a Leap Year

K.   76 trombones lead the big parade

L.   20,000 leagues under the sea

M.   7 days of the week

N.   12 eggs in a dozen

O.   3 blind mice (see how they run!)

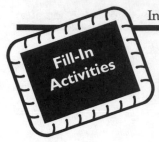

Early Finishers

In every class, every day, there will be several students who finish their assignments early. With nothing to do, even "good" students may behave inappropriately and disrupt the work of the whole class. The following sample activities are designed to keep "early finishers" involved in constructive activities that won't disrupt the rest of the class. They also provide great motivation for students to work hard, and finish their assignments so they can participate in these fun activities. After reviewing the next four pages of examples of *Early Finishers* you will find additional activities integrated into the content section of chapter 5. The implementation of *Early Finishers* will enable you to maintain a positive learning environment for students.
As you select activities to use as *Early Finishers*, remember to adjust each activity to meet the situational and individual needs of students.

At The Back Of The Room

- Set up a puzzle that students can work on throughout the day.

- Set up a reading corner where students can go and read silently after they have finished an assignment.

- Tangram puzzles (see page 128).

Name _____

All About Me

1. Draw a picture of your family.

2. Write the names of four friends in your class.

3. Draw three clocks. Show:
   A. when you got up.
   B. when you eat lunch.
   C. when you go to bed.

4. Draw a car using only circles.

5. Write the numbers counting by 5's to 50.

6. Write a sentence using six words that start with the letter B.

7. Make a list of everything you ate yesterday.

8. Close your eyes. Listen! Write down six things you hear.

9. What is your favorite color? List 5 things that color.

10. Write down 10 things you would like to get for your birthday.

11. If you were the teacher what would you do?

12. Write the numbers backwards from 25 to 0.

13. Write down 7 things that start with the same letter as your first name.

14. Draw an animal using only triangles.

15. Write down 5 things you will use today that start with the letter T.

16. How old are you?

17. If you smiled at everyone you saw for one whole day, what do you think would happen?

18. Write the days of the week.

19. What is your favorite animal?

20. If you could do anything you wanted, what would you do today?

NAME _____

Spot 20

Grades
6-12

Lulu is away at camp. She wrote the following letter to her best friend, after curfew, by the light of a flashlight, under the covers last night. Usually a very good writer, she made a few writing errors (20 to be exact) in her letter. Can you spot and circle all twenty errors?

July 12, 2002

Dear Emily;

Greatings from camp! You would not believe the awful time I am having! The first day, my bags were run over by the bus as it pulled out of the parking lot. All of the chips I had packed for late night snacks were crushed to dust and deposited throughout my clothes. It was an omen of badd things to come.

That night it rained, and wouldn't you know it, my cot was positioned directly below a leak in the cabin roof? Need less to say I woke up soggy and I've been sneezing ever since. By the time I hanged up my wet blankets and made it to breakfast, the only foold left was cold pancakes and orange juice with unidentified floating objects in it. Ugh!

The first morning we spent most of the time at the lake. Other than the fact that the water was icey cold, our canoe capsized, and my glases are now quietly resting somewhere at the bottom of Lake Wet. It was tons of fun! That afternoon I went on a nature hike. I can now identify two kinds of pinetrees, a three varieties of wild flowers, an edible berry, and poison oak. The poison oak I studied up close and personal, which left me trying not to scratch for the rest of of the evening.

The secon night passed without incident, unless you want to count the family of mice that spent the dark hours traversing the cabin floor to raid the cookies someone had left out. They were actully kindof cute.

Today it rained so we had to spend the entire day in the lodge. In the morning I tried to make a bird house out of craft sticks. It turned out looking more like a condemmed building than anything a bird would ever want to live in. I spent the afternoon learning how to weave a basket. It was looking great until the person next to me accidentally sat on it. After dinner we learned camp songs. you know, the kind that once you get in your head you can't get rid of. So now I'm breaking curfew to write to you from under my covers to the tune of "Row Row Row You Boat.

Just two more weeks and this joyous adventure will be over! I'll give you a call when I get home, if I survive that long

See you soon,

Lulu

SPOT 20
ANSWER KEY

Corrections in **BOLD**

July 12, 2002

Dear Emily**,**

Greetings from camp! You would not believe the awful time I am having! The first day, my bags were run over by the bus as it pulled out of the parking lot. All of the chips I had packed for late night snacks were crushed to dust and deposited throughout my clothes. It was an omen of **bad** things to come.

That night it rained, and wouldn't you know it, my cot was positioned directly below a leak in the cabin roof. **Needless** to say I woke up soggy and I've been sneezing ever since. By the time I **hung** up my wet blankets and made it to breakfast, the only **food** left was cold pancakes and orange juice with unidentified floating objects in it. Ugh!

The first morning we spent most of the time at the lake. Other than the fact that the water was **icy** cold, our canoe capsized, and my **glasses** are now quietly resting somewhere at the **bottom** of Lake Wet. It was tons of fun! That afternoon I went on a nature hike. I can now identify two kinds of **pine trees, a** three varieties of wild flowers, an edible berry, and poison oak. The poison oak I studied up close and personal, which left me trying not to scratch for the rest of **of** the evening.

The **second** night passed without incident, unless you want to count the family of mice that spent the dark hours traversing the cabin floor to raid the cookies someone had left out. They were **actually kind of** cute.

Today it rained, so we had to spend the entire day in the lodge. In the morning I tried to make a bird house out of craft sticks. It turned out looking more like a **condemned** building than anything a bird would ever want to live in. I spent the afternoon learning how to weave a basket. It was looking great until the person next to me accidentally sat on it. After dinner we learned camp songs. **You** know, the kind that once you get in your head you can't get rid of. So now I'm breaking curfew, to write to you from under my covers, to the tune of "Row Row Row **Your** Boat.**"**

Just two more weeks and this joyous adventure will be over. I'll give you a call when I get home, if I survive that long**.**

See you soon,

Lulu

Fill-In Activities

Short Activities

There may be occasions when you are faced with empty class time due to insufficient lesson plans or unexpected events. When this occurs, be ready to implement a short activity designed for the entire class. These activities are usually directed by the teacher and require various lengths of instructional time to complete, ranging from 20 to 40 minutes. Two effective *Short Activities* follow this introduction as examples. A larger selection of *Short Activities* and lesson plans are included in the *Activities* section of this chapter and are organized by subject area.

Poster Creation Review

Subject: Adaptable

Time: 30+ minutes

Materials Needed:

pencil, paper, crayons and other art supplies

Grades
K-8

Objective:

Students will create a poster which reflects something they have learned in a recent lesson.

Procedure:

1. Review concepts or ideas that students have studied in a lesson that day.
2. List these concepts and ideas on the board.
3. Set a time limit for having the posters completed.
4. Have students create a poster depicting some aspect of the lesson.
5. Collect posters for teacher evaluation and classroom display.

Extension:

Have volunteers explain their posters to the class.

Bingo Review

Subject: Adaptable

Time: 30+ minutes

Materials Needed:

Bingo Review worksheet, pencils, small objects to mark the bingo squares (pieces of colored paper, beans, etc.), and prizes for the winners

Advance Preparation:

Identify 25 terms that students have been studying recently. Science, spelling, or vocabulary words work well. Students can help you compile this list.

Objective:

Students will review terms or concepts they have been studying.

Procedure:

1. Establish that participating in this activity is a privilege and that anyone who behaves inappropriately (i.e. flipping their markers across the room or calling out answers), will not be allowed to participate.

2. Distribute one bingo sheet to each student.

3. List the 25 words on the board and have the students copy them randomly onto their bingo sheet.

    NOTE: Stress the importance of copying the words so that their sheet is like no one else's.

4. Distribute the bingo markers.

Fill-In Activities

5. Using your own list, randomly select a term and provide the class with a clue or definition of the word.

6. Students raise their hands to guess the answer.

7. When the correct answer is determined, everyone marks that spot on their sheet.

8. Steps 5-7 are repeated until someone has bingo with 5 squares marked in a row.

9. Continue play until three people have won.

10. Award prizes to the winners.

11. If time allows, have students clear their sheets and play again.

Extension:

At the conclusion of the game have students turn their sheets over and define each word or use it correctly in a sentence.

Notes For The Teacher:

Be firm, fair, and consistent in maintaining expected student behavior during this activity. It will make it more enjoyable for you and the other students in the class.

If time is limited, alter the game so that three or four in a row constitutes bingo.

If you are teaching in a middle or junior high school, save the bingo sheets from the first class and use them again and again throughout the day.

Name _____

Bingo Review

Place a word in the far left column, then write words in each of the subject areas that begin with the letter in that row. Use subject words that are part of a lesson or unit being taught.

Fill-In
Activities

Reference Guide
for Activities

Fill-In
Activities

Activities and Lessons

The activities and lessons in the following section have been developed for whole class, teacher directed instruction. The section is organized according to subject and each type of lesson is easily identified by the corresponding icon shown below. Within each subject there are activities for every grade level. Activities may be adapted into *Five-Minute Fillers* and *Early Finishers*.

Activity Pages:

Copy some of the activities in this handbook to keep in your *SubPack*. At the beginning of the day explain that these fun worksheets will be available for students who finish assignments early throughout the day. You may want to set out a couple of different sheets and let students choose which ones they would like to do. Be prepared with enough worksheets for each student in the class to have one, because students who don't get to do them in class will often want to take one home to do "just for fun." As you leave the school at the end of the day, ask if you can make copies to replace those the students used.

Geo Art Gallery

Subject: Art

Time: 30 minutes

Materials Needed:

Several sets of tangrams (ideally one set for each student). These can either be purchased commercially or made using colored card stock and the templates found at the end of this lesson. (See page 144.)

Advance Preparation:

Objective:

Students will use basic geometric shapes to create a work of art.

Procedure:

1. Divide the class into six groups.

2. Show the class the tangram pieces and explain that they will be using these colored geometric shapes to create a work of art.

3. Stress that any student who behaves inappropriately (i.e. throwing the tangram pieces) will be removed from his or her group and not be allowed to participate in the activity.

4. Allow students to decide if their group wants to work together and use all of the pieces in one big design, or divide the pieces up and make individual designs.

5. Tell the students how much time they will have to create their masterpiece. This will vary depending on the situation but try to allow at least 10 minutes.

6. Distribute tangram sets to each group. Try not to give any group two sets of the same color.

7. Have students begin working. Provide updates on how much time is left.

8. When the allotted time is up explain that they will spend the last five minutes of the lesson touring the "classroom gallery" and seeing the work of other artists.

9. When touring time is finished have students separate the pieces back into the original tangram sets. (If each set is a different color this process is a lot easier!). Ask one student from each group to collect the tangrams and return them to the teacher.

Extension:

Have the students make an artist information card to be displayed by their work. Things to put on the card may include the names of the artists, the number of each color used, the number of each shape used, the total number of pieces used, and a name for the work of art.

Notes For The Teacher:

Classroom management may get a little hectic during the "touring" portion of the lesson. Here are some suggestions of things to do before the tour begins to help keep things under control.

1. Review classroom rules.

2. State the expected student behavior (walking, whispering, look but don't touch, etc.).

3. Ask if anyone in the class has ever been to an art gallery or museum. Discuss the atmosphere and behavior that they observed there.

4. Compare the touring time to a trip to the library or school media center.

Art

Tangram Puzzles

Subject: Art

Time: 15-30 minutes

Materials Needed:

Tangram sets (one for each student or pair of students—see *Notes About Tangrams* page 133)

puzzle worksheets (one for each student or pair of students)

Advance Preparation:

Photocopy puzzle worksheets

Objective:

Students will practice their spatial thinking skills.

Procedure:

1. Distribute to each student or pair of students a set of tangram pieces and copy of a tangram puzzle such as those found on page 129-131.

2. Encourage students as they rearrange the tangram pieces to construct the puzzle.

3. Students who finish early can make their own puzzles by arranging the tangram pieces on plain paper then tracing around the outside of the design. These student puzzles can be exchanged among class members.

Notes For The Teacher:

There are many books and educational activity sets with lessons similar to *Tangram Puzzles* which can be purchased through educational supply companies. For information about requesting current catalogs see page 133.

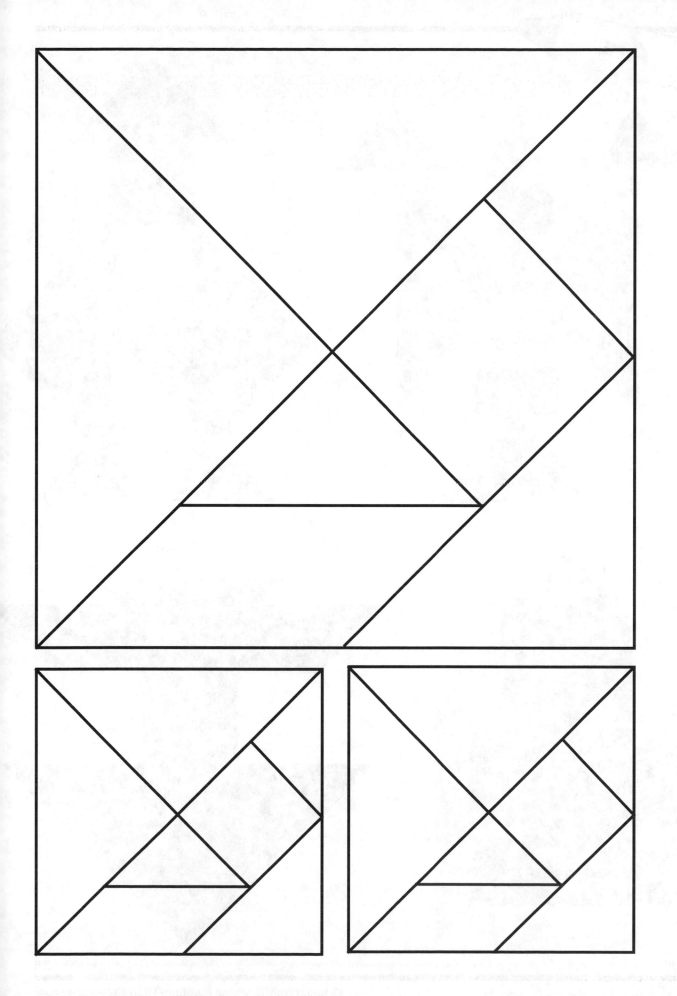

1.

2.

3.

4.

5.

6.

7.

8.

Art

Answers to Puzzles

1.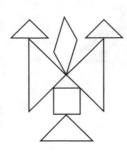

2.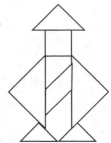

3.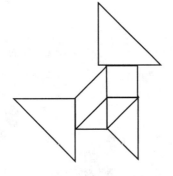

4.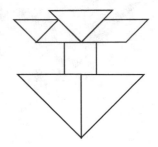

5.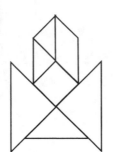

6.

7.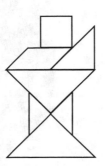

8.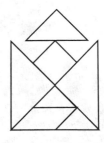

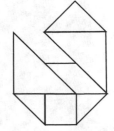

Notes About Tangrams

Used in the Geo-Art Gallery Activity page 126 and Tangram Puzzles page 128.

If you want to purchase commercial tangrams they are available through several school supply companies at costs between $1.00-$2.00 per set (remember that ideally each student will have their own set). Listed below are several companies with the telephone numbers for requesting a copy of their catalog.

- Summit Learning   1-800-500-8817
- Delta Education   1-800-442-5444
- Cuisenaire   1-800-237-3142

These companies also sell numerous activity packets for use with tangrams as well as many other educational materials.

If you choose to make your own tangrams here are a few suggestions:

1. Copy tangrams onto **DIFFERENT COLORS** of **HEAVY** card stock.

2. Be sure the template sheet is flat against the copier, otherwise the shapes will be distorted and not fit together properly.

3. Laminate the sheets of printed card stock before cutting the shapes apart.

4. Take the copied, laminated sheets, along with a few extra pair of scissors to school with you and let students, who finish early, cut them apart. Another option is to turn it into a class project. Have students cut them apart and then experiment making shapes while you read aloud from a good book.

5. Keep sets in sturdy zip-lock bags for storage and distribution purposes.

Purchasing or making tangrams may seem like a lot of work, but they are a versatile tool that can be used for many activities at any grade level and are well worth the effort.

Name _____

Hole Punch Art

Directions: Attach this sheet to a piece of colored paper. Use a pin or push tack to punch out
the dots, then hang the colored paper up in the window!

Grid Drawings

Grades
4-8

Subject: Art

Time: 15-30 minutes

Materials Needed:

pencils, crayons, *Grid Worksheets*

Advance Preparation:

Make one copy of each worksheet for each student in the class.

Objective:

Students will use grids to help them complete or enlarge an image.

Procedure:

1. Distribute worksheets.

2. Explain directions and give helpful hints for completing the assignment. (Hints: draw in pencil first, look at the picture block by block, etc.)

3. Have students complete and color worksheets.

4. Turn in drawings for teacher evaluation.

Art

Extension:

Collect student drawings and have students vote for their favorite. Award a prize to the class winner.

Notes For The Teacher:

Students often enjoy sitting in small groups and talking quietly while they work on their drawings. If a group gets too noisy they can always be separated.

These worksheets can be copied back to back and students can choose which one they would like to complete. Students who finish early can then turn the paper over and begin working on the other activity.

You may want to create your own *Graph Art Worksheets* using holiday or lesson content themes.

Name _____

Grid Enlargement

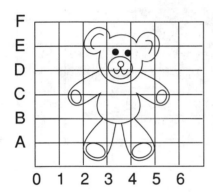

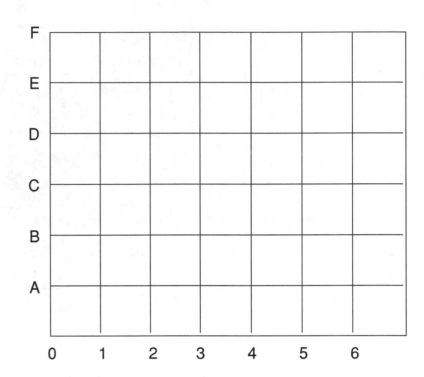

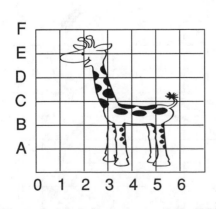

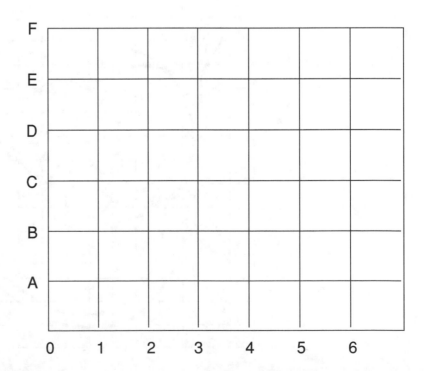

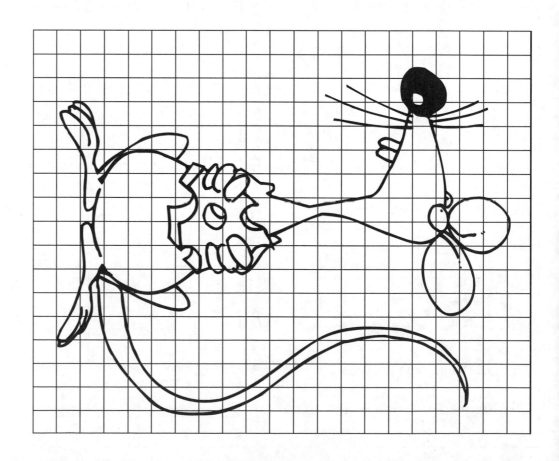

NAME _____

Grid Drawings

Name _____

Grid Completion

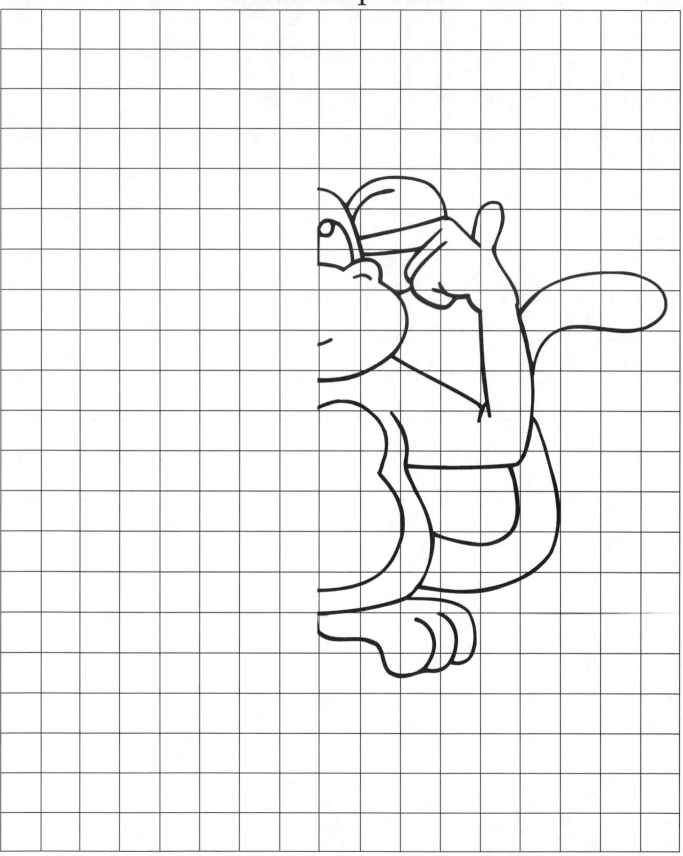

Under Construction

Grades
4-12

Time: 30+ min.

Materials: sketch paper, pencils,

Objective: Students will develop a sketch for a teacher-assigned construction project.

Optional Materials: colored pencils, rulers, compasses, templates etc.

Advance Preparation: Determine the specific details of the project to be assigned.

In this activity students will be asked to complete a sketch for a construction project. The details, specifications, areas of emphasis, difficulty level, and nature of the project will be determined by the teacher.

Possible construction projects include the following:

- a kitchen
- a house
- a school
- a shopping mall

- a hotel
- a flower garden
- a new city park
- a new 100 home community

Potential areas of emphasis could include the following:

- drawing to scale
- color schemes
- cost efficiency

- creativity
- practicality

Procedure:

1. Make sure all students are equipped with paper and pencils.

2. Explain the nature of the assignment, details of the construction project, and set a time limit.

Example: *Today's assignment is to complete a sketch for a new resort hotel to be built in Las Vegas. The International Boating Association wants to develop a boat-theme resort featuring a 300-room hotel, swimming pool, tropical aquarium, large sand box, and outdoor restaurant. The resort wants to become "the" place for families to stay in Las Vegas. Your preliminary sketches need to be turned in by the end of the class hour and will be evaluated on the creativity of incorporating the "boat-theme" into the design.*

Distributing copies of the instructions or outlining key information on the board will eliminate the need for repeating the details of the assignment over and over again.

3.   Monitor student work.

4.   Collect and evaluate the finished projects.

You may want to photocopy or request permission to keep samples of excellent work to use as examples in other classes.

NAME _____

The Obscure Words of Art

Like any other discipline, Art has a vocabulary of its own. How savvy are you at deciphering its obscure terminology?
Try to match the words below with the correct definition or description.

Tools of the Trade

_____	1.	stump	A. a rod shaped engraving tool
_____	2.	rigger	B. a tool used in shaping ceramic pots
_____	3.	rib	C. cigar-shaped tool used to blend or smudge charcoal, pencil, chalk, or crayon
_____	4.	adze	D. a cutting tool used in sculpture to rough shape wood
_____	5.	mahlstick	E. a light wooden rod three or four feet long which painters use as a rest or support when executing detailed work
_____	6.	spline	F. a device used to copy, enlarge, or reduce a work of art
_____	7.	graver	G. narrow strip of flexible, transparent plastic used in mechanical drawings as a ruler for curved surfaces
_____	8.	pantograph	H. a lettering brush half the width of a standard lettering brush of the same numbered size

Colors of Art

_____	1.	ceruse	A. a brilliant yellow green
_____	2.	cyan	B. a yellow to reddish brown dyestuff
_____	3.	magenta	C. a brown pigment made by burning beech wood
_____	4.	bistre	D. deep blue
_____	5.	chay	E. white lead
_____	6.	tumeric	F. deep dark purplish blue, or bluish maroon
_____	7.	weld	G. a natural red dyestuff obtained from the root of an East Indian plant
_____	8.	chartreuse	H. a bright yellow dye

Miscellaneous Art Terms

_____	1.	taboret	A. a rough sketch of very small proportions
_____	2.	cachet	B. small cabinet kept near an artist's drawing table or easel
_____	3.	blot drawing	C. an artistic invention made up of discarded materials (old bus tickets, candy wrappers, etc.)
_____	4.	mastic	D. an accidental blot or stain on a paper used to construct an imaginary landscape
_____	5.	interlace	E. a monogram or symbol used in place of a signature
_____	6.	merz	F. the technique of painting in transparent water color
_____	7.	putto	G. a chubby nude infant often depicted in art since the 15th century
_____	8.	thumbnail sketch	H. resin obtained from a tree used in the 19th century as a picture varnish
_____	9.	aquarelle	I. a pattern of art in which elements intercross and intertwine with one another

The Obscure Words of Art
ANSWER KEY

Like any other discipline, Art has a vocabulary of its own. How savvy are you at deciphering its obscure terminology? Try to match the words below with the correct definition or description.

Tools of the Trade

C	1.	stump	A.	a rod shaped engraving tool
H	2.	rigger	B.	a tool used in shaping ceramic pots
B	3.	rib	C.	cigar-shaped tool used to blend or smudge charcoal, pencil, chalk, or crayon
D	4.	adze	D.	a cutting tool used in sculpture to rough shape wood
E	5.	mahlstick	E.	a light wooden rod three or four feet long which painters use as a rest or support when executing detailed work
G	6.	spline	F.	a device used to copy, enlarge, or reduce a work of art
A	7.	graver	G.	narrow strip of flexible, transparent plastic used in mechanical drawings as a ruler for curved surfaces
F	8.	pantograph	H.	a lettering brush half the width of a standard lettering brush of the same numbered size

Colors of Art

E	1.	ceruse	A.	a brilliant yellow green
D	2.	cyan	B.	a yellow to reddish brown dyestuff
F	3.	magenta	C.	a brown pigment made by burning beech wood
C	4.	bistre	D.	deep blue
G	5.	chay	E.	white lead
B	6.	tumeric	F.	deep dark purplish blue, or bluish maroon
H	7.	weld	G.	a natural red dyestuff obtained from the root of an East Indian plant
A	8.	chartreuse	H.	a bright yellow dye

Miscellaneous Art Terms

B	1.	taboret	A.	a rough sketch of very small proportions
E	2.	cachet	B.	small cabinet kept near an artist's drawing table or easel
D	3.	blot drawing	C.	an artistic invention made up of discarded materials (old bus tickets, candy wrappers, etc.)
H	4.	mastic	D.	an accidental blot or stain on a paper used to construct an imaginary landscape
I	5.	interlace	E.	a monogram or symbol used in place of a signature
C	6.	merz	F.	the technique of painting in transparent water color
G	7.	putto	G.	a chubby nude infant often depicted in art since the 15th century
A	8.	thumbnail sketch	H.	resin obtained from a tree used in the 19th century as a picture varnish
F	9.	aquarelle	I.	a pattern of art in which elements intercross and intertwine with one another

NAME _____

Masters of the Trade

You probably recognize the names of the artists listed below. Can you match the artist to one of their well known works and an event or characteristic of their life? In front of the artist column write both the Work of Art letter and Trivia number.

		Artist	Work of Art	Trivia
____	____	Rembrandt	A. The Marriage of Giovanni	1. A persian known as the master of the miniature.
____	____	Monet	B. Sistine Madonna	2. Luncheon guests sometimes waited several hours while he painted the cook.
____	____	Da Vinci	C. Anatomy Lesson of Dr. Tulp	3. He painted more than 100 self-portraits throughout his life.
____	____	Picasso	D. Book of Victory	4. He always signed his pictures in letters of the Greek alphabet.
____	____	Degas	E. Water-lily Series	5. The local barber came to the open field and cut his hair while he painted.
____	____	Renoir	F. The Three Dancers	6. Shot himself in a field and died two days later.
____	____	El Greco	G. Mona Lisa	7. He was forbidden to see his mother after the age of five.
____	____	Michelangelo	H. The Dancing Class	8. During World War I he designed scenery for Diaghilev's Ballets Russes.
____	____	David	I. The Burial of Count Orgaz	9. Before death he walked the streets of Paris alone, blind, and terrified of automobiles.
____	____	Rousseau	J. David	10. He played the violin for his friends and flute in the French Army Infantry Band.
____	____	Raphael	K. The Coronation	11. As a nobleman and aristocrat he could not accept money for his work.
____	____	Velazquez	L. Gabrielle With a Rose	12. He worked in Rome off and on for 70 years for seven different Popes.
____	____	Van Eych	M. Starry Night	13. Made distant and secret journeys to paint portraits of princesses for Philip the Good.
____	____	Bihzad	N. The Sleeping Gypsy	14. Drew 10 cartoons depicting scenes from the acts of the apostles; made tapestries.
____	____	Van Gogh	O. The Spinners	15. Twice his wife plead for and gained his freedom from prison.

Masters of the Trade
ANSWER KEY

		Artist	Work of Art	Trivia
C	3	Rembrandt	The Anatomy Lesson of Dr. Tulp	He painted more than 100 self-portraits throughout his life.
E	5	Monet	Water-lily Series	The local barber came to the open field and cut his hair while he painted.
G	7	Da Vinci	Mona Lisa	He was forbidden to see his mother after the age of five.
F	8	Picasso	The Three Dancers	During World War I he designed scenery for Diaghilev's Ballets Russes.
H	9	Degas	The Dancing Class	Before death he walked the streets of Paris alone, blind, and terrified of automobiles.
L	2	Renoir	Gabrielle With a Rose	Luncheon guests sometimes waited several hours while he painted the cook.
I	4	El Greco	The Burial of Count Orgaz	He always signed his pictures in letters of the Greek alphabet.
J	12	Michelangelo	David	He worked in Rome off and on for 70 years for seven different Popes.
K	15	David	The Coronation	Twice his wife plead for and gained his freedom from prison.
N	10	Rousseau	The Sleeping Gypsy	He played the violin for his friends and flute in the French Army Infantry Band.
B	14	Raphael	Sistine Madonna	Drew cartoons depicting scenes from the acts of the apostles; made into tapestries.
O	11	Velazquez	The Spinners	As a nobleman and aristocrat he could not accept money for his work.
A	13	Van Eych	The Marriage of Giovanni	Made distant and secret journeys to paint portraits of princesses for Philip the Good.
D	1	Bihzad	Book of Victory	A persian known as the master of the miniature.
M	6	Van Gogh	Starry Night	Shot himself in a field and died two days later.

NAME _____

Business by Design

You have been selected to design the business cards for *Tropical Island*, a company which grows and sells tropical plants.

The following information must be included on the card:

- Company Name

- Company Logo (which you design)

- Employee Name

- Employee Title

- Mailing Address

- Fax Number

- Telephone Number

- E-mail Address

The actual card size is:

2" by 3 1/2" but you can complete your design in the larger box below.

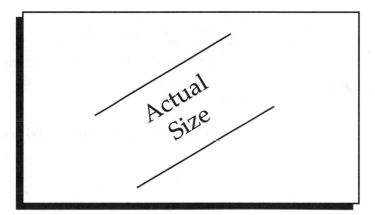

Your Design:

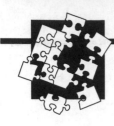

Following Directions

Subject: Critical Thinking

Time: 15-30 minutes

Materials Needed:

Teacher Directed Instructions, Student Activity Sheet, crayons

Advance Preparation:

Photocopy one *Student Activity Sheet* for each student.

Objective:

Students will follow oral directions and develop their listening skills.

Procedure:

1. Ask the following questions to discuss the importance of following directions:

    A. When is it important to follow directions?

    B. Why is it important to follow directions?

    C. What could happen if you did not follow directions?

2. Hand out a worksheet to each student and have them write their names in the specified place.

3. Distribute crayons to each student.

4. Instruct the students to listen carefully as you read each set of instructions twice. Tell them not to do anything until they have listened carefully both times.

5. Read the instructions 1-5 found on the *Teacher Directed Instructions.* Make sure that students do not begin until the instructions have been read twice.

6. Collect worksheets for teacher evaluation.

Extension:

Hand out blank pieces of paper and have students follow simple oral directions as the teacher gives them (i.e. put your name at the top, draw a circle in the center of the paper, make a line across the bottom of the paper, etc.).

Teacher Directed Instructions

Following Directions:

Distribute to each student a copy of the *Student Activity Sheet* and crayons. Tell them to listen carefully while you read the instructions out loud.

Say: *Listen carefully to what I say to do. I will repeat each direction only two times. Do exactly what I say.*

1. Find the square with the butterfly in the corner. Put your finger on the butterfly. Color the triangle with your crayon. Put an X in the circle. Draw a circle inside of the square.

2. Find the square with the umbrella in the corner. Put your finger on the smallest square. Color the umbrella. Write the letter A in the biggest square. Draw a line through the middle square.

3. Find the square with the apple in it. Put your finger on the apple. Now look carefully at the triangle. Draw a line above the triangle. Draw a square inside the triangle. Outline the triangle with your crayon.

4. Find the square with the flower in the corner. Put your finger on the flower. Look carefully at the circles. Draw a triangle inside the top circle. Write the letter your name begins with in the biggest circle. Color the smallest circle.

5. Turn your paper over. Draw a big circle. Can you make this circle into a happy face?

NAME _____

Following Directions Activity Sheet

Guess the Object Grades 2-6

Subject: Critical Thinking

Time: 30+ minutes

Materials Needed:

pencil and paper

Advance Preparation:

Objective:

Students will practice their listening and oral direction skills.

Procedure:

1. Have the class draw an object as the teacher gives an oral description. The object should be simple like a toothbrush, pencil, basketball, key, flowers, umbrella, etc.

2. Do not identify the object by name until students have had a chance to guess what it is and share their pictures with class members.

3. Repeat the activity with students giving oral directions for the class to draw and guess at.

4. Discuss the importance of listening carefully and giving good directions during this activity.

5. Discuss other situations when it is important to listen carefully or communicate clearly.

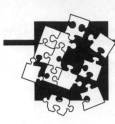

Extension:

1. Divide the class into teams of two and have them practice giving descriptions and listening to one another to guess what is being described.

2. Have students draw a simple picture using geometric shapes (see examples). If time allows, have them color their pictures.

3. Organize the students into partners and instruct them to sit back-to-back.

4. Have one student give directions about how to draw his picture while the other follows the directions and completes a drawing on the back of his paper.

   NOTE: The student giving directions cannot look at the drawing in progress and the student drawing cannot ask questions.

5. Have the students change roles.

6. When they are finished, have the students compare pictures and discuss which directions were easy to follow and which were confusing.

7. Have the students complete the activity again with a different partner. Compare the second partner's drawing with the one done by the first partner to determine which time they gave better directions.

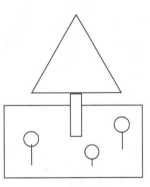

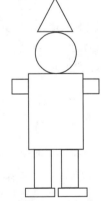

Notes For The Teacher:

Give directions for drawing the object rather than saying it is like something else. For example, if the object was a basketball you could say, " *Draw a circle. Draw lines across it and put dots all over the inside of the circle,*" rather than saying, "*It is like a baseball only bigger.*"

Brain Teasers and Riddles

Grades
3-8

1. What is full of holes, yet holds water? **A sponge**

2. What is bought by the yard, yet worn by the foot? **Carpet**

3. What is the longest word in the English language? **Smiles. There is a mile between the first and last letter.**

4. If eight birds are on a roof and you shoot at one, how many remain? **None. They all fly away.**

5. Why can't it rain for two days continually? **Because there is always a night in between.**

6. What speaks every language? **An echo**

7. Why is a nose in the middle of a face? **Because it is the scenter.**

8. What table is completely without legs? **A time-table**

9. What is the difference between a jeweler and a jailer? **One sells watches, the other watches cells.**

10. What is black and white and read all over? **A newspaper.**

11. Can a man living in Chicago be buried west of the Mississippi? **No. He is still alive.**

12. How far can a dog run into the woods? **Halfway. The other half he is running out.**

13. A farmer had seventeen sheep. All but nine died. How many did he have left? **Nine.**

14. A man has two coins in his hand. The two coins total thirty cents. One is not a nickel. What are the two coins? **A nickel and a quarter. (The other is a nickel.)**

15. Why is Ireland the wealthiest country? **Because its capital is always Dublin.**

16. If a telephone and a piece of paper had a race, who would always win? **The telephone, since the paper will always remain stationery.**

17. Why should fish be well-educated? **They are found in schools.**

18. Which takes the least time to get ready for a trip: An elephant or a rooster? **The rooster . . . He only takes his comb, but the elephant has to take a whole trunk.**

19. Do they have a Fourth of July in England? **Yes. (But it is not a holiday.)**

20. Take two apples from three apples. What have you got? **Two apples.**

21. Four men can build four boats in four days. How long will it take one man to build one boat? **Four days. (Four men building four boats is the same as one man working sixteen days.)**

22. Can you measure out exactly two gallons of water using only two unmarked containers? One of the containers will hold eight gallons and the other will hold five gallons. **Pour five gallons into the eight gallon can. Then repeat this until the eight gallon can is full. (Two gallons will be remaining in the five gallon can.)**

Minute Mysteries

"Minute Mysteries" are stories that are told within a minute and then require the listeners to solve a mystery. Students generate questions that can be answered with a simple "yes" or "no" in order to solve the mystery. These stories are fun and teach children to use critical thinking skills while they sort through the information to figure out the answer.

1. A cowboy left town on Tuesday and was gone three days, coming back on Tuesday.

   Q. How is that possible?

   A. His horse was named Tuesday.

2. A man is found dead in a cabin in the ocean.

   Q. What could have happened?

   A. The man is in the cabin of an airplane which crashed in the ocean.

3. A person lived on the 15th floor of a high-rise apartment building. Everyday he got on the elevator, rode down to the lobby and went to work. Every evening he came home from work, rode the elevator to the 13th floor and walked up the stairs to his apartment.

   Q Why?

   A. The person is very short and can only reach the elevator button to the 13th floor.

4. A man was lonely and wanted a talking parrot to keep him company. He went to the pet store and found a beautiful bird that was for sale at a bargain price. He asked the store owner if the bird could be trained to talk. The owner said, *"This bird is absolutely guaranteed to repeat everything it hears."* So the man bought the bird and took it home. But two weeks later he returned to the store, demanding his money back, saying, *"The bird refused to talk."* The store owner said, *"I stand by my guarantee and will not give your money back."*

   Q. How could he say that, considering the bird wouldn't talk?

   A. The parrot was deaf.

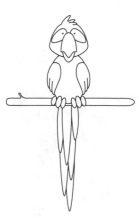

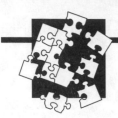

Mind Benders

1. The Shopping Trip

One day last week my brother went to town with only $10 in his pocket, but returned in the evening with $20.

He bought a pair of shoes at Chipmans and some meat at the meat market. He also had his eyes examined. It so happens that my brother gets paid every Thursday by check and the banks in this town are open on Tuesday, Friday, and Saturday only. The eye doctor is not in his office on Saturday and there is no market on Thursday or Friday. What day did my brother go to town?

2. The Chess Tournament Dilemma

Four men named P.F. Smith, C.J. Smith, Reynolds, and Fellows played in a chess tournament.

The Smiths were the famous Smith brothers, twins who played opposite ends on the Princeton football team.

Reynolds surprised everyone when he defeated Fellows.

The man who finished third said graciously to the winner at the conclusion of the matches, "I've heard a great deal about you and I am happy to meet you. May I congratulate you."

The runner-up was terribly crippled, having had infantile paralysis when he was four years old. As a result he had never married, but had lived a sheltered life with his widowed mother, making chess his chief diversion.

P.F. Smith sometimes talked too much. He had disgraced himself when he was an usher at Fellow's wedding by making the bride's mother late to the wedding.

In what order did the men finish?

3. The Artisans

There are three men, named James, John, and Jake, each of whom is engaged in two occupations. Their occupations classify each of them as two of the following: chauffeur, electrician, musician, painter, gardener, and barber. From the following facts, find in what two occupations each man is engaged.

1. The chauffeur offended the musician by laughing at his long hair.
2. Both the musician and the gardener used to go fishing with James.
3. The painter had the electrician wire his new house.
4. The chauffeur dated the painter's sister.
5. John owed the gardener $5.00.
6. Jake beat both John and the painter at horse shoes.

4. The Stolen Antique

Three men, Mr. White, Mr. Black and Mr. Brown and their wives were entertained at the home of their friend one evening. After the departure of the guests, the host and hostess discovered that a valuable antique had been stolen. It was later discovered that one of the six guests was the thief. From the facts given, see if you can discover who it was.

1. The spouse of the thief lost money at cards that evening.
2. Because of partial paralysis of his hands and arms, Mr. Brown was unable to drive his car.
3. Mrs. Black and another female guest spent the entire evening doing a jigsaw puzzle.
4. Mr. Black accidentally spilled a drink on Mrs. White when he was introduced to her.
5. Mr. Brown gave his wife half of the money that he had won to make up for her loss.
6. Mr. Black had beaten the thief in golf that day.

Solutions to Mind Benders:

1. ***The Shopping Trip***
    My brother went to town on Tuesday.

2. ***Chess Tournament Dilemma***
    Winner-C.J. Smith
    Runner-up- Reynolds
    Third- Fellows
    Fourth- P.F. Smith

3. ***The Artisans***
    James- barber and painter
    John- musician and electrician
    Jake- chauffeur and gardener

4. ***The Stolen Antique***
    Mrs. Black was the thief.

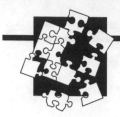

The Plimpton Hold Up

If you were present for three minutes at the scene of the hold up pictured below and later were questioned as a witness, how many questions relating to it could you answer? Study this picture carefully for three minutes and without referring to the picture again, answer as many of the questions as you can.

The Plimpton Hold Up Questions

1.	In what town did the hold-up occur?

2.	What was held up?

3.	What is its correct address?

4.	On the corner of what two streets is it?

5.	Is the thief in the picture?

6.	Where is he?

7.	How much money did he steal?

8.	Did the policeman see the hold-up?

9.	What is he doing about it?

10.	What is the name of the taxi company?

11.	What is the number of the taxi?

12.	In what direction is the taxi going?

13.	What time did the hold-up take place?

14.	What is the date?

15.	How many people are shown?

16.	How many are aware of the hold-up?

17.	What kind of store is next to the bank?

18.	Who owns it?

19.	What is its correct address?

20.	What kind of store is on the corner?

21.	Who owns it?

22.	What is the number of this store?

23.	At the intersection of what two streets is it?

24.	Which of these two is the one-way street?

25.	In what direction does traffic go on this street?

26.	Where is the hydrant?

27.	What does the sign on 20th Street advertise?

28.	What is the price of the advertised product?

29.	Is there a mailbox shown?

30.	On what street are the car tracks?

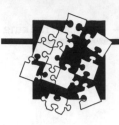

Desert Dilemma

Subject: Critical Thinking

Time: 15-30 minutes

Materials Needed:

Desert Dilemma worksheet for each student or group

Advance Preparation:

Make photocopies of the student worksheets.

Objective:

Students will practice critical thinking skills as they analyze and discuss different priorities in a difficult situation.

Procedure:

1. Distribute to the class the *Desert Dilemma* worksheets, either individually or in small groups.

2. Review the situation and instructions as a class.

3. Allow students 10 minutes to rank the items listed.

4. Have a class discussion on how they ranked the items allowing students to justify or revise their own choices.

Extension:

Have the students list the objects on the back of their paper and put a star next to each of the objects they plan to carry. Then explain in writing how they plan to use each of these items.

Notes For The Teacher:

This activity can be done as a class with one student giving directions, and the other students doing the drawing at their own desks.

Name _____

Grades
4-12

Desert Dilemma

Situation: While driving through the desert you take a wrong turn and drive 50 miles before your car runs out of gas. You are stranded wearing shorts, a t-shirt and tennis shoes. There is nothing around you but cactus and sand. The temperature is about 110 degrees in the shade. Your only hope for rescue is to make it back to the main road.

You rummage around in the car and find the 20 items listed below. You realize that you will not be able to carry all of them with you so you rank the items according to how important you think they will be in ensuring your survival and rescue. Place the number 1 by the most important item, 2 by the second most important, and so on, with 20 being the least important item.

Remember that you are in the desert and that the three essential things for survival are food, clothing, and shelter. Work individually, and later we will discuss your choices with the rest of the class.

_____	any part of the car	_____	sling shot
_____	sun glasses	_____	50 ft of nylon rope
_____	AM/FM radio	_____	boots
_____	blanket	_____	first aid kit
_____	lipstick	_____	pencil and paper
_____	a candy bar	_____	flash light
_____	box of matches	_____	plastic garbage bag
_____	silk scarf	_____	hammer
_____	an apple	_____	a pack of gum
_____	a map of the state		

Name _____

Word Puzzles I

Directions:

These puzzles represent common expressions and phrases. Solve them by carefully noticing the positions of the words and letters. Are they under, over, mixed-up, inside, or a certain size?

E K A KISSM	search and	NEFRIENDED	$\dfrac{\text{wear}}{\text{long}}$
egsg gesg segg sgeg	S M O K E	GIVE GET GIVE GET GIVE GET GIVE GET	$\dfrac{\text{cover}}{\text{agent}}$
NOT GUILTY STANDER	$\dfrac{\text{man}}{\text{board}}$	$\dfrac{\text{EZ}}{\text{iiii}}$	LM AL EA AE EM ML
$\dfrac{\text{BELT}}{\text{HITTING}}$	A D S L A	he ⦃ art	**T.V.**
ar up ms	**CHAIR**	**TIRE**	T O W N

Answers found on page 164.

Name _____

Word Puzzles II

Directions:

These puzzles represent common expressions and phrases. Solve them by carefully noticing the positions of the words and letters. Are they under, over, mixed-up, inside, or a certain size?

S O C K	1,000, **1**000	C O S T S	ground / feet feet / feet feet / feet feet
g°i g n / a r o u d n n	time time	stand / I	T O U C H
FRIENDS standing / miss FRIENDS	WALKING	SOUP	ter very esting
r|e|a|d|i|n|g	b sick ed	LO head / heels VE	knee / lights
g r u / the block / n i n n	every|right|thing	R R O O A D D S S	i / 8

Answers found on page 164.

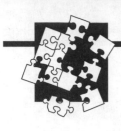

Answers to Word Puzzles

Word Puzzles I:

1. kiss and make up
2. search high and low
3. friend in need
4. long underwear

5. scrambled eggs
6. up in smoke
7. forgive and forget
8. undercover agent

9. innocent bystander
10. man overboard
11. easy on the eyes
12. three square meals

13. hitting below the belt
14. tossed salad
15. broken heart
16. black and white TV

17. up in arms
18. high chair
19. flat tire
20. downtown

Word Puzzles II:

1. sock in the eye
2. one in a million
3. rising costs
4. six feet underground

5. going around in circles
6. time after time
7. I understand
8. touchdown

9. mis-understanding between friends
10. walking tall
11. split pea soup
12. very interesting

13. reading between the lines
14. sick in bed
15. head over heals in love
16. neon lights

17. running around the block
18. right in the middle of everything
19. cross roads
20. I over ate

Foreign Language Five-Minute Fillers

Grades
8-12

Similar to the Five-Minute filler activities in the general interest section at the beginning of this chapter, the following sponge activities have been adapted to challenge students' foreign language skills. Whenever possible, have students write or speak their responses in the language they are studying.

1. Name as many cities as you can where _____ (language) is spoken.
2. List as many colors as you can.
3. Write the names of the months and days of the week.
4. List the numbers from one to one hundred.
5. Write the alphabet.
7. Describe what you are wearing.
8. List 15 objects you can see from where you are sitting.
9. Write down the names of all of the holidays you know.
10. Suppose a friend who doesn't speak _____ (language) was going on vacation to _____ (country where language is spoken), what would be the 10 most useful words you think they should learn before leaving.

Additional Foreign Language Activities

Grades
8-12

Beginner's Crossword Puzzle:
> Make a crossword puzzle in French, Spanish, German, Latin, or another foreign language you are studying. The clues may be in English.

Advanced Crossword Puzzle:
> Make a crossword puzzle in the language you are studying. The clues must be in the same language.

Floor Plan:
> Draw the floor plan of a house. Label the rooms, doors, windows, and furniture in Spanish, French, German, or any other non-English language.

"Buzz":

Play a game of "buzz," speaking only German, Spanish, or French. The first person calls out the word for "one" the second, "two"; the third "three"; and so on around the room. Every time a number that contains seven or is a multiple of seven (i.e., 7, 14, 17, 21) comes up call out "buzz" instead of the number. Remember, "buzz" is the only English word allowed!

Telephone:

Play a game of telephone, using only the language you are studying. The first person chooses a phrase or sentence in Spanish, French, or German and whispers it to the person next to him. That person, without asking him to repeat it, whispers the same phrase, as he understands it, to the next person, and so on. The last person in the row says the phrase out loud and translates it into English.

Calendar:

Make a calendar for this month, using only the foreign language you are studying. No abbreviations are permitted.

20 Questions:

Play twenty questions. One student chooses an object and tells the class whether it is animal, plant, or mineral. The rest of the class takes turns asking questions that can be answered only "yes" or "no" until they guess the object, or until they have asked twenty questions and still can't guess. Both the object and the questions must be stated in the foreign language the class is studying.

Stump the Experts:

Play "stump the experts." Three students volunteer or are chosen as experts. Members of the class take turns giving them words in the foreign language for one of the experts to translate into English. If he can do it, he remains as expert. If he can't, the one who stumped him becomes the expert. Later, class members give words in English and the experts translate it into the language being studied.

Writing Directions:

In the language you are studying, write directions explaining step-by-step how to do a simple task, such as putting on a hat and coat, cooking an egg, or sawing a board. Select a volunteer and without telling him what the task is or using any English, read your directions to him and have him carry out the instructions.

Writing a Limerick:

Write a limerick in the language you are studying. Remember, the first, second, and fifth lines rhyme and the third and fourth lines rhyme.

Spelling Bee:

Select one student as moderator and hold a spelling bee entirely in the language you are studying. Use words from the foreign language text used by the class.

Vocabulary Bee:

Select one student as moderator and hold a vocabulary bee. The moderator, using the foreign language text, gives words in English. Students must translate the words.

About the Country:

In English, write a description of a major country where the language you are studying is spoken. Include any small details you may know.

Display:

Arrange a display of several items from around the room on a desk while a volunteer is out of the room. Have him come in and study the display for one minute, then, without looking at it again, list everything on the desk from memory. The student must use the language being studied.

Concentration:

Play "concentration." Divide into teams of two. Cut paper into 3-by-5-inch pieces and make a set of concentration cards, using antonyms in the language you are studying. For instance, if Spanish is your language, one card might read "si", its match would be "no," one card might read "noche," its match "dia," one card might read "caliente," its match "frio," and so on. Make ten to twenty pairs.

To play, spread out all the cards, face down. The first player turns over any two cards and shows them to the other player. If they should be a matching pair of antonyms, he then puts them face up at his side of the table. The first player may then have another try at finding a matched pair. If the first player does not find a match, the second player tries to remember where and what has been turned up and attempts to find a matched pair. Both players must see the cards turned up each time to help them locate matches. The game continues until the last card has been picked up. One point is given for each matched pair. The high score wins.

Traveling Game:

Play a traveling game; each student must think of some item to go in a suitcase, using only the language being studied. The first person in the first row must pack something beginning with the letter "a," the second with "b," the third must start with "c," and so on. Begin by saying, "I am going to visit relatives, so I will get out my big suitcase and pack it with my..."

Examples in Spanish:

First student—"Abrigos"   Second student—"Botas"

If a student makes a correct addition—it doesn't need to be a sensible one—he earns one point. If he cannot think of one, he loses two points.

Super Sentence:

Play super sentence. Let one student choose ten or twelve words from the dictionary in the language being studied and write them on the board. In ten minutes, the rest of the class tries to write a sentence using all the words or as many as they can. Read the sentence aloud.

Slapstick:

Arrange student desks in a circle. Each student is assigned a word in the language they are studying (recent vocabulary lists work great). One student is selected to stand in the center of the circle with a rolled up newspaper. The teacher calls out one of the assigned words and the student to whom the word has been assigned must quickly call out another word before the student in the center can "slap" their desk with the newspaper. Play continues until someone doesn't say a word before having their desk slapped, or mispronounces a word. In either event, the student assumes the role of the person in the center, who returns to their desk. Play resumes until class is over or students lose interest.

In large classes it may be beneficial to create two circles, thus allowing for more student involvement and interaction. Changing the assigned words halfway through the class will help to keep things interesting and challenging.

NAME _____

State Nicknames

Every state in the United States has a nickname. How many states can you correctly match with their nicknames.

	State		Nickname
_____ 1.	Alabama	A.	The Heart of Dixie
_____ 2.	Alaska	B.	Palmetto State
_____ 3.	Arizona	C.	The First State or Diamond State
_____ 4.	Arkansas	D.	Empire State of the South or Peach State
_____ 5.	California	E.	Show Me State
_____ 6.	Colorado	F.	Peace Garden State
_____ 7.	Connecticut	G.	Badger State
_____ 8.	Delaware	H.	The Last Frontier
_____ 9.	Florida	I.	The Sunflower State
_____ 10.	Georgia	J.	Green Mountain State
_____ 11.	Hawaii	K.	Garden State
_____ 12.	Idaho	L.	Sooner State
_____ 13.	Illinois	M.	Volunteer State
_____ 14.	Indiana	N.	Old Line State or Free State
_____ 15.	Iowa	O.	The Prairie State
_____ 16.	Kansas	P.	The Pelican State
_____ 17.	Kentucky	Q.	The Golden State
_____ 18.	Louisiana	R.	Sage Brush State or Silver State
_____ 19.	Maine	S.	Old Dominion
_____ 20.	Maryland	T.	The Hoosier State
_____ 21.	Massachusetts	U.	Keystone State
_____ 22.	Michigan	V.	Tar Heel State or Old North State
_____ 23.	Minnesota	W.	The Grand Canyon State
_____ 24.	Mississippi	X.	The Centennial State
_____ 25.	Missouri	Y.	The Gem State
_____ 26.	Montana	Z.	North Star State or Gopher State

(Continued on reverse side.)

_____ 27.	Nebraska	AA.	Cornhusker State
_____ 28.	Nevada	BB.	Granite State
_____ 29.	New Hampshire	CC.	Equality State
_____ 30.	New Jersey	DD.	The Evergreen State
_____ 31.	New Mexico	EE.	Beaver State
_____ 32.	New York	FF.	The Bay State or Old Colony
_____ 33.	North Carolina	GG.	The Hawkeye State
_____ 34.	North Dakota	HH.	The Sunshine State
_____ 35.	Ohio	II.	The Constitution State or Nutmeg State
_____ 36.	Oklahoma	JJ.	Lone Star State
_____ 37.	Oregon	KK.	The Blue Grass State
_____ 38.	Pennsylvania	LL.	Mountain State
_____ 39.	Rhode Island	MM.	Beehive State
_____ 40.	South Carolina	NN.	The Empire State
_____ 41.	South Dakota	OO.	Treasure State
_____ 42.	Tennessee	PP.	Little Rhody or Ocean State
_____ 43.	Texas	QQ.	The Aloha State
_____ 44.	Utah	RR.	The Land of Opportunity
_____ 45.	Vermont	SS.	The Pine Tree State
_____ 46.	Virginia	TT.	Mount Rushmore State or Coyote State
_____ 47.	Washington	UU.	Buckeye State
_____ 48.	West Virginia	VV.	The Land of Enchantment
_____ 49.	Wisconsin	WW.	Magnolia State
_____ 50.	Wyoming	XX.	The Great Lakes State or Wolverine State

State Nicknames
ANSWER KEY

	State		**Nickname**
1.	Alabama	A.	The Heart of Dixie
2.	Alaska	H.	The Last Frontier
3.	Arizona	W.	The Grand Canyon State
4.	Arkansas	RR.	The Land of Opportunity
5.	California	Q.	The Golden State
6.	Colorado	X.	The Centennial State
7.	Connecticut	II.	The Constitution State or Nutmeg State
8.	Delaware	C.	The First State or Diamond State
9.	Florida	HH.	The Sunshine State
10.	Georgia	D.	Empire State of the South or Peach State
11.	Hawaii	QQ.	The Aloha State
12.	Idaho	Y.	The Gem State
13.	Illinois	O.	The Prairie State
14.	Indiana	T.	The Hoosier State
15.	Iowa	GG.	The Hawkeye State
16.	Kansas	I.	The Sunflower State
17.	Kentucky	KK.	The Blue Grass State
18.	Louisiana	P.	The Pelican State
19.	Maine	SS.	The Pine Tree State
20.	Maryland	N.	Old Line State or Free State
21.	Massachusetts	FF.	The Bay State or Old Colony
22.	Michigan	XX.	The Great Lakes State or Wolverine State
23.	Minnesota	Z.	North Star State or Gopher State
24.	Mississippi	WW.	Magnolia State
25.	Missouri	E.	Show Me State

State Nicknames
ANSWER KEY (*Continued*)

26.	Montana	OO.	Treasure State
27.	Nebraska	AA.	Cornhusker State
28.	Nevada	R.	Sage Brush State or Silver State
29.	New Hampshire	BB.	Granite State
30.	New Jersey	K.	Garden State
31.	New Mexico	VV.	The Land of Enchantment
32.	New York	NN.	The Empire State
33.	North Carolina	V.	Tar Heel State or Old North State
34.	North Dakota	F.	Peace Garden State
35.	Ohio	UU.	Buckeye State
36.	Oklahoma	L.	Sooner State
37.	Oregon	EE.	Beaver State
38.	Pennsylvania	U.	Keystone State
39.	Rhode Island	PP.	Little Rhody or Ocean State
40.	South Carolina	B.	Palmetto State
41.	South Dakota	TT.	Mount Rushmore State or Coyote State
42.	Tennessee	M.	Volunteer State
43.	Texas	JJ.	Lone Star State
44.	Utah	MM.	Beehive State
45.	Vermont	J.	Green Mountain State
46.	Virginia	S.	Old Dominion
47.	Washington	DD.	The Evergreen State
48.	West Virginia	LL.	Mountain State
49.	Wisconsin	G.	Badger State
50.	Wyoming	CC.	Equality State

NAME _____

Locations and Associations
Activity One: Locating the States

Use the list of states below to locate and correctly label as many states as you can on the blank map. Do not "cross-out" the states on the list. You will use the list again in activity two. Use a map to check your work.

Alabama

Alaska

Arizona

Arkansas

California

Colorado

Connecticut

Delaware

Florida

Georgia

Hawaii

Idaho

Illinois

Indiana

Iowa

Kansas

Kentucky

Louisiana

Maine

Maryland

Massachusetts

Michigan

Minnesota

Mississippi

Missouri

Montana

Nebraska

Nevada

New Hampshire

New Jersey

New Mexico

New York

North Carolina

North Dakota

Ohio

Oklahoma

Oregon

Pennsylvania

Rhode Island

South Carolina

South Dakota

Tennessee

Texas

Utah

Vermont

Virginia

Washington

West Virginia

Wisconsin

Wyoming

Activity Two: State Associations

Grades
5-12

Next to each state on the list in activity one, write down one or two words which you associate with that state. For example you might associate "orange juice" with the state of Florida or "igloos" with the state of Alaska.

When you have finished, share your association words with a partner while they try and guess which state you are referring to. Then switch roles and you try to guess the states from their associations.

© Substitute Teaching Institute/Utah State University

Name _____

How Well Can You
Follow Directions?

Start in the United States and follow the directions to see where you end up.

1. Write down: THE UNITED STATES OF AMERICA

2. Take out all of the E's.

3. Take out every fifth letter.

4. Change the F to an A.

5. Move the S's to the front of the word.

6. Take out all of the T's.

7. Take out the first vowel and the last consonant.

8. Move the fourth and fifth letter to the end of the word.

9. Replace the S's with L's.

10. Remove the sixth, seventh, and eighth letters.

11. Move the double L's to be the third and fourth letters.

12. Where did you end up? _____

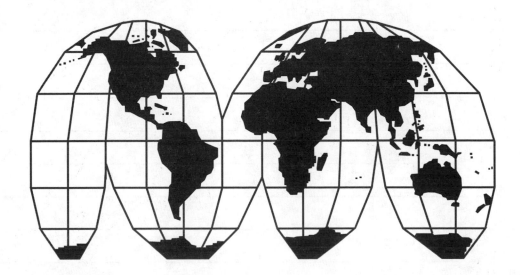

Answer: *Holland*

NAME _____

Where in the World

Listed below are 10 famous events and 10 well known places. Fill in the blanks as accurately and completely as you can.

Where did it happen?

1.   Writing of the Declaration of Independence _____

2.   First Olympics held _____

3.   Abraham Lincoln died _____

4.   Columbus first landed _____

5.   Treaty of Versailles signed _____

6.   Custer's Last Stand _____

7.   President John F. Kennedy assassinated _____

8.   Surrender papers of the Civil War signed _____

9.   Wright brothers first airplane flight _____

10. Martin Luther King shot and killed _____

Where is it located?

1.   Westminster Abbey _____

2.   Grand Canyon _____

3.   Louvre _____

4.   Taj Mahal _____

5.   Pyramids _____

6.   Rodeo Drive _____

7.   Leaning Tower of Pisa _____

8.   Mount Rushmore _____

9.   Eiffel Tower _____

10. Statue of Liberty _____

Where in the World
ANSWER KEY

Where did it happen?

1. Writing of the Declaration of Independence   Philadelphia , PA

2. First Olympics held   Olympia in Southern Greece (776 BC)

3. Abraham Lincoln died   Peterson Boarding House across the street from Ford's Theater in Washington DC

4. Columbus first landed   a small island in the Bahamas

5. Treaty of Versailles signed   Versailles, France (a suburb of Paris)

6. Custer's Last Stand   Indian encampment along the Little Big Horn River in Montana

7. President John F. Kennedy assassinated   Dallas, TX

8. Surrender papers of the Civil War signed   Mclean House near the Appomattox Courthouse in Appomattox, VA

9. Wright brothers first airplane flight   Kitty Hawk, NC

10. Martin Luther King shot and killed   balcony of the Lorraine Motel in Memphis, TN

Where is it located?

1. Westminster Abbey   London, England

2. Grand Canyon   Arizona

3. Louvre   Paris, France

4. Taj Mahal   Agra, India

5. Pyramids   four miles south of Cairo, Egypt

6. Rodeo Drive   Beverly Hills, CA

7. Leaning Tower of Pisa   Pisa, Italy

8. Mount Rushmore   South Dakota

9. Eiffel Tower   Paris, France

10. Statue of Liberty   Ellis Island, geographically a part of New Jersey but thought of as belonging to New York

NAME _____

A Citizenship Test

What does it take for a person from a foreign land to become an American citizen? In addition to being a person of good moral character, they must be at least 18 years old, have a solid grasp of the English language, and pass a citizenship test. Each year about one million immigrants take this test. They know their American history. Do you?

Below are 30 questions taken from the Immigration and Naturalization Service (INS) citizenship question pool. Write down the answer, or your best guess, then check your answers. You need to answer at least 18 of the 30 questions correctly to pass.

1. How many stars are there on our flag?

2. What do the stars on the flag mean?

3. What color are the stripes?

4. What do the stripes on the flag mean?

5. What is the date of Independence Day?

6. Independence from whom?

7. What do we call a change to the Constitution?

8. How many branches are there in our government?

9. How many full terms can a president serve?

10. Who nominates judges of the Supreme Court?

11. How many Supreme Court justices are there?

12. Who was the main writer of the Declaration of Independence?

13. What holiday was celebrated for the first time by American colonists?

14. Who wrote the Star-Spangled Banner?

15. What is the minimum voting age in the United States?

16. Who was president during the Civil War?

17. Which president is called the "Father of our Country?"

18. What is the 50th state of the Union?

19. What is the name of the ship that brought the Pilgrims to America?

20. Who has the power to declare war?

21. What were the 13 original states of the United States called?

22. In what year was the Constitution written?

23. What is the introduction to the Constitution called?

24. Which president was the first Commander in Chief of the United States Army and Navy?

25. In what month do we vote for the president?

26. How many times may a senator be re-elected?

27. Who signs bills into law?

28. Who elects the president of the United States?

29. How many states are there in the United States?

30. Who becomes president if both the president and vice president die?

Citizenship Test
ANSWER KEY

1. 50

2. One for each state in the Union.

3. Red and white

4. They represent the 13 original states.

5. July 4th

6. England

7. Amendments

8. Three

9. Two

10. The president

11. Nine

12. Thomas Jefferson

13. Thanksgiving

14. Francis Scott Key

15. 18

16. Abraham Lincoln

17. George Washington

18. Hawaii

19. The Mayflower

20. The Congress

21. Colonies

22. 1787

23. The Preamble

24. George Washington

25. November

26. There is no limit at the present time.

27. The president

28. The Electoral College

29. 50

30. Speaker of the House of Representatives

NAME _____

If History Were Altered

1. How would the world be different today if the colonists had not won the Revolutionary War and the new country had remained under British rule?

_____
_____
_____
_____

2. How would the world be different today if electricity had never been invented?

_____
_____
_____
_____

3. How would the world be different today if the atomic bomb had not been used against the Japanese in World War II?

_____
_____
_____
_____

4. How would the world be different today if Columbus and his ships had perished at sea and never reached the American Continents?

_____
_____
_____
_____

5. How would the world be different today if travel by airplane had never been developed?

_____
_____
_____
_____

NAME _____

The Constitution

Ratified in 1788 the Constitution of the United States has served as the basis for U.S. government ever since. It set up a federal government system with three branches, legislative, executive, and judicial, while allowing states to retain many rights and responsibilities. Try to correctly fill in the blanks to complete the preamble to this historical document.

Preamble

We the _____ of the United States, in order to _____ a more perfect _____, establish _____, insure domestic _____, provide for the common _____, promote the general _____, and secure the blessings of _____ to ourselves and our _____, do ordain and _____ this _____ for the _____ States of _____.

Throughout the 200+ years the constitution has been in place, relatively few amendments have been added to the original document. However, the amendments to the constitution, and rights guaranteed by them, are perhaps the most critical documentation of citizen rights in our society today. Can you match the amendment number and date to the responsibility, right, or law it secures.

_____ Amendment 1 (1791)   A.   Voting rights for blacks.

_____ Amendment 2 (1791)   B.   Lowered the voting age to eighteen.

_____ Amendment 4 (1791)   C.   Prohibition of alcohol.

_____ Amendment 5 (1791)   D.   Limited presidential terms of office.

_____ Amendment 13 (1865)   E.   Presidential succession outlined.

_____ Amendment 15 (1870)   F.   Do not have to testify against oneself.

_____ Amendment 18 (1919)   G.   Freedom of religion, speech, press, assembly, and petition.

_____ Amendment 19 (1920)   H.   Right to bear arms.

_____ Amendment 21 (1933)   I.   Warrants needed for searches and seizures.

_____ Amendment 22 (1951)   J.   Voting rights for women.

_____ Amendment 25 (1967)   K.   The repeal of the prohibition amendment.

_____ Amendment 26 (1971)   L.   The abolition of slavery.

The Constitution
ANSWER KEY

Preamble

We the people of the United States, in order to form a more perfect union, establish justice, insure domestic tranquillity, provide for the common defense, promote the general welfare, and secure the blessings of liberty to ourselves and our posterity, do ordain and establish this Constitution for the United States of America.

Constitutional Amendments

Amendment 1 (1791)	G.	Freedom of religion, speech, press, assembly, and petition.
Amendment 2 (1791)	H.	Right to bear arms.
Amendment 4 (1791)	I.	Warrants needed for searches and seizures.
Amendment 5 (1791)	F.	Do not have to testify against oneself.
Amendment 13 (1865)	L.	The abolition of slavery.
Amendment 15 (1870)	A.	Voting rights for blacks.
Amendment 18 (1919)	C.	Prohibition of alcohol.
Amendment 19 (1920)	J.	Voting rights for women.
Amendment 21 (1933)	K.	The repeal of the prohibition amendment.
Amendment 22 (1951)	D.	Limited presidential terms of office.
Amendment 25 (1967)	E.	Presidential succession outlined.
Amendment 26 (1971)	B.	Lowered the voting age to eighteen.

NAME _____

Presidential Trivia

Matching

_____ 1. George Washington

_____ 2. John Tyler

_____ 3. Grover Cleveland

_____ 4. Harry S. Truman

_____ 5. Gerald R. Ford

_____ 6. Woodrow Wilson

_____ 7. Theodore Roosevelt

A. Made the decision to use the atomic bomb against Japan.

B. The only president to serve two terms which did not follow each other.

C. Became the first president to hold regular press conferences to explain his policies.

D. As president, he created more than one million acres of national forests and parks.

E. Became the first vice-president to take over after a president had died in office.

F. Left school around the age of 14 to become a surveyor.

G. The only man to be both president and vice-president without being elected to either office.

True or False

_____ 1. President Lyndon B. Johnson was sworn into office aboard the presidential airplane.

_____ 2. President James Madison is referred to as "the father of the Declaration of Independence."

_____ 3. President John Quincy Adams was a poor public speaker with only an elementary knowledge of English.

_____ 4. President William H. Taft began the tradition of throwing out the first baseball of the major league baseball season.

_____ 5. Prior to becoming president, George Bush served as director of the Central Intelligence Agency.

_____ 6. President James Garfield amazed people by writing Latin with one hand and Greek with the other, at the same time.

_____ 7. President Andrew Johnson spent his childhood evenings reading books by the fire.

Which Does Not Belong

1. James Monroe   A. Monroe Doctrine   B. Louisiana Purchase   C. Civil War Soldier

2. Abraham Lincoln   A. Cherry Tree   B. Emancipation Proclamation C. Assassination

3. Ronald Reagan   A. Movie Star   B. Barbara   C. I don't remember

4. John F. Kennedy   A. Oldest President   B. Bay of Pigs   C. Lee Harvey Oswald

5. Dwight D. Eisenhower   A. I like Ike   B. Career Soldier   C. Wheelchair

6. George W. Bush   A. War on Terrorism   B. White House birds   C. Texas

Presidential Trivia Answers

Matching

F	1. George Washington	A.	Made the decision to use the atomic bomb against Japan.
E	2. John Tyler	B.	The only president to serve two terms which did not follow each other.
B	3. Grover Cleveland	C.	Became the first president to hold regular press conferences to explain his policies.
A	4. Harry S. Truman	D.	As president, he created more than one million acres of national forests and parks.
G	5. Gerald R. Ford	E.	Became the first vice-president to take over after a president had died in office.
C	6. Woodrow Wilson	F.	Left school around the age of 14 to become a surveyor.
D	7. Theodore Roosevelt	G.	The only man to be both president and vice-president without being elected to either office.

True or False

T 1. President Lyndon B. Johnson was sworn into office aboard the presidential airplane.

F 2. President James Madison is referred to as "the father of the Declaration of Independence."

F 3. President John Quincy Adams was a poor public speaker with only an elementary knowledge of English.

T 4. President William H. Taft began the tradition of throwing out the first baseball of the major league baseball season.

T 5. Prior to becoming president, George Bush served as director of the Central Intelligence Agency.

T 6. President James Garfield amazed people by writing Latin with one hand and Greek with the other, at the same time.

F 7. President Andrew Johnson spent his childhood evenings reading books by the fire.

Which Does Not Belong

1. James Monroe	A. Monroe Doctrine	B. Louisiana Purchase	C. ~~Civil War Soldier~~
2. Abraham Lincoln	A. ~~Cherry Tree~~	B. Emancipation Proclamation	C. Assassination
3. Ronald Reagan	A. Movie Star	B. ~~Barbara~~	C. I don't remember
4. John F. Kennedy	A. ~~Oldest President~~	B. Bay of Pigs	C. Lee Harvey Oswald
5. Dwight D. Eisenhower	A. I like Ike	B. Career Soldier	C. ~~Wheelchair~~
6. George W. Bush	A. War on Terrorism	B. ~~White House birds~~	C. Texas

This Year in History

Time: 30 minutes

Objective: Students will attempt to identify the things for which the current year will be remembered.

Materials: paper and pencils

Optional Materials:

news magazines, news papers, etc.

Advance Preparation: none

Procedure:

1.   Divide the class into small groups.
2.   List categories in which to identify specific events or fads of the year, such as the ones listed below.
   A. World Events
   B. National Events
   C. Political Events
   D. Music
   E. Commercials
   F. TV Shows
3.   Have students brainstorm as many items as they can for each category.
4.   As a class, compile a master list with one or two items in each category which best represents the time period.
5.   Discuss how students think the events and fads of this year will change or affect society in the years to come.

NAME _____

20 Events

Listed below are 20 events that changed American History. Match them with their description on the right.

_____ 1. Plymouth Colony

_____ 2. Slavery

_____ 3. Declaration of Independence

_____ 4. Ratification of the Constitution

_____ 5. 1800 Election

_____ 6. Louisiana Purchase

_____ 7. Seneca Falls Convention

_____ 8. Secession

_____ 9. Emancipation Proclamation

_____ 10. Transcontinental Railroad

_____ 11. Pullman Strike

_____ 12. Spanish-American War

_____ 13. Treaty of Versailles

_____ 14. National Origins Act, 1924

_____ 15. The Great Depression

_____ 16. Attack on Pearl Harbor

_____ 17. Montgomery Bus Boycott

_____ 18. Cuban Missile Crisis

_____ 19. Vietnam War

_____ 20. The Reagan Election

A. This protest set the civil rights movement in motion.

B. Marked the United States' arrival as a major world power.

C. Launched the movement that would help women win full citizenship, including the right to vote.

D. The establishment of a blueprint for American government.

E. Colonists began importing Africans to meet a severe labor shortage.

F. This legislation closed America's open door to immigrants.

G. A long bloody war that divided America and helped create a generation that mistrusted the government.

H. Presidential decree abolishing slavery.

I. The first major confrontation between the federal government and the labor movement.

J. Pilgrim settlers established a new settlement in North America.

K. Doubled the size of the United States and accelerated territorial expansion.

L. A confrontation with the Soviet Union that threatened to turn the Cold War into a nuclear war.

M. Economic crisis which left millions of Americans without jobs, homes, or food.

N. A decisive election in which the American people rejected big government and the welfare state.

O. The creation of a nation by the South and beginning of a long and terrible war.

P. Proclamation of the independence of a new nation which would be ruled by the people rather than a king.

Q. Marked the official beginning of the two party system with a peaceful, and orderly transfer of power.

R. A surprise Japanese attack that brought the United States into a Second World War.

S. Ended the First World War and set the conditions that led to the Second.

T. Transformed the social and economic life of America by linking the regions of the nation.

Select one of the events from the above list. Turn this paper over and write about how American life would be different today if this event had not occurred, or write a brief summary elaborating on the details of the event. You may want to use your textbook as a reference.

© Substitute Teaching Institute/Utah State University

20 Events
ANSWER KEY

1. Plymouth Colony

   J. Pilgrim settlers established a new settlement in North America.

2. Slavery

   E. Colonists began importing Africans to meet a severe labor shortage.

3. Declaration of Independence

   P. Proclamation of the independence of a new nation which would be ruled by the people rather than a king.

4. Ratification of the Constitution

   D. The establishment of a blueprint for American government.

5. 1800 Election

   Q. Marked the official beginning of the two party system with a peaceful, and orderly transfer of power.

6. Louisiana Purchase

   K. Doubled the size of the United States and accelerated territorial expansion.

7. Seneca Falls Convention

   C. Launched the movement that would help women win full citizenship, including the right to vote.

8. Secession

   O. The creation of a nation by the South and beginning of a long and terrible war.

9. Emancipation Proclamation

   H. Presidential decree abolishing slavery.

10. Transcontinental Railroad

    T. Transformed the social and economic life of America by linking the regions of the nation.

11. Pullman Strike

    I. The first major confrontation between the federal government and the labor movement.

12. Spanish-American War

    B. Marked the United States' arrival as a major world power.

13. Treaty of Versailles

    S. Ended the First World War and set the conditions that led to the Second.

14. National Origins Act, 1924

    F. This legislation closed America's open door to immigrants.

15. The Great Depression

    M. Economic crisis which left millions of Americans without jobs, homes, or food.

16. Attack on Pearl Harbor

    T. A surprise Japanese attack that brought the United States into a Second World War.

17. Montgomery Bus Boycott

    A. This protest set the civil rights movement in motion.

18. Cuban Missile Crisis

    L. A confrontation with the Soviet Union that threatened to turn the Cold War into a nuclear war.

19. Vietnam War

    G. A long bloody war that divided America and helped create a generation that mistrusted the government.

20. The Reagan Election

    N. A decisive election in which the American people rejected big government and the welfare state.

NAME _____

Are They for Real?

Some literary characterizations have been so vivid that they have almost taken a place in history. On the other hand, some real people have lived such legendary lives that they seem almost fictional. Can you identify the following men and explain if they are fact or fiction?

1. Alexander the Great

2. King Arthur

3. Paul Bunyan

4. Lloyd George

5. Johnny Appleseed

6. Robin Hood

7. Sherlock Holmes

8. Paul Revere

9. Mark Twain

10. Mike Fink

11. Marco Polo

12. Ivan the Terrible

Who Invented That?

Some of the men who invented things you use every day are familiar to you, but some of them may not be at all. Below is a list of familiar items used everyday. To the right is a list of inventors. Can you match the inventors with their invention?

1. The sewing machine

2. The phonograph

3. The television

4. The material called plastic

5. The sandwich

6. The pin

Elias Howe

Isaac M. Singer

Thomas Edison

Emile Berliner

John Wesley Hyatt

Alexander Parks

John Montagu

Lemuel W. Wright

Are They for Real?
ANSWER KEY

1. Alexander the Great is fact, he was the King of Macedonia, lived 356-323 B.C., and was considered a military genius for his conquests of Greece, Egypt, and the Middle East.

2. King Arthur is fiction, the legendary King of Britain who presided over the Roundtable.

3. Paul Bunyan is fiction, a tall-tale hero of early-American fiction.

4. Lloyd George is fact, he was the Prime Minister of Great Britain during WWI.

5. Johnny Appleseed's real name was John Chapman. One of the original ecologists, who walked over the American countryside planting apple seeds.

6. Robin Hood is fiction, though some authorities say the legendary charitable bandit of Sherwood Forest was based on a historical person, little evidence has been found.

7. Sherlock Holmes is the fictional detective to whom the solutions to tangled problems were "Elementary, my dear Watson." He was created by Sir Arthur Conan Doyle.

8. Paul Revere is fact, a silversmith and patriot of the American Revolution.

9. Mark Twain is fact, though his real name was Samuel Clemens, he was an American humorist and the author of *Tom Sawyer* and *The Adventures of Huckleberrry Finn*.

10. Mike Fink, though based on a real person, had so many tall-tales built around his career as a keel boat man that he must be considered fiction.

11. Marco Polo is fact, he was a Venetian who traveled through most of Asia on his trips in the thirteenth and fourteenth centuries.

12. Ivan the Terrible is fact, he was a Russian Czar who became noted for brutality and tyranny.

Who Invented That?
ANSWER KEY

1. Elias Howe received credit for this invention after a lengthy patent dispute with Isaac M. Singer.

2. Thomas Edison is credited with the invention of the phonograph, but Emile Berliner developed the flat disc record, the lateral-cut groove, and a method of duplicating records.

3. There is no single inventor of television. It is the result of many discoveries in electricity, electromagnetism, and electrochemistry.

4. Celluloid was the first of the synthetic plastics and was invented by John Wesley Hyatt following experiments done by Alexander Parkes. Hyatt was seeking material with which to make a better billiard ball.

5. The sandwich was invented by John Montagu, the Earl of Sandwich, because he was too busy gambling to take time out to eat a regular meal.

6. The ordinary pin with a solid head was first made on a machine invented by Lemuel W. Wright in 1824 in New Hampshire. Until then, the head of a pin was made by twisting fine wire into a ball and soldering it to one end of a sharpened wire.

Literature in the Classroom

Grades
K-12

Literature can enhance learning at every grade level. When sharing literature books:

- Use creative questioning to keep students interested. A question which requires a single right answer does little to keep students involved. Questions which have a variety of answers will keep students engaged in discussion and move learning forward.

- Have students reflect on what they would do in a similar situation, what else the character might have done, what would be different if the setting or era were changed in the story, etc.

- Ask students to justify actions and evaluate occurrences.

- Have trials of story predators.

- Write letters to the author. If you can get students involved in the story, positive behavior will be a natural result.

For a list of recommended children's literature see page 281.

Name Poetry

Subject: Language Arts

Time: 15-30 minutes

Materials Needed:

pencil and paper

Advance Preparation:

Create an example of a *Name Poem* to be used to teach the activity.

Objective:

Students will create a poem which is an expression of their own traits and personal characteristics.

Procedure:

1. Discuss different types of poetry. Ask students to share some poems that are familiar to them.

2. Tell the students that today they are going to create a poem about themselves.

3. Demonstrate an example of a *Name Poem* (acrostic poem) on the board.

Example:

C   is for chocolate chip cookies which are my favorite

Y   is for the yellow flowers that grow at my house

N   is for Nika my cat

T   is for the tree house I helped to build

H   is for happy thoughts

I   is for ice-cream on my birthday

A   is for all of the other things that make up me

4.   Ask the students to make a name poem using their own name.

5.   Share name poems with the class or in small groups.

6.   Collect poems for teacher evaluation and display.

Extension:

Create *Acrostic Poems* using other topics such as holidays, school subjects, sports, etc. Illustrate the poems by drawing and coloring pictures of the things written about in the poem.

Notes For The Teacher:

Younger students may have difficulty in completing this assignment with only one example for instruction. It may be helpful to create a second poem on the board, as a class, before they write their own.

Diamente Poetry

Subject: Language Arts

Time: 30+ minutes

Materials Needed:

pencil and paper

Advance Preparation:

Prepare a *Diamente Poem* pattern and example.

Objective:

Students will learn the *Diamente Pattern* for poetry and create a poem using this pattern.

Procedure:

1.   Talk about a specific topic (holiday, school subject, kind of food, famous person, etc.).

2.   Draw a chart on the board with the following categories: Smells, Tastes, Sounds, Sights, and Feelings.

3.   Fill in the chart with student suggestions for each category.

4.   Tell the students they will now use this information to write a diamente poem about this topic.

5.   Explain the pattern and put it on the board. See example.

	PATTERN	**EXAMPLE**
Line 1	subject	Fourth of July
Line 2	two adjectives or words that describe the subject	Fire Crackers, Bands
Line 3	three words that show action, usually "ing" words	Marching, Fighting, Picnicking
Line 4	two words that describe the subject	Flags, Sparklers
Line 5	a synonym (other name) for the subject	Independence Day

6.   As a class, compose a *Diamente Poem* about the selected topic using words from the chart on the board.

7.   Assign students to choose another topic and write a *Diamente Poem* on their own.

8.   Have volunteers share their poems with the class.

Extension:

Have students write a diamente about an upcoming holiday, then use the poem as the message in a greeting card.

Notes For The Teacher:

Students may have difficulty selecting their own topic to write on. You may wish to assign a specific topic to the whole class or brainstorm possible topics and suggest that students use one of the topics from the brainstorming session.

Writing and Revising

Time: 5-45 minutes

Objective: Students will practice writing and editing skills.

Advance Preparation:

Select a writing prompt for the students. Create a handout, write it on the board, or be prepared to give it verbally.

This activity can fill five minutes or an entire class hour depending on the complexity of the writing prompt, and at which step you want students to stop work and turn in their paper for teacher evaluation. There are no right or wrong answers, only an opportunity for students to explore their own thoughts, values, and beliefs. Encourage students to explain and justify their responses. Do not allow students to criticize the thoughts and opinions of others.

Procedure:

1. Provide the class with a writing prompt and time limit for completing the first draft of their work.

2. Have students exchange papers and edit one another's work for content and technical components.

3. Allow students time to discuss their editorial comments with one another, getting a second opinion from other students, if time permits.

4. After the editing process, have students complete a second draft of their work and hand it in for teacher evaluation.

Writing Prompts:

A. Write an invitation to a social event, real or imaginary, formal or casual.

B. Write a letter to a national news agency convincing them to cover a recent, or upcoming event at your school.

C. Write a menu for a new restaurant in town.

D.   Write a chronological report of everything you have done so far today.

E.   Write an outline of your life. Include events you anticipate will happen in the future.

F.   Write a letter to a music company explaining a billing mistake they made on your last order.

G.   Write a brief essay about what life as a street light would be like.

H.   Write a description of eating ice cream.

I.   Write an evaluation of the pen or pencil you are using.

J.   Write a memo to your boss asking him for a raise.

K.   Write a synopsis of a book you have recently read.

L.   Write a newspaper article about current fashion trends or a recent sporting event.

M.   If this weekend you could do anything you wanted to, what would you do?

N.   If you were a teacher and the students in your class wouldn't stop talking what would you do? What if you did that and they still didn't stop talking?

O.   If there was a poster contest coming up, would you rather create a poster all by yourself and get all of the credit, or work with a group and share the credit with the other group members.

P.   If you could be invisible for one day, what would you do?

Q.   If your parents were going to be living in a foreign country for the next year, would you rather go with them or stay in your own neighborhood with a friend? Why?

R.   What would the perfect day at school be like?

S.   If you could change just one thing about school, what would you change?

T.   Pretend you could only have one pair of shoes for the next year. Would you choose shoes which are really comfortable but look kind of goofy, or shoes that look really cool but are uncomfortable to wear?

U.   What are two things you don't like now, but ten years from now you don't think will be so bad?

V.   Suppose your dad forgot that he had promised to drive you and a friend to the movies one Saturday afternoon; he went golfing instead. If you could choose a punishment for your dad, what would it be? Do you think it would make him not do this again?

W.   What subjects in school do you think are really important to study? Why?

X.   If you could pick any age, and be that age for the rest of your life, what age would you want to be? Why?

Y.   If you could choose new jobs for your parents, what would you choose and why?

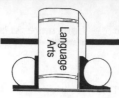

Sparkle

Subject: Language Arts

Time: 10-40 minutes

Materials Needed:

A list of level appropriate words to be used for spelling practice, pencil and paper

Objective:

Students will review the spelling of vocabulary or spelling list words through a group game.

Procedure:

1. This activity can be played as an entire class or in smaller groups. Start by having the students sit at their desks or stand next to them.

2. Give the class a word to spell. (You may choose to have them write the word on a piece of paper.)

3. Going row by row, have them spell the word one letter at a time. Everyone must listen so they know what letter when it becomes their turn.

4. After the last letter is said, the following person says "sparkle" and the next person sits down in their desk, indicating they are out. If someone misses a letter along the way, they too are asked to sit at their desk.

5. Those who are out will continue to write the words that are given on their paper and check them against those who are still in the game. The game can end at any point, but may continue until there is a final player.

NAME _____

Grades
3-8

Cold Words

Brr. . . . Can you s~~elbrmacnu~~ unscramble these cold words?

1. anmnsow _____
2. eci beuc _____
3. inretw _____
4. kewosflna _____
5. didnslge _____
6. odlc _____
7. bcierge _____
8. ngiisk _____
9. leccii _____
10. cie _____

11. lcreiag _____
12. oloig _____
13. eci rcaem _____
14. radzizlb _____
15. strof _____
16. zenorf _____
17. ushls _____
18. cie kasting _____
19. wnos _____
20. lalownsb _____

How many words can you think of that end in "ice" **There are at least 75!**

_____
_____
_____
_____
_____
_____
_____
_____
_____

Cold Scrambled Words:
1. snow man
2. ice cube
3. winter
4. snowflake
5. sledding
6. cold
7. iceberg
8. skiing
9. icicle
10. ice
11. glacier
12. igloo
13. ice cream
14. blizzard
15. frost
16. frozen
17. slush
18. ice skating
19. snow
20. snowball

Name _____

Let's Play Baseball

Grades
3-8

Use the following clues to help you identify 25 words associated with the game of baseball.

1. A summer pest. _____

2. Something you get in a nylon stocking. _____

3. Used to stay cool in hot weather. _____

4. A mistake. _____

5. Type of bird served at a holiday dinner. _____

6. A successful song or CD. _____

7. Container for storing orange juice. _____

8. A good foundation. _____

9. A famous Greek poet, also Bart Simpson's dad. _____

10. Not married. _____

11. To take something that isn't yours. _____

12. A quick visit. _____

13. The man at the dog pound. _____

14. You should slow down for these on a highway. _____

15. Giving up something you really like. _____

16. To multiply by two. _____

17. It flies only at night. _____

18. Used to make pancakes. _____

19. A disguise. _____

20. To boycott going to work. _____

21. The results of a test. _____

22. Not in. _____

23. Used to serve food on. _____

24. Found on the playground. _____

25. An expensive jewel. _____

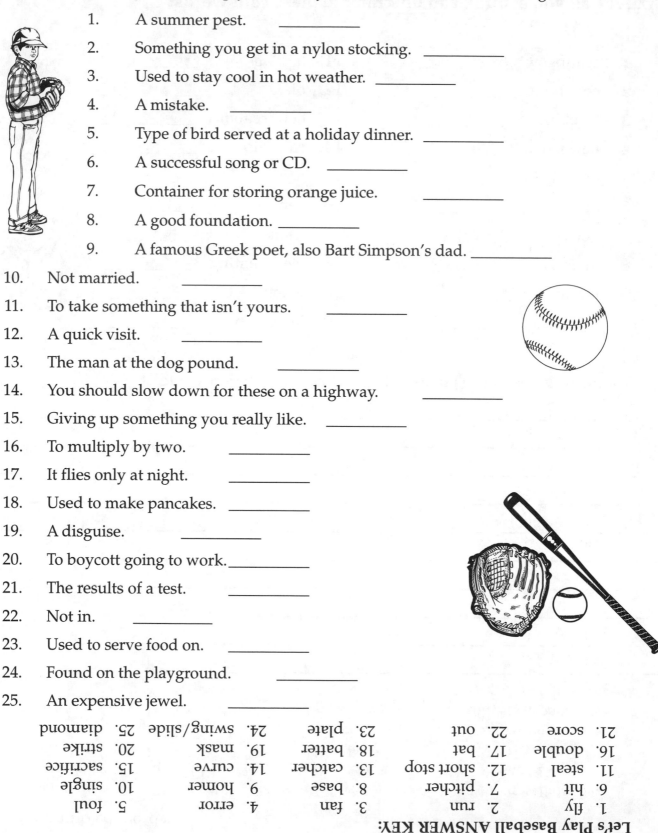

Let's Play Baseball ANSWER KEY:

1. fly	2. run	3. fan	4. error	5. foul
6. hit	7. pitcher	8. base	9. homer	10. single
11. steal	12. short stop	13. catcher	14. curve	15. sacrifice
16. double	17. bat	18. batter	19. mask	20. strike
21. score	22. out	23. plate	24. swing/slide	25. diamond

200

© Substitute Teaching Institute/Utah State University

My Awful, Terrible, Horrible, No Good, Very Bad Day

Grades
4-8

Subject: Language Arts

Time: 30+ minutes

Materials Needed:

pencils, paper, a copy of the book *Alexander and the Terrible Horrible No Good Very Bad Day* by Judith Viorst. Available for check-out at most libraries or for purchase at most bookstores.

Advance Preparation:

Objective:

Students will identify and express their experiences and feelings in writing.

Procedure:

1. Read the book *Alexander and the Terrible Horrible No Good Very Bad Day*. If the book is not available you may tell about a time when you had a bad day.

2. Have students discuss things that have happened and caused them to have a bad day. Try to discourage the discussion of morbid or disturbing events. (To learn more about brainstorming strategies, see page 72.)

3. Ask students to name feelings that they have when things go wrong (you may want to list these on the board).

4. Have students write about their own *Awful, Terrible, No Good, Very Bad Day*. Remind them to include feelings in their narration.

5. Ask volunteers to share their writing with the class.

6. Collect stories for the teacher to review.

Extension:

If there is time, have the students illustrate their writing. With student permission, place the illustrated experiences in a three ring binder for students to read at their leisure.

Notes For The Teacher:

Giving students specific writing guidelines will help insure quality work. For example you may require that younger students write at least six sentences and that older students write at least three paragraphs. Providing an example you have written about a very bad day of your own will also help to get them started on the right track.

Most students enjoy listening to a good story, so classroom management should not be much of a problem while you are reading. However, it is always a good idea to explain exactly the kind of behavior you expect during an activity before you begin (feet on the floor, pencils down, eyes on the teacher, facing forward, etc.).

Silly Stories

Grades
4-8

Subject: Language Arts

Time: 15 minutes

Materials Needed:

Silly Story worksheets and pencils

Advance Preparation:

Copy student worksheets.

Objective:

Students will practice naming nouns, verbs, adjectives, adverbs, and other words as they work cooperatively to compose *Silly Stories*.

Procedure:

1. Review with students the following parts of speech:

    A. Noun   = name of a person, place, or thing

    B. Verb   = shows action

    C. Adjective   = describes a noun (color, size, etc.)

    D. Adverb   = describes a verb (often ends in <u>ly</u>)

2. Explain that students are going to practice naming examples of these parts of speech as they work with a partner to complete a *Silly Story.*

3. Complete the example *Silly Story* as a class.

4. Read the completed example aloud to the class.

5. Divide the class into partners and distribute the *Silly Story* worksheets.

6. Have one student provide the words for one story with the other acting as scribe and narrator. Then switch roles to complete the second *Silly Story.*

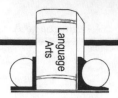

7. If time allows, students may volunteer to read their *Silly Stories* to the class.

Extension:

Trade partners and reuse the same worksheets to create new stories with a different person's input. Students in older grades may also enjoy writing their own *Silly Story* worksheets for classmates to complete.

Notes For The Teacher:

Detailed instructions and a reminder of classroom rules and expectations will help insure good classroom management during this fun activity.

Silly Story — Trip Into Outer Space

Grades
4-8

Directions: Ask a student for the part of speech or type of word as indicated. Write the word on the space provided. Repeat the process until all the spaces are filled. Read the completed *Silly Story* aloud to the class.

Last night I had a dream about you. At the age of (1) _____ you were good looking and

the captain of the spaceship (2) _____. In the dream you and a crew of (3)

_____ traveled to the planet (4) _____. The flight began at

(5) _____ a.m. "10... 9... 8... 7... 6... 5... 4... 3... 2... 1...(6)_____ ," the controller

called as the space ship blasted off from (7) _____. During take off the ship started to (8)

_____ but quick action from the crew kept it on course and prevented you from

crashing into (9) _____. Outer space was (10) _____ as you (11)

_____ past the moon everyone

(12) _____ to the windows to take a look. Finally the planet (13) _____ was in

sight. After orbiting the planet (14) _____ times, while you were looking for your (15)

_____ , the space ship finally landed. Everyone got off and began collecting (16)

_____ (17) _____ that were all over the surface of the planet, until you started

hearing (18) _____ noises. You were afraid the planet was going to explode so you

hurried back on board the ship and took off (19) _____. The last thing I remember

is your spaceship heading straight for the (20)_____ in my house. Boy was I ever

(21) _____ to wake up!

1.	number	12.	verb (past tense)
2.	proper name	13.	same planet as #4
3.	animal (plural)	14.	number
4.	planet	15.	personal belonging
5.	time of day	16.	adjective
6.	exclamation	17.	noun (plural)
7.	geographical location	18.	verb ending in "ing"
8.	verb	19.	adverb ending in "ly"
9.	geographical location	20.	room in a house
10.	adjective	21.	feeling
11.	verb (past tense)		

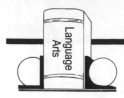
Silly Story — Getting to School

Directions: Ask a student for the kind of word indicated. Write the word on the space provided. Repeat the process until all the spaces are filled. Read the completed *Silly Story* aloud to the class.

You would not believe the (1) _____ time I had getting to school today. First of all my alarm went off at (2) _____ a.m. instead of (3) _____ a.m., which is the time I usually get up. When I (4)_____ my closet to decide what to wear the only clothes I could find were (5) _____ (6) _____ and (7) _____ (8) _____. Luckily the outfit I'd been wearing for the past (9) _____ days was still in the laundry basket so I put it on. Then I went to the (10) _____ to eat breakfast but, the only food I could find was (11) _____ and week old (12) _____ so I (13) _____ them together and ate it (14) _____. As if that wasn't bad enough, when I went to brush my teeth (15) _____ came out of the faucet instead of water. I was not having a (16) _____ day. Then my (17) _____ couldn't find the (18) _____ to the car, so I had to walk all the way to school carrying the (19) _____ (20) _____ I had made for my (21) _____ class project. Halfway to school a (22) _____ started chasing me so I (23) _____ ran the rest of the way. I rushed inside the front (24) _____ just as the late bell rang. I sure do hope the rest of my day goes (25) _____.

1. adjective
2. time
3. time
4. past tense verb
5. color
6. piece of clothing
7. adjective
8. piece of clothing
9. number
10. room in a house
11. food
12. food
13. past tense verb
14. adverb ending in "ly"
15. liquid
16. adjective
17. member of a family
18. part of a car
19. adjective
20. noun
21. school subject
22. animal
23. adverb ending in "ly"
24. part of a building
25. adverb

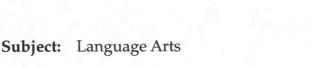

Writing for an Audience

Subject: Language Arts

Time: 15-30 minutes

Materials Needed:

pencil, paper, and a classroom object

Advance Preparation:

Make a list of potential audiences and purposes for writing to that audience on the chalkboard.

Objective:

Students will practice writing for different audiences.

Procedure:

1. Hold up a common object in the classroom (ruler, tape dispenser, key, tablet, etc.)

2. Discuss what the object is and what it is used for.

3. Ask the students to choose an audience and purpose for writing from the board then briefly write to that audience.

4. Instruct students to not tell anyone the audience they have selected.

5. Have volunteers read their paragraphs aloud and have the class members guess which audience they selected.

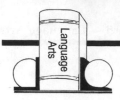
Samples of Audiences and Purposes:

1. Tell a story about the object to a kindergarten class.

2. Write in a journal as though you were an archeologist who dug up this object two hundred years from now.

3. You are from another planet and you are writing home to explain how the object is used on earth.

4. Write a memo to the principal explaining why this object should be purchased for every student in the school.

5. Explain to someone who has never seen this object how it is used.

6. Write specific details about this object so that the reader could walk into the classroom and pick it out from other similar objects.

Extension:

Have students select another object in the classroom and write about it without mentioning it by name. Trade papers among class members and have them try to figure out what object the person is writing about.

Notes For The Teacher:

Setting specific guidelines for the writing assignment will help with this activity. Specify that it should be at least five sentences or that ten minutes will be all the time available for writing. The younger the students the more specific instructions they will need.

Establishing guessing procedures for step five will help with classroom management. Students will want to call out their guesses as the volunteers read their paragraphs. Establish that no one is to guess until the reader has read their entire paper and that the reader will call on someone who is raising their hand when they have finished.

The Newspaper

Grades
K-12

Subject: Language Arts

Time: 15-30 minutes

Materials Needed:

newspaper, pencil, and paper

Advance Preparation:

None

Objective:

Apply real life examples to learning that occurs in the classroom.

The newspaper can be a lifesaver when substitute teaching. If there were no plans left for a classroom, the newspaper can be used to teach anything!

- In a kindergarten class, students can circle letters of the alphabet to learn upper and lower case concepts.

- In first grade, students could circle words they recognize or discuss the emotions depicted in pictures.

- At various grade levels, students can:

  —create a shopping list from ads and use math skills to create a total cost

  —forecast weather and discuss climate

  —work out statistics for sporting events

  —write a want ad or cartoon to expand writing skills to different audiences

  —create a budget using data from job opportunities, apartment rental, and food advertisement sections

Use some creativity and you can teach anything!

NAME _____

Pieces of a Puzzle

In many ways a story is like a puzzle. A story can be broken down into individual pieces such as good guys, bad guys, supporting characters, settings, beginning, ending, conflict, etc. Until all of the pieces are arranged correctly they may not make a lot of sense, but skillfully pieced together to form a complete picture, they can tell a powerful story. Choose one story piece from each column in the chart below and then put them together to create an original story of your own.

Protagonist (Good Guy)	Antagonist (Bad Guy)	Supporting Character	Setting	Conflict	Conclusion
chef	dentist	doctor	New York City	man vs. self	tragedy
nurse	father	best friend	beach	man vs. nature	to be continued
lawyer	college student	dog	foreign country	man vs. society	happy
teacher	athlete	waitress	hotel	good vs. evil	bad guy wins
cowboy	politician	movie star	ranch	something stolen	everyone dies
computer expert	thief	artist	cemetery	young vs. old	guy gets girl
detective	jockey	zoo keeper	used car lot	man vs. machine	only a dream
author	sister	computer	school	a dying request	the butler did it

Great Minds Think Alike

Time: 30 minutes

Objective: Students will write the ending to a short story then compare their conclusion with that of the original author.

Materials:

Copy of an original short story, paper, pencils

Advance Preparation:

Procedure:

1. Explain to students that you are going to read the beginning of a short story by Guy De Maupassant (or author of your choice) and then have them write the ending to the story. When everyone has finished writing, they will have the opportunity to share their writings and compare them to the conclusion written by the original author.

2. Read the beginning of *The Necklace* (or other short story of your choice) aloud to the class (see page 212).

3. Allow students 15 minutes to write a conclusion to the story.

4. If time permits, invite students to share their conclusions with the class or in small groups.

5. Read aloud the original ending to the story.

6. Ask students to list similarities and differences between their conclusion and the author's conclusion at the bottom of their page and then turn it in for teacher evaluation.

THE NECKLACE

GUY DE MAUPASSANT

She was one of those pretty, charming young ladies, born, as if through an error of destiny, into a family of clerks. She had no dowry, no hopes, no means of becoming known, appreciated, loved and married by a man either rich or distinguished; and she allowed herself to marry a petty clerk in the office of the Board of Education.

She was simple, not being able to adorn herself, but she was unhappy, as one out of her class; for women belong to no caste, no race, their grace, their beauty and their charm serving them in the place of birth and family. Their inborn finesse, their instinctive elegance, their suppleness of wit, are their only aristocracy, making some daughters of the people the equal of great ladies.

She suffered incessantly, feeling herself born for all delicacies and luxuries. She suffered from the poverty of her apartment, the shabby walls, the worn chairs and the faded stuffs. All these things, which another woman of her station would not have noticed, tortured and angered her. The sight of the little Breton, who made this humble home, awoke in her sad regrets and desperate dreams. She thought of quiet antechambers with their oriental hangings lighted by high bronze torches and of the two great footmen in short trousers who sleep in the large armchairs, made sleepy by the heavy air from the heating apparatus. She thought of large drawing rooms hung in old silks, of graceful pieces of furniture carrying bric-a-brac of inestimable value and of the little perfumed coquettish apartments made for five o'clock chats with the most intimate friends, men known and sought after, whose attention all women envied and desired.

When she seated herself for dinner before the round table, where the tablecloth had been used three days, opposite her husband who uncovered the tureen with a delighted air, saying; "Oh! the good potpie! I know nothing better than that," she would think of the elegant dinners of the shining silver, of the tapestries peopling the walls with ancient personages and rare birds in the midst of fairy forests; she thought of the exquisite food served on marvelous dishes, of the whispered gallantries, listened to with the smile of the Sphinx while eating the rose-colored flesh of the trout or a chicken's wing.

She had neither frocks nor jewels, nothing. And she loved only those things. She felt that she was made for them. She had such a desire to please, to be sought after, to be clever and courted.

She had a rich friend, a schoolmate at the convent, whom she did not like to visit; she suffered so much when she returned. And she wept for whole days from chagrin, from regret, from despair and disappointment.

One evening her husband returned, elated, bearing in his hand a large envelope.

"Here," he said, "here is something for you."

She quickly tore open the wrapper and drew out a printed card on which were inscribed these words:

The Minister of Public Instruction and Madame George Ramponneau ask the honor of M. and Mme Loisel's company Monday evening, January 18, at the Minister's residence.

Instead of being delighted, as her husband had hoped, she threw the invitation spitefully upon the table, murmuring:

"What do you suppose I want with that?"

"But my dearie, I thought it would make you happy. You never go out, and this is an occasion, and a fine one! I had a great deal of trouble to get it. Everybody wishes one, and it is very select; not many are given to employees. You will see the whole official world there."

She looked at him with an irritated eye and declared impatiently:

"What do you suppose I have to wear to such a thing as that?"

He had not thought of that; he stammered:

"Why, the dress you wear when we go to the theater. It seems very pretty to me."

He was silent, stupefied, in dismay, at the sight of his wife weeping. Two great tears fell slowly from the corners of her eyes toward the corners of her mouth; he stammered:

"What is the matter? What is the matter?"

By a violent effort she had controlled her vexation and responded in a calm voice, wiping her moist cheeks:

"Nothing. Only I have no dress and consequently I cannot go to this affair. Give your card to some colleague whose wife is better fitted out than I."

He was grieved but answered;

"Let us see, Matilda. How much would a suitable costume cost, something that would serve for other occasions, something very simple?"

She reflected for some seconds, making estimates and thinking of a sum that she could ask for without bringing with it an immediate refusal and a frightened exclamation from the economical clerk.

Finally she said in a hesitating voice:

"I cannot tell exactly, but it seems to me that four hundred francs ought to cover it."

He turned a little pale, for he had saved just this sum to buy a gun that he might be able to join some hunting parties the next summer, on the plains at Nanterre, with some friends who went to shoot larks up there on Sunday. Nevertheless, he answered:

"Very well. I will give you four hundred francs. But try to have a pretty dress."

The day of the ball approached, and Mme Loisel seemed sad, disturbed, anxious. Nevertheless, her dress was nearly ready. Her husband said to her one evening:

"What is the matter with you? You have acted strangely for two or three days."

And she responded: "I am vexed not to have a jewel, not one stone, nothing to adorn myself with. I shall have such a poverty-laden look. I would prefer not to go to this party."

He replied: "You can wear some natural flowers. At this season they look very chic. For ten francs you can have two or three magnificent roses."

She was not convinced. "No," she replied, "there is nothing more humiliating than to have a shabby air in the midst of rich women."

Then her husband cried out: "How stupid we are! Go and find your friend Madame Forestier and ask her to lend you her jewels. You are well enough acquainted with her to do this."

She uttered a cry of joy. "It is true!" she said. "I had not thought of that."

The next day she took herself to her friend's house and related her story of distress. Mme Forestier went to her closet with the glass doors, took out a large jewel case, brought it, opened it and said; "Choose, my dear."

She saw at first some bracelets, then a collar of pearls, then a Venetian cross of gold and jewels and of admirable workmanship. She tried the jewels before the glass, hesitated, but could neither decide to take them nor leave them. Then she asked:

"Have you nothing more?"

"Why, yes. Look for yourself. I do not know what will please you."

Suddenly she discovered in a black satin box a superb necklace of diamonds, and her heart beat fast with an immoderate desire. Her hands trembled as she took them up. She placed them about her throat, against her dress, and remained in ecstasy before them. Then she asked in a hesitating voice full of anxiety:

"Could you lend me this? Only this?"

"Why, yes, certainly."

She fell upon the neck of her friend, embraced her with passion, then went away with her treasure.

The day of the ball arrived. Mme Loisel was a great success. She was the prettiest of all, elegant, gracious, smiling and full of joy. All the men noticed her, asked her name and wanted to be presented. All the members of the Cabinet wished to waltz with her. The minister of education paid her some attention.

She danced with enthusiasm, with passion, intoxicated with pleasure, thinking of nothing, in the triumph of her beauty, in the glory of her success, in a kind of cloud of happiness that came of all this homage and all this admiration, of all these awakened desires and this victory so complete and sweet to the heart of woman.

She went home toward four o'clock in the morning. Her husband had been half asleep in one of the little salons since midnight, with three other gentlemen whose wives were

enjoying themselves very much.

He threw around her shoulders the wraps they had carried for the coming home, modest garments of everyday wear, whose poverty clashed with the elegance of the ball costume. She felt this and wished to hurry away in order not to be noticed by the other women who were wrapping themselves in rich furs.

Loisel detained her. "Wait," said he. "You will catch cold out there. I am going to call a cab."

But she would not listen and descended the steps rapidly. When they were in the street they found no carriage, and they began to seek for one, hailing the coachman whom they saw at a distance.

They walked along toward the Seine, hopeless and shivering. Finally they found on the dock one of those old nocturnal coupes that one sees in Paris after nightfall, as if they were ashamed of their misery by day.

It took them as far as their door in Martyr Street, and they went wearily up to their apartment. It was all over for her. And on his part he remembered that he would have to be at the office by ten o'clock.

She removed the wraps from her shoulders before the glass for a final view of herself in her glory. Suddenly she uttered a cry. Her necklace was not around her neck.

Her husband, already half undressed, asked: "What is the matter?"

She turned toward him excitedly:

"I have—I have—I no longer have Madame Forestier's necklace."

He arose in dismay: "What! How is that? It's not possible."

And they looked in the folds of the dress, in the folds of the mantle in the pockets, everywhere. They could not find it.

He asked: "You are sure you still had it when we left the house?"

"Yes, I felt it in the vestibule as we came out."

"But if you had lost it in the street we should have heard it fall. It must be in the cab."

"Yes. It is probable. Did you take the number?"

"No. And you, did you notice what it was?"

"No."

They looked at each other, utterly cast down. Finally Loisel dressed himself again.

"I am going," said he, "over the track where we went on foot, to see if I can find it."

And he went. She remained in her evening gown, not having the force to go to bed, stretched upon a chair, without ambition or thoughts.

Toward seven o'clock her husband returned. He had found nothing.

He went to the police and to the cab offices and put an advertisement in the newspapers, offering a reward; he did everything that afforded them a suspicion of hope.

She waited all day in a state of bewilderment before this frightful disaster. Loisel returned at evening, with his face harrowed and pale, and had discovered nothing.

"It will be necessary," said he, "to write to your friend that you have broken the clasp of the necklace and that you will have it repaired. That will give us time to turn around."

She wrote as he dictated.

At the end of a week they had lost all hope. And Loisel, older by five years, declared:

"We must take measures to replace this jewel."

The next day they took the box which had inclosed it to the jeweler whose name was on the inside. He consulted his books.

"It is not I, Madame," said he, "who sold this necklace; I only furnished the casket."

Then they went from jeweler to jeweler, seeking a necklace like the other one, consulting their memories, and ill, both of them, with chagrin and anxiety.

In a shop of the Palais-Royal they found a chaplet of diamonds which seemed to them exactly like the one they had lost. It was valued at forty thousand francs. They could get it for thirty-six thousand.

Stop reading at this point and assign students to write their own conclusion.

THE NECKLACE — concluded

GUY DE MAPASSANT

They begged the jeweler not to sell it for three days. And they made an arrangement by which they might return it for thirty-four thousand francs if they found the other one before the end of February.

Loisel possessed eighteen thousand francs which his father had left him.

He borrowed the rest.

He borrowed it, asking for a thousand francs of one, five hundred of another, five louis of this one and three louis of that one. He gave notes, made ruinous promises, took money of usurers and the whole race of lenders. He compromised his whole existence, in fact, risked his signature without even knowing whether he could make it good or not, and, harassed by anxiety for the future by the black misery which surrounded him and the prospect of all physical privations and moral torture, he went to get the new necklace, depositing on the merchant's counter thirty-six thousand francs.

When Mme Loisel took back the jewels to Mme Forestier the latter said to her in a frigid tone:

"You should have returned these to me sooner, for I might have needed them."

She did open the jewel box as her friend feared she would. If she should perceive the substitution what would she think? What should she say? Would she take her for a robber?

Mme Loisel now knew the horrible life of necessity. She did her part, however, completely, heroically. It was necessary to pay this frightful debt. She would pay it. They sent away the maid; they changed their lodgings they rented some rooms under a mansard roof.

She learned the heavy cares of a household, the odious work of a kitchen. She washed the dishes, using her rosy nails upon the greasy pots and the bottoms of the stewpans. She washed the soiled linen, the chemises and dishcloths, which she hung on the line to dry; she took down the refuse to the street each morning and brought up the water, stopping at each landing to breathe. And, clothed like a woman of the people, she went to the grocer's, the butcher's and the fruiterer's with her basket on her arm, shopping, haggling to the last sou her miserable money.

Every month it was necessary to renew some notes, thus obtaining time, and to pay others.

The husband worked evenings, putting the books of some merchants in order, and nights he often did copying at five sous a page.

And this life lasted for ten years.

At the end of ten years they had restored all, all, with interest of the usurer, and accumulated interest, besides.

Mme Loisel seemed old now. She had become a strong, hard woman, the crude woman of the poor household. Her hair badly dressed, her skirts awry, her hands red, she spoke in a loud tone and washed the floors in large pails of water. But sometimes, when her husband was at the office, she would sear herself before the window and think of that evening party of former times, of that ball where she was so beautiful and so flattered.

How would it have been if she had not lost that necklace? Who knows? Who knows? How singular is life and how full of changes! How small a thing will ruin or save one!

One Sunday, as she was taking a walk in the Champs Elysees to rid herself of the cares of the week, she suddenly perceived a woman walking with a child. It was Mme Forestier, still young, still pretty, still attractive. Mme Loisel was affected. Should she speak to her? Yes, certainly. And now that she had paid, she would tell her all. Why not?

She approached her. "Good morning, Jeanne."

Her friend did not recognize her and was astonished to be so familiarly addressed by this common personage. She stammered:

"But, Madame—I do not know—You must be mistaken."

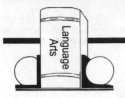

THE NECKLACE — concluded

GUY DE MAPASSANT

"No, I am Matilda Loisel."

Her friend uttered a cry of astonishment: "Oh! my poor Matilda! How you have changed!"

"Yes, I have had some hard days since I saw you, and some miserable ones—and all because of you."

"Because of me? How is that?"

"You recall the diamond necklace that you loaned me to wear to the minister's ball?"

"Yes, very well."

"Well, I lost it."

"How is that, since you returned it to me?"

"I returned another to you exactly like it. And it has taken us ten years to pay for it. You can understand that it was not easy for us who have nothing. But it is finished, and I am decently content."

Mme Forestier stopped short. She said:

"You say that you bought a diamond necklace to replace mine?"

"Yes. You did not perceive it then? They were just alike."

And she smiled with a proud and simple joy. Mme Forestier was touched and took both her hands as she replied:

"Oh, my poor Matilda! Mine were false. They were not worth over five hundred francs!"

How Many are There?

Grades
K-5

Subject: Math

Time: 15-30 minutes

Materials:

chalkboard and chalk

Advance Preparation:

This lesson works well with *Survey Your Friends* on page 226.

Objective:

Students will categorize and count their classmates in various ways.

Procedure:

1. Discuss ways that class members are alike and different (eye color, hair color, number of siblings, number of places lived, month they were born, number of letters in their name, favorite food, color, candy, book, etc.).

2. Make a grid on the board similar to the one below using one of the categories mentioned above.

3. Complete the grid as a class.

When We Were Born

Jan	Feb	Mar	Apr	May	June	July	Aug	Sept	Oct	Nov	Dec

4. Have the students determine which column has the most and which has the least.

5. Summarize by explaining that all things can be categorized in different ways.

6. Have the students decide another way to categorize the class and complete a second grid.

Extension:

Discuss situations where the information from the grids may be useful.

Extension:

Assign students to independently make a grid categorizing the members of their family in some way.

Notes For The Teacher:

Developing an organized method for determining and recording grid information will help significantly with classroom management during this activity. For example, fill in the columns one by one by having students who should be counted for each column raise their hand as you come to it. Ask another student, who is not being counted, to count the hands raised and enter the number on the grid.

Name _____

Addition Facts

7 + 5	4 + 4	6 + 3	3 + 2	5 + 1	9 + 4	8 + 6	6 + 5	3 + 3	9 + 8
8 + 7	7 + 7	3 + 1	6 + 2	7 + 4	5 + 3	10 + 9	6 + 6	7 + 3	6 + 1
5 + 4	4 + 3	9 + 2	10 + 3	9 + 9	10 + 6	8 + 5	6 + 4	4 + 2	10 + 5
5 + 5	8 + 3	9 + 7	7 + 6	8 + 8	9 + 6	2 + 1	7 + 2	10 + 7	8 + 4
10 + 8	2 + 5	9 + 3	8 + 1	2 + 2	10 + 4	9 + 5	9 + 1	10 + 2	8 + 2

Name _____

Subtraction Facts

7 − 5	4 − 4	6 − 3	3 − 2	5 − 1	9 − 4	8 − 6	6 − 5	3 − 3	9 − 8
8 − 7	7 − 7	3 − 1	6 − 2	7 − 4	5 − 3	10 − 9	6 − 6	7 − 3	6 − 1
5 − 4	4 − 3	9 − 2	10 − 3	9 − 9	10 − 6	8 − 5	6 − 4	4 − 2	10 − 5
5 − 5	8 − 3	9 − 7	7 − 6	8 − 8	9 − 6	2 − 1	7 − 2	10 − 7	8 − 4
10 − 8	2 − 5	9 − 3	8 − 1	2 − 2	10 − 4	9 − 5	9 − 1	10 − 2	8 − 2

Math

Name _____

Grades
3-6

Multiplication Facts

7	4	6	3	5	9	8	6	3	9
x 5	x 4	x 3	x 2	x 1	x 4	x 6	x 5	x 3	x 8

8	7	3	6	7	5	10	6	7	6
x 7	x 7	x 1	x 2	x 4	x 3	x 9	x 6	x 3	x 1

5	4	9	10	9	10	8	6	4	10
x 4	x 3	x 2	x 3	x 9	x 6	x 5	x 4	x 2	x 5

5	8	9	7	8	9	2	7	10	8
x 5	x 3	x 7	x 6	x 8	x 6	x 1	x 2	x 7	x 4

10	2	9	8	2	10	9	9	10	8
x 8	x 5	x 3	x 1	x 2	x 4	x 5	x 1	x 2	x 2

Name _____

Grades
3-6

Division Facts

5)35 4)16 3)18 2)6 1)5 4)36 6)48 6)30 3)9 8)72

7)56 7)49 1)3 2)12 4)28 3)15 9)90 6)36 3)21 1)6

4)20 3)12 2)18 3)30 9)81 6)60 5)40 4)24 2)8 5)50

5)25 3)24 7)63 6)42 8)64 6)54 1)2 2)14 7)70 4)32

8)80 5)10 3)27 1)8 2)4 4)40 5)45 1)9 2)20 2)16

© Substitute Teaching Institute/Utah State University

Salute

Subject: Math

Time: 5-30 minutes

Materials Needed:

One deck of numbered cards per group. Scratch paper, if needed.

Objective:

Students will enjoy a fast paced review of addition, subtraction, multiplication, and division math facts. Salute is a small group math facts activity that requires two players and one dealer.

Procedure:

1. Three students work as a group. The dealer holds the deck of cards and deals one card, face down, to each player.

2. Both players "salute" with the card by placing the card face out while holding it on their foreheads. This process should allow the dealer to see both cards and the players to see each others cards, but not his/her own card.

3. After the players "salute," the dealer adds or multiplies the cards together and tells the players the answer.

4. When the players hear the answer, they will use an opposite operation and orally respond with the number on the card s/he is holding.

Graph Art

Subject: Math

Time: 15-30 minutes

Materials Needed:

Graph Art worksheets, pencils, and crayons

Advance Preparation:

Copy worksheets and determine six points to be used in the art activity.

Objective:

Students will learn to plot points on a graph and create an image which incorporates several plotted points.

Procedure:

1. Teach or review with students how to plot a point on a graph (see *Notes For The Teacher*).

2. Distribute graph worksheets and have students plot six pre-determined points.

3. Make sure the points are dark enough to be seen on the back side of the paper.

4. Demonstrate or show examples of graph art (see next page).

5. Explain the rules for *Graph Art*.

    A. All dots must be connected.

    B. A dot may connect more than once.

C. All dots must be used.

D. Other lines may be added to create the picture.

6. Have the students turn their paper over and use the dots to create their own graph art.

7. If time allows, color the artwork.

8. Turn in artwork for classroom display. It is fun to see different pictures that all contain the same six dots.

Graph Art Examples

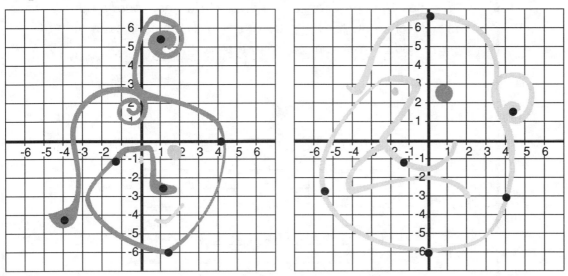

Extension:

Number and display pictures without the students' names visible. Have each class member vote by secret ballot for their three favorite works of art. Tally the votes on the board and award a prize to the classroom winner.

Notes For The Teacher:

Making copies of or keeping graph art done by previous classes is a great way to collect a portfolio of examples. Often students who finish early are more than willing to make another picture for you to keep and show to other classes.

Background Information On Plotting Points

A point on a graph can be found using a pair of numbers. The number pair for a point is called its coordinates. The *first* number in the pair tells how far to go right or left. The *second* number in the pair tells how far to go up or down. Below are examples of how to find points from coordinates.

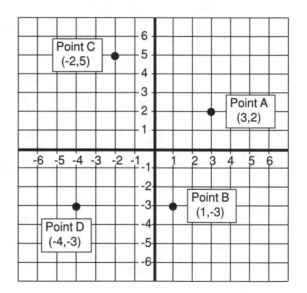

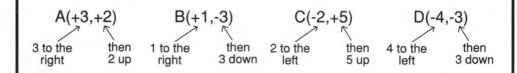

A(+3,+2)   B(+1,-3)   C(-2,+5)   D(-4,-3)

3 to the   then   1 to the   then   2 to the   then   4 to the   then
right   2 up   right   3 down left   5 up   left   3 down

Name _____

Graph Art

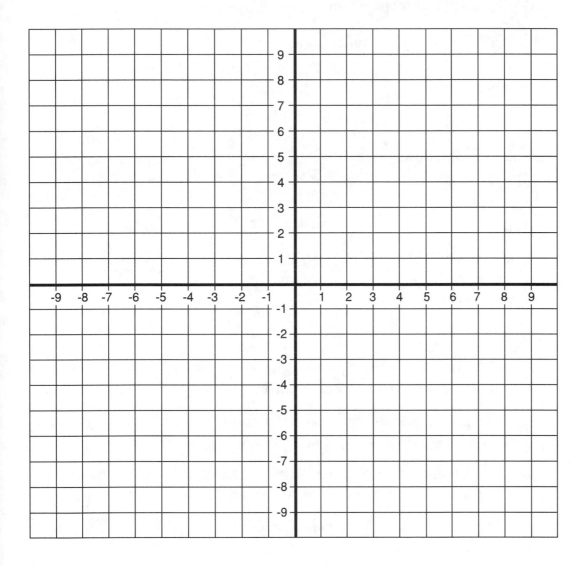

Survey Your Friends

Subject: Math

Time: 30+ minutes

Materials Needed:

pencil and paper

Advance Preparation:

Objective:

Students will survey the class on a topic of interest, create a bar graph to illustrate the results, and develop questions relating to the information collected.

Procedure:

1. Conduct a class survey on a topic of interest. (Favorite candy bar, color, professional football team, etc.)

2. Have the students construct a bar graph illustrating the results of the survey. (See example on next page.)

3. Have students write three questions that require using the bar graph to determine the correct answer. (See example below.)

4. Exchange papers among classmates and have them answer each other's questions.

5. Be sure that both the student who wrote the questions and the student who answered them are clearly identified on the paper, then hand in for teacher evaluation.

Example Bar Graph and Questions

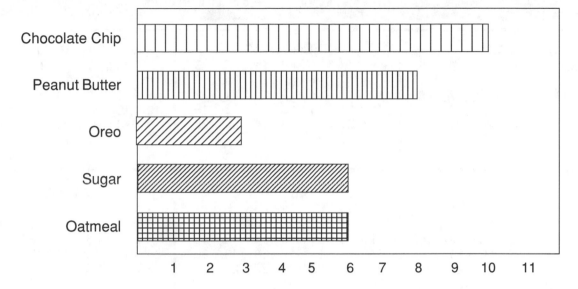

Favorite Cookie Graph

Questions:

1. How many more students voted for Oatmeal than Oreo Cookies? _____

2. What were the total number of votes for Peanut Butter and Sugar cookies combined? _____

3. Which kind of cookie got the most votes? _____

Extension:

Have students develop individual surveys to conduct outside of class. Assign them to survey 30 people, at lunch, during recess, etc. After the surveys are complete, assign students to construct bar graphs to be compiled in a book or displayed in the classroom for other students to see.

Notes For The Teacher:

Finding an organized way to conduct the class survey will help with classroom management during this activity. One method is to have students write their answers on a piece of paper. Collect the papers and have one student read the results while another tallies the information on the board. The students love to participate like this and it leaves the teacher free to monitor the class and deal with any disruptive behavior without interrupting the progress of the lesson.

It is also helpful in classrooms where students have not had much graph experience to model the bar graph on the board while they construct their own on paper.

Name _____

Calendar Math

JANUARY
S	M	T	W	Th	F	S
						1
2	3	4	5	6	7	8
9	10	11	12	13	14	15
16	17	18	19	20	21	22
23	24	25	26	27	28	29
30	31					

FEBRUARY
S	M	T	W	Th	F	S
		1	2	3	4	5
6	7	8	9	10	11	12
13	14	15	16	17	18	19
20	21	22	23	24	25	26
27	28	29				

MARCH
S	M	T	W	Th	F	S
			1	2	3	4
5	6	7	8	9	10	11
12	13	14	15	16	17	18
19	20	21	22	23	24	25
26	27	28	29	30	31	

APRIL
S	M	T	W	Th	F	S
						1
2	3	4	5	6	7	8
9	10	11	12	13	14	15
16	17	18	19	20	21	22
23	24	25	26	27	28	29
30						

MAY
S	M	T	W	Th	F	S
	1	2	3	4	5	6
7	8	9	10	11	12	13
14	15	16	17	18	19	20
21	22	23	24	25	26	27
28	29	30	31			

JUNE
S	M	T	W	Th	F	S
				1	2	3
4	5	6	7	8	9	10
11	12	13	14	15	16	17
18	19	20	21	22	23	24
25	26	27	28	29	30	

JULY
S	M	T	W	Th	F	S
						1
2	3	4	5	6	7	8
9	10	11	12	13	14	15
16	17	18	19	20	21	22
23	24	25	26	27	28	29
30	31					

AUGUST
S	M	T	W	Th	F	S
		1	2	3	4	5
6	7	8	9	10	11	12
13	14	15	16	17	18	19
20	21	22	23	24	25	26
27	28	29	30	31		

SEPTEMBER
S	M	T	W	Th	F	S
					1	2
3	4	5	6	7	8	9
10	11	12	13	14	15	16
17	18	19	20	21	22	23
24	25	26	27	28	29	30

OCTOBER
S	M	T	W	Th	F	S
1	2	3	4	5	6	7
8	9	10	11	12	13	14
15	16	17	18	19	20	21
22	23	24	25	26	27	28
29	30	31				

NOVEMBER
S	M	T	W	Th	F	S
			1	2	3	4
5	6	7	8	9	10	11
12	13	14	15	16	17	18
19	20	21	22	23	24	25
26	27	28	29	30		

DECEMBER
S	M	T	W	Th	F	S
					1	2
3	4	5	6	7	8	9
10	11	12	13	14	15	16
17	18	19	20	21	22	23
24	25	26	27	28	29	30
31						

1. How many days are there between March 5th and October 30th? _____

2. How many months have names with four or less letters in their name? _____

3. How many days are in these "short name" months combined? _____

4. How many days are there in the month you were born? _____

5. Laws require that there are 180 days in a school year. If school started on August 15 and you went seven days a week without any days off for holidays or weekends, when would summer vacation begin? _____

6. Suppose there was a law that allowed you to attend school only on odd numbered dates, Monday through Friday. How many days would you attend school in the month of October? _____

7. There are 24 hours in one day. How many hours are there in the month of June? ____

8. There are 365 days in a year (excluding leap year). Figure out, as of today, how many days old you are. _____

9. Which months have 30 days?   Which have 31 days?

_____ _____   _____ _____

_____ _____   _____ _____

_____ _____   _____ _____

_____ _____   _____ _____

10. Which month did you not list in the previous question? _____

11. If you left on April 26th for a 14 day vacation to Hawaii, on what day would you return home? _____

12. How many school days are there between February 26 and April 19? _____

13. What is something you remember from last year?_____

14. If school lets out for summer vacation on June 1 and begins again on August 28, how many days of summer vacation do you get?_____

15. How many Mondays are there in the month of October?_____

16. How many days are there between Christmas Day and New Years Day? _____

17. Do any months in the calendar have a Friday the 13th? _____ Which one(s)? _____

_____

18. How many days are there between Valentine's Day and Independence Day? _____

19. Suppose you only went to school on Monday, Wednesday, and Friday. How many days would you go to school in the month of March? _____

20. Think up your own Calendar Math Question and have someone else answer it.

Question: _____

_____

Answer: _____

Calendar Math
ANSWER KEY

1. 238 days

2. 3 months

3. 92 days

4. answers will vary

5. February 10

6. 11 days

7. 720 hours

8. answers will vary

9. 30 Days: April, June, September, November / 31 Days: January, March, May, July, August, October, December

10. February

11. May 9

12. 37 days

13. answers will vary

14. 88 days

15. 5 Mondays

16. 6 days

17. Yes; October

18. 140 days

19. 14 days

20. answers will vary

NAME _____

Number Patterns

Find the next three numbers in the sequences below.

1.   150, 200, 250, 300,   _____ , _____ , _____

2.   1, 7, 49, 343,   _____ , _____ , _____

3.   654, 641, 628, 615,   _____ , _____ , _____

4.   13312, 3328, 832, 208,   _____ , _____ , _____

5.   72, 78, 84, 90,   _____ , _____ , _____

6.   23, 27.5, 32, 36.5,   _____ , _____ , _____

7.   123, 234, 345, 456,   _____ , _____ , _____

8.   115, 105, 96, 88,   _____ , _____ , _____

9.   86, 84, 80, 74,   _____ , _____ , _____

10.   2, 3, 4.5, 6.75,   _____ , _____ , _____

11.   99, 98, 96, 93,   _____ , _____ , _____

12.   11, 43, 75, 107,   _____ , _____ , _____

13.   2, 5, 11, 20,   _____ , _____ , _____

14.   842, 759, 676, 593,   _____ , _____ , _____

15.   1, 2, 4, 7,   _____ , _____ , _____

16.   5, 16, 38, 82,   _____ , _____ , _____

17.   12, 18, 27, 40.5,   _____ , _____ , _____

18.   2, 3, 5, 8, 13,   _____ , _____ , _____

19.   4, 13, 40, 121,   _____ , _____ , _____

20.   888, 448, 228, 118,   _____ , _____ , _____

Number Patterns
ANSWER KEY

1. 150, 200, 250, 300, **350, 400, 450**   (+ 50)

2. 1, 7, 49, 343, **2401, 16807, 117649**   (x 7)

3. 654, 641, 628, 615, **602, 589, 576**   (– 13)

4. 13312, 3328, 832, 208, **52, 13, 3.25**   (÷ 4)

5. 72, 78, 84, 90, **96, 102, 108**   (+ 6)

6. 23, 27.5, 32, 36.5, **41, 45.5, 50**   (+ 4.5)

7. 123, 234, 345, 456, **567, 678, 789**
   drop the first number, add the next consecutive
   counting number on the end

8. 115, 105, 96, 88, **81, 75, 70**   (– 10, – 9, – 8, – 7 …)

9. 86, 84, 80, 74, **66, 56, 44**   (– 2, – 4, – 6, – 8, – 10 …)

10. 2, 3, 4.5, 6.75, **10.125, 15.1875, 22.78125**   (x 1.5)

11. 99, 98, 96, 93, **89, 84, 78**   (– 1, –2, – 3, – 4, – 5 …)

12. 11, 43, 75, 107, **139, 171, 203**   (+ 32)

13. 2, 5, 11, 20, **32, 47, 65**   (+ 3, + 6, + 9, + 12)

14. 842, 759, 676, 593, **510, 427, 344**   (– 83)

15. 1, 2, 4, 7, **11, 16, 22**   (+ 1, +2, +3, +4, +5)

16. 5, 16, 38, 82, **170, 346, 698**   (+ 3 then x 2)

17. 12, 18, 27, 40.5, **60.75, 91.125, 136.6875**   (÷2 then + the original number)

18. 2, 3, 5, 8, 13, **21, 34, 55**   (add the two previous
                                                            numbers together)

19. 4, 13, 40, 121, **364, 1093, 3280**   (x 3 then + 1)

20. 888, 448, 228, 118, **63, 35.5, 21.75**   (÷ 2 then + 4)

A Dozen Puzzlers

1. A lady goes to the well with two jugs. One holds exactly nine quarts and the other holds exactly five quarts. She needs exactly three quarts of water for her soup. Using only two jugs, which she cannot mark in any way, how can she get the three quarts?

Answer She fills the nine-quart jug and pours five quarts from it into the five-quart jug. She empties the five-quart jug and pours the remaining four-quarts left in the nine-quart jug into the five-quart jug. Now she fills the nine-quart jug again and pours one quart in to fill up the five-quart jug. Then she empties the five-quart jug and fills it again with five quarts from the eight quarts that are in the nine-quart jug. And now, she has three quarts left in the nine-quart jug—just enough to make her soup!

2. Five hundred people shopped in a candy store and spent a total of $500. The women each spent $1, the children spent one cent each, and the men each spent $5. How many men shopped in the store? How many women? How many children?

Answer Four hundred children, one woman, ninety-nine men.

3. The zoo just bought exactly one ton of animals (2000 pounds): a zebra, a wolf, a Lynx, a peacock, and a buffalo. The zebra makes up forty-five percent of the total weight, and the wolf weighs nine times the combined weight of the Lynx and the peacock. The average weight of the Lynx and the peacock is five-tenths percent of the weight of the zebra. How much does the buffalo weigh?

Answer 1,010 pounds.

4. Millie, the marble packer, arranged all her marbles in one solid square and found that she had two hundred marbles left over. She then received a new shipment of one thousand marbles. She increased two sides of her original square by five marbles and found she was twenty-five marbles short of completing the second square. How many marbles did Millie have to start with?

Answer 14,600 marbles.

5. If you had just bought the real estate pictured below and wanted to subdivide it into eight lots, each of the exact same size and shape, how would you do it?

Answer

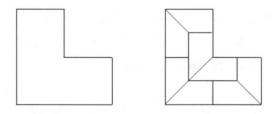

6. Draw a square and divide it into nine smaller squares by drawing two vertical and two horizontal lines. Using each number only once, arrange the numbers one through nine in the squares so that they total fifteen across, down, and diagonally.

Answer

2	9	4
7	5	3
6	1	8

7. Without leaving any digit out or repeating a digit, arrange the numbers one through seven so that when added together, they equal one hundred.

Answer $15 + 36 + 47 + 2 = 100$

8.   Write down any number. Multiply by two. Add eighteen. Divide by two. Subtract your original number. No matter what you started with, your answer is nine!

Answer

43	x	2	=	86
86	+	18	=	104
104	÷	2	=	52
52	-	43	=	9

9.   Write down any three-digit number. Reverse the number—if you had one hundred twenty-three, write three hundred twenty-one—and subtract the smaller from the larger. Write down the answer. Now reverse the answer and add. Your answer is one thousand eighty-nine, no matter what number you started with!

Answer 873

-378

495

+594

1089

10.   If you will tell me which column or columns the age of your car is in, I will tell you how old it is.

A	**B**	**C**	**D**
1	2	4	8
3	3	5	9
5	6	6	10
7	7	7	11
9	10	12	12
11	11	13	13
13	14	14	14
15	15	15	15

Answer   Add the top number of the columns you find the age in. The total will give you the age.

11. The oldest mathematical puzzle in the world is said to be this four thousand year-old puzzler translated from the Ahmes Papyrus:

There is a number such that if the whole of it is added to one-seventh of it, the result will make nineteen.

Can you figure it out?

Answer x + $x/7$ =   19

            $7(x$ + $x/7)$ = 19×7

                        $8x$ =   133

                        x =   16 5/8

12. There are over forty patterns of four squares that add up to thirty-four in Durer's Magic Square. How many can you find?

16	3	2	13
5	10	11	8
9	6	7	12
4	15	14	1

Answer A few of them are: all rows, all columns, the two diagonals, four corner squares, four center squares. Carry on!

NAME _____

Musical Terms

Match the musical terms below with the correct definition on the right.

_____ 1. Concerto

_____ 2. Overture

_____ 3. Suite

_____ 4. Chamber Music

_____ 5. Choral Music

_____ 6. Ballet

_____ 7. Folksong

_____ 8. Quartet

_____ 9. Theme

_____ 10. Variations

_____ 11. Waltz

_____ 12. Requiem

_____ 13. Movement

_____ 14. Aubade

_____ 15. Chanterelle

A. singing on a grand scale often complete with massive choirs and orchestras

B. a musical composition in honor of the dead

C. the repetition of a theme with changes in rhythm or style

D. a long piece of music played by a solo performer and accompanied by a symphony orchestra

E. music to be played in the morning, perhaps to awaken someone

F. a dance rhythm of one strong beat followed by two lesser beats

G. short orchestral piece designed to precede and set the mood for an opera or play

H. a group of pieces either played separately one after the other or as one continuous piece of music

I. the main melody of a musical work

J. a traditional song, composer unknown, passed from one generation to the next

K. a section of a larger musical work with a distinct beginning and end

L. the name given to the highest string on any bowed instrument

M. a type of classical music played by small groups of musicians without any singing

N. a piece of music written for four musicians

O. an art form that uses dancing, scenery, and music to tell a story

Musical Terms
ANSWER KEY

1. Concerto   D.   a long piece of music played by a solo performer and accompanied by a symphony orchestra

2. Overture   G.   short orchestral piece designed to precede and set the mood for an opera or play

3. Suite   H.   a group of pieces either played separately one after the other or as one continuous piece of music

4. Chamber Music   M.   a type of classical music played by small groups of musicians without any singing

5. Choral Music   A.   singing on a grand scale often complete with massive choirs and orchestras

6. Ballet   O.   an art form that uses dancing, scenery, and music to tell a story

7. Folksong   J.   a traditional song, composer unknown, passed from one generation to the next

8. Quartet   N.   a piece of music written for four musicians

9. Theme   I.   the main melody of a musical work

10. Variations   C.   the repetition of a theme with changes in rhythm or style

11. Waltz   F.   a dance rhythm of one strong beat followed by two lesser beats

12. Requiem   B.   a musical composition in honor of the dead

13. Movement   K.   a section of a larger musical work with a distinct beginning and end

14. Aubade   E.   music to be played in the morning, perhaps to awaken someone

15. Chanterelle   L.   the name given to the highest string on any bowed instrument

NAME _____

Musical Directions

How well do you know your musical directions? The Italian terms below are often used to indicate the tempo, style, or expression with which a composition is to be played. How many can you match with the correct interpretation on the right?

_____ 1. Adagio	A. Get softer
_____ 2. Allegro	B. Whispered
_____ 3. Andante	C. Majestically
_____ 4. Crescendo	D. Pluck the string
_____ 5. Diminuendo	E. Repeat the note(s) rapidly (literally "trembling")
_____ 6. Forte	F. Moderately soft
_____ 7. Fortissimo	G. Medium Speed (literally "at a walking pace")
_____ 8. Largo	H. Short, detached notes
_____ 9. Legato	I. Fast
_____ 10. Maestoso	J. Play again from the start
_____ 11. Mezzo Forte	K. Smoothly, with long notes
_____ 12. Mezzo Piano	L. Loud
_____ 13. Pianissimo	M. Get slower
_____ 14. Pizzicato	N. Moderately loud
_____ 15. Prestissimo	O. Very, very fast
_____ 16. Presto	P. Slow
_____ 17. Staccato	Q. Get Louder
_____ 18. Vivace	R. Very loud
_____ 19. Sotto Voce	S. Slow
_____ 20. Ritardando	T. Very soft
_____ 21. Con Brio	U. Play with sliding notes
_____ 22. Da Capo	V. Soft
_____ 23. Glissando	W. Lively
_____ 24. Piano	X. Very fast
_____ 25. Tremolo	Y. Spirited

Musical Directions
ANSWER KEY

1. Adagio	P.	Slow
2. Allegro	I.	Fast
3. Andante	G.	Medium Speed (literally "at a walking pace")
4. Crescendo	Q.	Get Louder
5. Diminuendo	A.	Get softer
6. Forte	L.	Loud
7. Fortissimo	R.	Very loud
8. Largo	S.	Slow
9. Legato	K.	Smoothly, with long notes
10. Maestoso	C.	Majestically
11. Mezzo Forte	N.	Moderately loud
12. Mezzo Piano	F.	Moderately soft
13. Pianissimo	T.	Very soft
14. Pizzicato	D.	Pluck the string
15. Prestissimo	O.	Very, very fast
16. Presto	X.	Very fast
17. Staccato	H.	Short, detached notes
18. Vivace	W.	Lively
19. Sotto Voce	B.	Whispered
20. Ritardando	M.	Get slower
21. Con Brio	Y.	Spirited
22. Da Capo	J.	Play again from the start
23. Glissando	U.	Play with sliding notes
24. Piano	V.	Soft
25. Tremolo	E.	Repeat the note(s) rapidly (literally "trembling")

Name that Musical

Time: 30 minutes

Objective: Students will attempt to identify famous stage musicals from information about the music they are best-known for.

Materials Needed:

pencils, paper, *Musical Information* (see below)

Advance Preparation: none

Procedure:

1.   Divide the class into small groups.

2.   Explain that in this activity you (the teacher) will read some information about a famous stage musical. As a group, they will have two minutes to determine and write down the name of the musical you have described. At the end of the two minute discussion time, each group holds up a piece of paper with the name of a musical on it. If the name is correct, the group gets two points; if it is close, but not quite right, one point may be awarded.

3.   Play continues until all of the musicals have been described.

4.   Additional information about the musical such as the story line, may be provided by the teacher, to help students identify it, as is appropriate.

5.   The group with the most points at the end wins.

Musical Information:

This musical was first performed in New York, 1946. The music and lyrics were both written by Irving Berlin. Best-known songs include, *There's No Business Like Show Business*, and *Anything You Can Do I Can Do Better*. What is the title of this musical production? ***(Annie Get Your Gun)***

This musical was first performed in London, 1978. The music was written by Andrew Lloyd-Webber, with lyrics by Tim Rice. Best-known songs include, *Don't Cry For Me Argentina* and *Goodnight and Thank You*. What is the title of this musical production? *(Evita)*

This musical was first performed in New York, 1946. The music was written by Jim Jacobs, with lyrics by Warren Casey. Best-known songs include, *Summer Nights, Greased Lightning,* and *Beauty School Drop-Out*. What is the title of this musical production? *(Grease)*

This musical was first performed in New York, 1950. The music and lyrics were both written by Frank Loesser. Best-known songs include, *Luck Be A Lady*, *If I Were A Bell*, and *Sit Down You're Rocking The Boat*. What is the title of this musical production? *(Guys and Dolls)*

This musical was first performed in New York, 1957. The music was written by Leonard Bernstein with lyrics by Stephen Sondheim. Best-known songs include, *Maria*, *Tonight*, *America*, and *I Feel Pretty*. What is the title of this musical production? *(West Side Story)*

This musical was first performed in New York, 1956. The music was written by Frederick Loewe with lyrics by Alan Jay Lerner. Best-known songs include, *The Rain in Spain*, *On The Street Where You Live*, and *I Could Have Danced All Night*. What is the title of this musical production? *(My Fair Lady)*

This musical was first performed in New York, 1959. The music was written by Richard Rodgers with lyrics by Oscar Hammerstein. Best-known songs include, *My Favorite Things, Climb Every Mountain*, and *Do-Re-Mi*. What is the title of this musical production? *(The Sound of Music)*

This musical was first performed in New York, 1967. The music was written by Galt MacDermot, with lyrics by Gerome Ragni and James Rado. Best-known songs include, *Aquarius, Manchester England,* and *Good Morning Starshine.* What is the title of this musical production? *(Hair)*

This musical was first performed in New York, 1927. The music was written by Jerome Kern with lyrics by Oscar Hammerstein. Best-known songs include, *Old Man River, Can't Help Lovin' Dat Man,* and *Why Do I Love You.* What is the title of this musical production? *(Show Boat)*

This musical was first performed in New York, 1951. The music was written by Richard Rodgers and Oscar Hammerstein. Best-known songs include, *I Whistle A Happy Tune,* and *Getting to Know You.* What is the name of this musical production? *(The King and I)*

This musical was first performed in New York, 1943. The music was written by Richard Rodgers and Oscar Hammerstein. Best-known songs include, *Oh What A Beautiful Morning* and *The Surrey With The Fringe On Top.* What is the name of this musical production? *(Oklahoma)*

This musical was first performed in New York, 1949. The music was written by Richard Rodgers and Oscar Hammerstein. Best-known songs include, *Some Enchanted Evening, There Is Nothin' Like a Dame,* and *I'm Gonna Wash That Man Right Out Of My Hair.* What is the name of this musical production? *(South Pacific)*

This musical was first performed in New York, 1945. The music was written by Richard Rodgers and Oscar Hammerstein. Best-known songs include, *June Is Busting Out All Over, You'll Never Walk Alone,* and *Mister Show.* What is the name of this musical production. *(Carousel)*

NAME _____

Fascinating Facts About Famous Musicians

You probably know that Scott Joplin wrote *The Entertainer* and is considered the father of ragtime music, but did you know he didn't attend school until his teens, college until he was twenty-seven, and that when he died he was buried in an unmarked grave? Listed below are 10 famous musicians, a title of their work, and a fascinating fact about their life. Can you place the correct letter of their work and number of the fascinating fact about their life in the blanks before each musician?

_____ _____ Vivaldi

_____ _____ Bach

_____ _____ Mozart

_____ _____ Beethoven

_____ _____ Chopin

_____ _____ Brahms

_____ _____ Tchaikovsky

_____ _____ Gilbert & Sullivan

_____ _____ Stravinsky

_____ _____ Gershwin

A. *The Magic Flute*

B. *Four Seasons*

C. *Minute Waltz*

D. *Brandenburg Concertos*

E. *The Pirates of Penzance*

F. *1812 Overture*

G. *Moonlight Sonata*

H. *Rhapsody in Blue*

I. *The Rite of Spring*

J. *Lullaby and Goodnight*

1. He once held his wife's hand during childbirth and with his other hand wrote music.

2. At age seven he begged for piano lessons, but playing the piano made him too excited to sleep.

3. He once composed forty-six pieces of music while spending a month in jail.

4. As a boy he played violin duets with his father at church.

5. When in a new city he always visited the zoo first.

6. When he died one out of ten people in Vienna came to pay their respects.

7. Though not friends, they collaborated, mostly by correspondence for 20 years on 14 operettas.

8. At age sixteen he left school to work 10 hours a day in a music store, by nineteen he was rich and famous

9. He kept his pockets filled with candy and little pictures to give to neighborhood children on his walks.

10. His practical jokes included putting people to sleep with soft music then waking them up with a bang.

Fascinating Facts About Famous Musicians
ANSWER KEY

B. 4.	Vivaldi	*Four Seasons*	As a boy he played violin duets with his father at church.
D. 3.	Bach	*Brandenburg Concertos*	He once composed forty-six pieces of music while spending a month in jail.
A. 1.	Mozart	*The Magic Flute*	He once held his wife's hand during childbirth and with his other hand wrote music.
G. 6.	Beethoven	*Moonlight Sonata*	When he died one out of ten people in Vienna came to pay their respects.
C. 10.	Chopin	*Minute Waltz*	His practical jokes included putting people to sleep with soft music then waking them up with a bang.
J. 9.	Brahms	*Lullaby and Goodnight*	He kept his pockets filled with candy and little pictures to give to neighborhood children on his walks.
F. 2.	Tchaikovsky	*1812 Overture*	At age seven he begged for piano lessons, but playing the piano made him too excited to sleep.
E. 7.	Gilbert & Sullivan	*The Pirates of Penzance*	Though not friends, they collaborated, mostly by correspondence for 20 years on 14 operettas.
I. 5.	Stravinsky	*The Rite of Spring*	When in a new city he always visited the zoo first.
H. 8.	Gershwin	*Rhapsody in Blue*	At age sixteen he left school to work 10 hours a day in a music store, by nineteen he was rich and famous.

Experiments, Tricks, and Activities

The activities in this section can be used in a number of different ways. With little or no preparation they can fill an extra few minutes at the end of class or be presented as part of a comprehensive lesson. The information below provides insights and ideas for comprehensive lesson development.

The Learning Cycle

The Learning Cycle is a method of instruction which presents three types of activities in a specified order to accomplish effective learning. The three phases of the Learning Cycle are as follows:

1. **Exploration Phase:** Students explore what they already know about a topic. Questions are raised. Brainstorming and discovery activities are often used.

2. **Concept Development Phase:** This is the "gaining new knowledge" phase. Students learn the names of objects, events, and principles. The teacher gives an explanation and the student does research. This is part of gaining a general understanding of basic concepts.

3. **Concept Application Phase:** Students are asked to apply learned concepts to a new situation. The teacher poses a new problem or situation that can be solved on the basis of previous experiences. Posing a question, determining a possible answer, performing an experiment to verify the answer, then discussing the results are often part of this phase.

The Scientific Method

The scientific method is a structured set of science procedures often used in scientific study. Students will most likely be familiar with the process, but review never hurts.

1. Identify a question or problem.
2. Gather relevant information.

3. Form a hypothesis (an educated guess about the solution or outcome of the problem).
4. Test the hypothesis.
5. Formulate results.

Often the results of one activity or experiment will lead to additional questions. By changing one of the variables and reworking the same basic experiment, additional hypotheses can be tested.

Ideas for Stretching a Science Lesson

- Have students brainstorm related questions generated by the activity and discuss possible ways of finding the answers.

- Have students write step-by-step instructions for completing the activity portion of the lesson.

- Ask students to list five things that they learned from the lesson.

- Challenge students to write a short worksheet or quiz for the lesson, then exchange papers and complete.

- Assign students to write about how the world would be different if the scientific principle studied did not exist or was altered.

- Have students use their textbooks or other classroom resources to do further research on the topic and write a brief report.

By selecting a few activities, assembling needed materials, and developing class-length lesson plans ahead of time, you will be prepared to successfully fill empty class time with exciting learning experiences.

The Slippery Bill

Equipment: A dollar bill or piece of paper measuring about three-by-five inches.

Procedure: Hold the bill vertically in your left hand and get ready to catch it with your right thumb and fingers on each side of the bottom edge but not quite touching it. Drop the bill and catch it with your right hand. Easy! Now challenge a student to catch it, poised the same way you were, with thumb and fingers just off the bottom edge, while you hold the bill and release it. He will miss it almost every time.

Explanation: When you are both releasing and catching the bill, your brain signals your right hand to catch as it signals your left to release. When someone else is catching, he must rely on a visual clue before he begins to catch, and that almost always takes a little too long.

Not a Knot?

Equipment: Two or three feet of string.

Procedure: Lay the string out on a table. Hold one end in each hand, and pose the problem of how to tie a knot in it without letting go of either end.

Solution: Fold your arms, pick up each end, and unfold your arms. There will be a knot in the string because there was a "knot" in your arms.

Big Things in Small Holes

Equipment: A dime, a quarter, paper, and pencil.

Procedure: Trace around the dime on a small piece of paper and cut out the circle. Now challenge someone to put the quarter through the hole without tearing the paper.

Solution: With the quarter inside, fold the paper in half across the hole. Now just push the coin through. As long as the diameter of the coin is a bit less than half the circumference of the hole, it will go through easily.

White Light

Equipment: A shallow pan or bowl, a pocket mirror, and a flashlight.

Procedure: Fill the bowl with water and put the mirror halfway in at an angle of about 30 degrees to the surface of the water. Shine the flashlight at the mirror. A spectrum of colors will appear on the ceiling.

Explanation: This parallels Isaac Newton's experiment with a prism that proved the "white" sunlight to be made up of many colors. In this case, the water acts as a prism, refracting each wave length at a slightly different angle to form a rainbow on the ceiling. If there is direct sunlight in the room, set a glass of water by a window and a spectrum of colors will appear on the windowsill.

To the Center

Equipment: A glass of water and a cork.

Procedure: Drop the cork in the glass of water. It will float to one side. Challenge someone to make the cork float in the center of the glass. If they are not able to—and the cork will probably head right back to the edge every time—carefully fill the glass with more water until it "bulges" over the top. The cork will move to the center.

Explanation: Surface tension creates the "bulge" and changes the surface of the water into a convex shape. The light cork floats to the center where the water is highest.

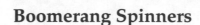

Boomerang Spinners

Equipment: Index cards and scissors.

Procedure: Cut a boomerang from an index card—A widespread V with legs about four inches long. Round all the corners slightly. Put the boomerang flat on a book with one leg projecting over the edge. Strike that projecting leg with a sharp forward motion of your pencil along the edge of the book. The boomerang will whirl up and away, then come back to you.

Explanation: The spinning of the boomerang makes it work like a gyroscope. While it spins, it maintains the same rotation plane. As it falls, the force of air on the now inclined blades pushes it back along its own path.

Chimes

Equipment: knife, fork, spoon, string, rubber bands

Procedure One: Tie the pieces of silverware at intervals on a length of the string so that they do not touch each other. Hold the ends of the string to the ears. As the head is moved the silver pieces will clang together and chimes can be heard.

Explanation: The sounds heard are very much like the sounds of ordinary clanking of the silver, except that each sound lasts longer since the silver is free to vibrate. The string conducts the sounds to the ears, making them louder and more mellow. The vibrations in the individual pieces are at regular frequencies and produce musical tones. Irregular vibrations would make noise.

Procedure Two: Replace the string with rubber bands tied together. Hold the rubber to the ears as the string was held. There will likely be no sound at all, certainly not chimes. This is because rubber is not elastic in the scientific sense.

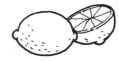

Explanation: Vibrations from the silverware are fed into the string, and travel up the string to the ears. The string is elastic enough to transmit the vibrations with a little loss. In the rubber bands the sound energy is absorbed. The sound waves get weaker as they travel up and soon die out completely. The common definition of "elastic" is "stretchable-but-finally-coming-back." So in common usage a rubber band and things woven of rubber are elastic. In the scientific sense, glass and hard steel are very elastic, while rubber is not.

Lemon Fireworks

Equipment: a candle flame, lemon, and flour

Procedure One: Squeeze the lemon peel near the flame and small displays of "fireworks" may be seen shooting from the flame.

Explanation: As the lemon peel is bent, some of the oil and water in it squirt out into the flame. Some of the oil burns as it passes through the flame, and some of the water vaporizes and sputters.

Procedure Two: Sprinkle flour on the candle flame. Tiny sparkles will be seen as the flour particles catch fire. The particles must be fine, with a large part of their surfaces exposed to the oxygen of the air, to produce the effect.

The Rising Arms

Equipment: doorway

Procedure: Stand in the doorway with hands resting at side. Press outward against the door frame, with the backs of your hands, as if trying to raise your arms. Slowly count to 25. Step away from the door frame and arms will begin to rise mysteriously.

Explanation: This is an example of the workings of mind and muscle. The count to 25 is sufficient to produce a persistent attempt to raise the arms. The door frame prevents this, but as soon as you step out of the doorway, the persistent effort to raise the arms becomes a possible reality.

The Goofy Ping-Pong Ball

Equipment: ping-pong ball, hard rubber comb, and a piece of wool cloth

Procedure: Rub the comb briskly against the cloth. Move it in circles around the ping-pong ball, it is not necessary to touch the ball. The ball will follow the comb.

Explanation: Rubbing places a charge of static electricity on the comb. The uncharged ball is attracted by the charge on the comb.

Getting a Rise

Equipment: sheet of paper and two books

Procedure: Suspend the paper by placing the books under each end. Blow straight across, just under the paper, and it will bend downward, not upward as expected.

Explanation: Air in motion exerts less lateral or side pressure than air at rest or moving more slowly. When air is blown under the paper, it exerts less pressure than the still air above it. The still air then pushes the paper down. This is the principle by which airplanes fly.

NAME _____

Things I Like To . . .

_____
_____
_____

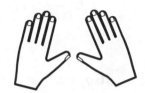 **TOUCH**

SMELL

  SEE

_____
_____

TASTE

HEAR

_____
_____

Touchy Feely Scavenger Hunt

Subject: Science

Time: 15-30 minutes

Materials Needed:

paper and pencil

Advance Preparation:

Objective:

The students will be able to identify the five senses, and will become aware of the different textures that make up various objects through a scavenger hunt.

Procedure:

1. Have students identify the five senses (sight, touch, taste, smell, and hearing).

2. Discuss the sense of touch and how it is used.

3. Brainstorm 15-20 words that describe how things feel (soft, fuzzy, hard, cold, rough, etc.)

4. Have students, either individually or in groups, list these words on their papers. Then conduct a scavenger hunt around the classroom listing objects that *"feel"* like the word when they *"touch"* it.

5. Discuss the following as a class:

    A. What was the most difficult *"feel"* to find?

    B. What textures do you like best?

    C. Why are different textures used for different things?

Extension:

Conduct a second scavenger hunt outside the classroom such as on the playground. Compare the differences in textures found outside with those found inside.

Extension:

Have students write a creative story about what the world would be like if everything "felt" the same.

Notes For The Teacher:

Be sure to remind students of expected classroom behavior during the scavenger hunt (i.e. walking and talking quietly, keeping hands, feet, and objects to yourself).

Balloon Reactions

Grades
2-8

Subject: Science

Time: 15 minutes

Materials Needed:

two balloons of the same size, two pieces of string 60 cm (2 ft.) long, wool cloth

Advance Preparation:

Procedure:

1.   Inflate balloons and tie the ends with string.

2.   Hold the balloons so that they hang about one to two inches apart.

3.   Rub one of the balloons with the wool cloth and repeat step two.

4.   Observe what happens. (The balloons attract then repel each other after touching.)

5.   Rub the other balloon with the wool cloth and repeat step two again.

6.   Observe what happens. (The balloons repel each other.)

7.   Ask the students if they can explain what they observed.

8.   Teach about static electricity to complete or correct student explanations as needed (see *Notes For The Teacher/Background Information*).

Extension:

Complete the activity again substituting strips of plastic for balloons. Ask the students to predict and explain the outcome of each step.

Notes For The Teacher:

Static electricity works best on cool clear days, but success should be attainable except perhaps on an extremely hot and muggy day. As you select the wool cloth for this activity make sure it has not been treated with anti-cling products which would inhibit the production and transfer of static electricity.

Background Information:

As in many other aspects of life, when dealing with static electricity opposites attract. When the balloons in this activity are placed near one another in step two they are both neutral and so there is no reaction. The wool cloth used in step three gives up electrons to the balloon and causes it to be negatively charged. Thus in step four the balloons attract each other until they touch. Upon contact the negatively charged balloon gives up some of its electrons and causes the other to also be negatively charged and so they begin to repel one another. When both balloons have been rubbed with the wool in step five they are both negatively charged and will repel each other.

Eco-Mural

Subject: Science

Time: 30+ minutes

Materials Needed:

four large mural size sheets of paper, eco-cards, pencils, and crayons or markers

Advance Preparation:

Copy and cut apart the eco-cards.

Objective:

Students will learn about the components of different ecosystems as they exist in various environments.

Procedure:

1. Discuss that an ecosystem is a group of things, both living and nonliving, which exist together in an area and help one another to survive.

2. Explain that students are going to work in groups to draw a mural of an ecosystem by depicting the parts of the ecosystem listed on a set of cards given to each group.

3. Explain the rules for the activity.

    A. Everyone must participate.

    B. All cards must be represented in the mural.

    C. Other things that could be found in the ecosystem may be added to the picture.

    D. The name of the ecosystem must be printed on the mural.

    E. The names of those who created the mural should also appear on the picture.

4. Divide the class into four groups.

5.   Assign a group captain from each group.

6.   Distribute the mural paper, pencils, and art supplies to each group.

7.   Give the group captain the eco-cards for each group to distribute among the group members.

8.   Assign group captains the responsibility of making sure that everyone participates and that all of the eco-cards are represented in the mural.

9.   Set a time limit for the completion of the murals (students will need 25-30 minutes).

10.   Have students complete the *Eco-Murals*.

11.   Collect the eco-cards for future use.

12.   Have volunteers from each group explain their ecosystem.

13.   Turn in *Eco-Murals* for classroom display.

Extension:

Discuss what would happen if one or more parts of the ecosystem were destroyed. How would it affect the rest of the ecosystem? Allow the students time to complete a writing activity in which they express what would happen if a piece of the eco-system was removed.

Notes For The Teacher:

Students may have difficulty organizing and completing their murals. You may wish to suggest the following steps for groups to follow:

1.   Group Captain reads the cards out loud.

2.   The group decides what kind of an ecosystem they will be drawing.

3.   The mural is outlined by placing the cards on the paper where the pictures will be.

4.   Everyone then begins replacing the cards with pictures.

ECO-CARDS

OCEAN	DESERT	WETLAND	FOREST
sun	sun	sun	sun
water	sand	ponds	waterfall
starfish	rocks	marshy ground	fallen logs
fish	snakes	frogs	deer
sharks	camels	fish	birds
octopus	spiders	birds	chipmunks
seaweed	cactus	tall grass	pine trees
algae	sage brush	water lilies	bushes
whale	lizards	moss covered rocks	lake

Name _____

Weather Words

If you can unscramble these weather words, then you're hot stuff!

1. nira _____
2. hsnusnie _____
3. ucloyd _____
4. fownaslke _____
5. ouownpdr _____
6. nynsu _____
7. dunhtre _____
8. doanort _____
9. ryd _____
10. zaribdlz _____
11. locd _____
12. morthmerete _____
13. yic _____
14. zidzrel _____
15. emarptreuet _____

16. taterpoincpii _____
17. mwra _____
18. owrinab _____
19. idmuh _____
20. hgignnlit _____
21. etw _____
22. toh _____
23. ndywi _____
24. aifanllr _____
25. gogfy _____
26. stacvoer _____
27. wnos _____
28. stacrefo _____
29. ialh _____
30. morts _____

Weather Words Answers:

1. rain
2. sunshine
3. cloudy
4. snowflake
5. downpour
6. sunny
7. thunder
8. tornado
9. dry
10. blizzard
11. cold
12. thermometer
13. icy
14. drizzle
15. temperature
16. precipitation
17. warm
18. rainbow
19. humid
20. lightning
21. wet
22. hot
23. windy
24. rainfall
25. foggy
26. overcast
27. snow
28. forecast
29. hail
30. storm

NAME _____

Interesting Water Facts

Grades
6-12

Did you know that growing food for one person for one day requires about 1,700 gallons of water? Just think how many gallons are needed to grow the food for all of the students at your school. In completing this worksheet you will compute and learn many interesting facts about water

FACT: Americans use an average of 130 gallons of water, per person, per day.

1. How many gallons would a family of five use in one day? _____

2. How many gallons are used by the people in your household? _____

3. How many gallons will be used by the people in this class today? _____

4. How many gallons would one person use in a year's time? _____

5. Approximately how many gallons have you used in your lifetime? _____

FACT: Water is a bargain.

The average cost for a gallon of water is less than one cent per gallon. The average cost for a gallon of milk is $2.34. Complete the chart below to illustrate how much more daily activities would cost if the price of water was similar to that of milk.

Daily Activity	Water Used	Current Cost	Cost at $2.34 / gal	Difference Between Costs
6. washing a car	100 gallons	< $1.00		
7. doing a load of laundry	47 gallons	< 47 ¢		
8. running the dishwasher	60 gallons	< 60 ¢		
9. brushing your teeth	3 gallons	< 3 ¢		
10. a 10 minute shower	55 gallons	< 55 ¢		

FACT: It takes a lot of water to produce things we use and consume everyday.

Match the amount of water needed for production for each item below.

11. water needed to grow one ear of corn	136 gallons
12. water a cow needs to drink to produce a gallon of milk	1,400 gallons
13. water used to produce a family car	3 gallons
14. water used to produce a loaf of bread	26 gallons
15. water used to prepare a hamburger, fries, and drink	100,000 gallons

Fact: Every drip counts!

16. If a dripping faucet drips a cup of water every hour, how many gallons of water will "drip" down the drain every year? (HINT: THERE ARE 16 CUPS IN A GALLON) _____

17. Many houses in America have toilets that leak. A leaking toilet can waste as much as 60 gallons of water everyday. Suppose that one-third of the students in your class had one leaky toilet in their home. How much water would be wasted in the homes of your classmates every year? _____

18. Turning off the water while brushing your teeth can save as much as two gallons of water every time you brush. If you turn off the faucet as you brush your teeth two times each day, how much water would be saved over the course of one year? _____

Interesting Water Facts
ANSWER KEY

1. 650 gallons

2. no. in household x 130

3. no. in class x 130

4. 47,450 gallons

5. 130 x 365 x age in years

6. $234.00; $233.00

7. $109.98; $109.51

8. $140.40; $139.80

9. $7.02; $6.99

10. $128.70; $128.15

11. 26 gallons

12. 3 gallons

13. 100,000 gallons

14. 136 gallons

15. 1,400 gallons

16. 547.5 gallons

17. no. in class ÷ 3 x 60 x 365

18. 1,460 gallons

NAME _____

Science Fact and Fiction

Science fiction loves to predict the future. While it often seems impossible that things described in today's science fiction will ever become a reality, many things that science fiction writers wrote about long ago really do exist today. Can you guess the year when science fiction became a reality?

Year	Invention	Predicted By
_____	1. Air-conditioned Skyscrapers	Jules Verne, *In the Twenty-Ninth Century—The Day of an American Journalist* (1875)
_____	2. Artificial Intelligence	Aaron Nadel, *The Thought Machine* (1927)
_____	3. Atomic Energy	H.G. Wells, *The World Set Free* (1914)
_____	4. Credit Cards	Edward Bellamy, *Looking Backward*, 2000-1887 (1888)
_____	5. Lasers	Sir Francis Bacon (1626)
_____	6. Long-distance Submarines	Jules Verne, *Twenty Thousand Leagues Under the Sea* (1870)
_____	7. Microfilm	Hugo Gernsback, *Ralph 125C 41+* (1911)
_____	8. Navigational Satellites	Edward Everett Hale (1870)
_____	9. News Broadcasts	Jules Verne, *In the Twenty-Ninth Century* (1875)
_____	10. Robots	Karel Capek, *R. U. R. (Rossum's Universal Robots)* (1921)
_____	11. Space Suits	Frank R. Paul, *Amazing Stories Magazine* (1939)
_____	12. Spacecraft that carry people to the Moon	Jules Verne, *From the Earth to the Moon* (1865) H.G. Wells, *The First Men in the Moon* (1901)
_____	13. Tape Recorders	Hugo Gernsback, *Ralph 125C 41+* (1911)
_____	14. Television	Jules Verne, *In the Twenty-Ninth Century* (1875) H.G. Wells, *The Time Machine* (1895)
_____	15. Test-tube Babies	Aldous Huxley, *Brave New World* (1931)

Science Fact and Fiction
ANSWER KEY

	Invention	Predicted By
1930	1. Air-conditioned	Jules Verne, *In the Twenty-Ninth Century—The Day of an American Journalist* (1875)
1950+	2. Artificial Intelligence	Aaron Nadel, *The Thought Machine* (1927)
1942	3. Atomic Energy	H.G. Wells, *The World Set Free* (1914)
1952	4. Credit Cards	Edward Bellamy, *Looking Backward, 2000-1887* (1888)
1960	5. Lasers	Sir Francis Bacon (1626)
1950+	6. Long-distance	Jules Verne, *Twenty Thousand Leagues Under the Sea* (1870)
1920	7. Microfilm	Hugo Gernsback, *Ralph 125C 41+* (1911)
1959	8. Navigational Satellites	Edward Everett Hale (1870)
1920	9. News Broadcasts	Jules Verne, *In the Twenty-Ninth Century* (1875)
1920+	10. Robots	Karel Capek, *R. U. R. (Rossum's Universal Robots)* (1921)
1950-1960's	11. Space Suits	Frank R. Paul, *Amazing Stories* Magazine (1939)
1960	12. Spacecraft	Jules Verne, *From the Earth to the Moon* (1865) H.G. Wells, *The First Men in the Moon* (1901)
1936	13. Tape Recorders	Hugo Gernsback, *Ralph 124C 41+* (1911)
1920's	14. Television	Jules Verne, *In the Twenty-Ninth Century* (1875) H.G. Wells, *The Time Machine* (1895)
1978	15. Test-tube Babies	Aldous Huxley, *Brave New World* (1931)

Extension: Have students compute the number of years between the science fiction prediction and the actual invention.

Making an Announcement

Grades
5-12

Time: 30+ minutes

Objective: Students will practice making an announcement to a group of people.

Materials: none

Advance Preparation: none

Directions:

Assign each student to write a list of four school-related announcements which they will present to the class. Announcements can be fact or fiction, but remind students that they will have to deliver them in a serious and business like manner. Share some examples, and set a time limit (5-10 minutes) for writing the list of announcements.

Randomly select students to exit the classroom, knock on the door, request permission to make an announcement, receive permission, and deliver the announcements they have prepared. Repeat this process until all members of the class have delivered their announcements.

Note: Applause after announcements is appropriate.

Example:

Student exits the classroom and knocks on the door.

Teacher opens the door.

Student: Excuse me Mr./Ms._____, could I make some announcements to your class?

Teacher: Yes. Please come in.

Student: I have been asked to make the following announcements:

1. The French Club wishes to announce their upcoming field trip to Paris next week. Please turn in permission slips at the office.

2. The Calculus Social will be today after school. Remember to bring your graphing calculator.

3. The media center will be closed to all students for the rest of the week.

4. Due to lack of interest, this year's high school graduation has been cancelled.

Applause

An Occasional Speech   Grades 6-12

Time: 30+ minutes

Objective: Students will prepare and deliver an appropriate speech for a specified occasion.

Materials: none

Advance Preparation: Prepare a scenario for the speech.

Directions:

Explain to students that different events call for different types of speeches. Share the scenario you have selected with the class and discuss the purpose or necessary elements of the speech. For example, does the speech need to persuade, share information, console, express appreciation, etc.

Allow students 10-15 minutes to prepare a short (3 minutes or less) speech for the designated occasion.

As time permits, allow volunteers, or select students at random, to share their speech with the class.

NOTE: Applause at the end of each speech is appropriate.

Possible Speech Scenarios:

1. An acceptance speech after winning a $1,000,000 sweepstakes contest.
2. A speech given by a city official to announce the construction of a new city park.
3. A speech announcing to employees the closing of the business where they work.
4. A speech to honor the contributions of professional athletes to society.
5. A speech to persuade the school board to only hold classes four days a week.
6. A speech to inform the student body about the dangers of cafeteria food.
7. A speech to announce the assassination of the president of the United States.

Classroom Commercial

Time: 30+ minutes

Objective: Students will prepare a brief presentation designed to sell a product.

Materials: common classroom objects

Advance Preparation: none

Directions:

Arrange students in cooperative learning groups. Explain that each group will be assigned a classroom object and have 15 minutes to prepare a commercial or sales presentation. The goal of the presentation is to convince fellow classmates that they must have the object to be successful, popular, or survive at school.

Assign and distribute a different classroom object to each group of students. Allow students to use the object as a prop in their presentation. Remind students of the preparation time limit.

Have student groups take turns presenting their presentation/commercial before the class.

If time permits, discuss how current advertising or promotion campaign strategies were imitated in student presentations.

NOTE: Applause at the end of each presentation is appropriate.

Classroom Object Ideas:

desk	backpack	chair	pencil sharpener
pencil	chalk	tape	calculator
eraser	pen	stapler	teacher's edition of class textbook

Appendix

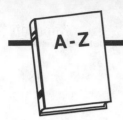

Glossary

Abuse
The physical, sexual, or emotional maltreatment of individuals.

Acknowledge and Restate
Classroom management strategy that involves verbally acknowledging student protests or outbursts, then restating expected behavior. Acknowledging a student's comment validates them as a person and will often diffuse an emotionally charged situation. Phrases such as, "I can tell that you" and "It is obvious that" can be used to acknowledge what the student said. Transition words such as "however," "but," and "nevertheless," bring the dialogue back to the expected behavior. Example: "I can tell that you are not very interested in this topic, nevertheless the assignment is to write a 500 word essay about music and you are expected to have it completed by the end of class." (See also I Understand.)

Active Response
A questioning response that requires thought, evaluation, or synthesis of information on the part of the student giving the response.

Active Viewer
A student who views a video, filmstrip, or other audio visual presentation while actively engaging in thought about what they are seeing and hearing. Two forms of active engagement include note taking during the presentation and watching for specific information to answer questions after the presentation.

Anecdotal Records
Records of the date, place, time, names of individuals involved, description of the situation, choices for action considered, action that was taken, and the outcome of specific incidents in which one is involved. Recommended in instances of illness, injury, severe student misbehavior and emotionally volatile situations.

Anecdotal Summary
See Anecdotal Records.

Authoritarian
Teaching style which demands immediate and unquestioning student obedience to teacher directives.

Blood Borne Pathogens
Bacteria, viruses, or other disease-causing agents that can be carried and transmitted from one person to another via blood.

Bloom's Taxonomy
Six levels of thinking organized by Dr. Benjamin Bloom. The levels are organized from the lowest level of thinking to the highest in the following order: knowledge, comprehension, application, analysis, synthesis, and evaluation. These levels of thinking are often used as a basis for developing and presenting thought-provoking questions to students.

Bodily Fluids
Term used for a number of fluids manufactured within the body. Usually used when referring to blood, semen, urine, and saliva.

Brainstorming
Teaching strategy to generate a lot of ideas in a short period of time. A prompt or topic is provided, then ideas are expressed freely and recorded within a given time limit. Evaluation of ideas is not a part of the brainstorming process. This strategy is often used as a springboard or starting point for other activities. (See also DOVE Rules.)

Captain (Cooperative Learning)
Cooperative learning student role of group leader responsible for keeping group members on-task and working towards the objective, sometimes also referred to as the Director or Manager.

Captivate and Redirect
Two-step strategy for focusing the attention of a group of students. The first step involves capturing the students' attention by whispering, turning out the lights, clapping your hands, ringing a bell, etc. The second step is to immediately provide concise instructions that direct student attention to the desired activity. This strategy is often used at the beginning of class or when making a transition from one activity to the next.

Clean-up Captain (Cooperative Learning)
Cooperative Learning student role responsible for supervising the clean-up of the group's area at the end of the activity or project.

Coerce
See Coercive.

Coercive
Interactions with students that attempt to achieve compliance to rules or instructions through the use of threats or force. Methods and practices intended to

compel students to behave out of a fear of what will happen to them if they don't.

Common Sense Trap
Behavior management trap which involves trying to motivate students to comply with expectations by restating facts they already know, i.e. "If you don't get started, you're never going to get done." Usually unsuccessful because students are not presented with any real incentive to change their behavior. (See also Traps.)

Concept Mapping
Strategy for organizing information about a central topic or theme. Key words and brief phrases are written down, circled, and connected to the main topic and each other by lines. Concept mapping can be used to introduce a topic, take notes, or summarize what students have learned. "Webbing" is another name for this strategy.

Confidentiality
Keeping personal information about students in confidence, i.e. not discussing student grades, disabilities, and/or behaviors with others, except on a need-to-know basis.

Consequences
A designated action or circumstance, either positive or negative, pre-determined to follow established student behavior. Example: A student completes their assignment, the consequence is they receive a sticker.

Consequential Behavior
Behavior which has significant impact on student learning or the classroom learning environment.

Cooperative Learning
Student learning strategy in which students work together in a small group (3-5 students) to complete a project or assignment. Typically each group member has a specific role or assignment and every member must contribute in order for the group to successfully complete the assigned task. Common student roles include captain, materials manager, recorder, procedure director, and clean-up captain. (See also Work Together.)

Correct Individuals
Refers to the philosophy of changing the behavior of individual students by addressing and working with them one-on-one, rather than reprimanding or punishing an entire group of students for the inappropriate behavior of a single person.

Criticism Trap
Classroom management trap that involves criticizing students in an attempt to "shame" them into behaving appropriately. In reality the more students are criticized for a behavior the more likely the behavior is to continue because of the attention students are receiving. Criticism not only perpetuates inappropriate behaviors, but it also creates a negative classroom atmosphere. (See also Traps.)

Cultural Diversity
Similarities and differences of groups and/or individuals that align themselves with others based on common racial and/or ethnic characteristics or affiliations. Typical associations often include language, customs, and beliefs. (See also Ethnic Diversity and Racial Diversity.)

Despair and Pleading Trap
Classroom management trap where a despondent teacher resorts to pleading with students to behave appropriately. This action communicates to students that the teacher doesn't know how to manage their behavior and that the classroom has pretty much been turned over to them. Rarely will students be compelled to behave appropriately in order to "help out" the teacher. (See also Traps.)

Disability
Term currently being used in place of handicap in reference to conditions experienced by individuals that result in the individual having special needs. (See also Disabled.)

Disabled
An individual with disabilities such as mental retardation, hard of hearing, deafness, speech impaired, visually impaired, seriously emotionally disturbed, orthopedically impaired, or having other health impairments or learning disabilities such that they need special services or considerations. (See also Disability.)

DOVE Rules (of Brainstorming)
Rules and guidelines for conducting a brainstorming session.
D – Don't judge ideas, evaluation comes later.
O – Original and offbeat ideas are encouraged.
V – Volume of ideas, get as many possible in the time limit.
E – Everyone participates.
(See also Brainstorming.)

Due Care and Caution
The expected level of care and caution that an ordinarily reasonable and prudent person would exercise under the same or similar circumstances.

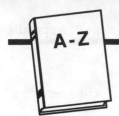

Early Finisher
Individual student learning activity designated as appropriate for students to be engaged in when they finish an assignment or project earlier than the rest of the class, or prior to the beginning of the next class activity. Examples: crossword puzzles, silent reading, art projects, etc.

Echo the Correct Response (Questioning/Risk-Free Environment)
Strategy used to generate a positive and risk-free classroom environment when a student responds incorrectly to a question. The incorrect response is acknowledged, then the question and the student's attention are directed to another student. Once a correct response has been given, the question is redirected to the student who gave the incorrect response. The student can now "echo" the correct response and feel positive about their ability to answer the question.

Emergency Situations
An unexpected situation requiring prompt action to maintain or secure the safety and well being of students. Examples: fire, earthquake, bomb threat, flood, tornado, chemical spill, etc.

Ethnic Diversity
Similarities and differences between groups of people classified according to common traits, values, and heritage. Examples may include food, clothing, music, and rituals. (See also Cultural Diversity and Racial Diversity.)

Evacuation Map
A map designating the closest and alternative emergency exits, as well as the recommended route for reaching these exits from a given location. Such a map should be posted in every classroom.

Evacuation Procedures
Specified actions to be taken in the event that students must leave the school building due to fire or other emergency situations. Often such procedures include recognizing the evacuation signal, escorting students out of the building to a designated safe zone, and accounting for students once the evacuation has taken place.

Expectations
Established levels or standards of student behavior. Traditionally referred to as classroom rules.

Facilitator
One who enables or assists another in accomplishing a goal or objective, i.e. a teacher facilitates student learning by providing instruction, materials, and assistance as needed.

Field Trip
An educational activity in which students travel to a location other than the usual classroom or designated learning area. Often field trips involve the transportation of students to and from school grounds. Special legal considerations and supervision responsibilities are associated with student participation in field trip activities. (See also Permission Slips and Supervision.)

Firm, Fair, and Friendly
Classroom management code of behavior which fosters a positive classroom atmosphere through firm, fair, and friendly teacher-to-student interactions.

Five-Minute Filler
A whole class learning activity that can be completed in approximately five minutes. Usually teacher directed and often used to fill empty class time while waiting for the bell, lunch, recess, etc.

Frequency
The rate at which an event or action occurs and/or reoccurs. Example: A student leaving their seat to sharpen their pencil three times in twenty minutes.

Gifted and Talented
A student ability classification which indicates exceptional students who demonstrate above average ability, a high level of task commitment, and advanced creativity. These students often function at a higher intellectual level than their peers of the same age. Special programs are often instituted to provide advanced learning opportunities for such students.

Handicap
See Disability.

Higher Level Questioning
Asking questions which require more than a recall of learned facts in response. Higher level questions require students to synthesize, summarize, classify, compare, apply, generalize, and/or evaluate known information before they answer the question.

Homework Assignments
Worksheets, projects, or other assignments which students are supposed to complete at home after school hours. Includes both the completion of assignments started in class and independent "at home" projects.

I Understand
Classroom management strategy used to acknowledge and stop student protests before redirecting the student's attention to appropriate on-task behavior, without becoming emotionally involved in the situation. Example: Student, "You are the worst teacher we've ever had." Teacher, "I understand. However as your teacher for today you are expected to follow my directions. Please open your science book to page 132 and begin silently reading the chapter." (See also Acknowledge and Restate.)

IDEA
Individuals with Disabilities, Education Act – Public Law 94-142. Established in 1975 and originally called "The Education for All Handicapped Children Act," this law provides that all disabled children between the ages of 3 and 21 are entitled to free public education.

IEP
Individual Education Plan established for students with special learning needs. The plan is developed by a team which includes the student, his/her parent(s), teachers, and professionals. It details the goals and objectives of educational services to be provided as well as listing the special and regular activities that the student will participate in.

Incentives
Student rewards that provide motivation for appropriate behavior. Examples: a fun activity after everyone finishes the assignment, a certificate recognizing student achievement, tickets for a drawing received for being on-task or working quietly, etc.

Inconsequential Behavior
Student behavior, that may or may not be annoying, which does not significantly detract from the learning environment or prevent students from achieving learning objectives and goals.

Instructive Language
Directions, expectations, or rules that instruct students regarding what they are supposed to do or how they are supposed to behave versus detailing what they are "not" supposed to do. Examples: work silently vs. no talking, walk down the hall vs. no running, quietly discuss this with your partner vs. don't talk too loud, etc. (See also Operational, Proactive, or Prohibitive.)

Intrinsic (Motivation)
Motivation based upon an internal and personal reward such as a sense of satisfaction or pride in a job well done.

Intensity
Relating to the degree of concentration or effort required. Example: The intensity of completing a challenging math assignment is greater than listening to the teacher read a chapter from a book after lunch.

KWL
A learning strategy that begins by identifying what the learner knows about a topic and what the learner wants to know about the topic. A teaching and/or learning experience then takes place and the activity concludes with the learner identifying what they have learned about the topic.

Learning Exercise
An activity, project, lesson or assignment implemented for the purpose of educating students.

Least Restrictive Environment
Regarding the education rights of students with disabilities, referring to their right to be educated and treated in an environment and manner similar to their nondisabled peers. This often involves mainstreaming students with disabilities into regular classes and making individual accommodations as needed to serve these students in a "regular" classroom environment.

Lesson Plans
A detailed set of instructions which outline classroom activities for the day, including lessons to be taught, materials to be used, schedules to be met, and other pertinent information relating to student instruction and classroom management.

Mainstream
The enrollment of a student with disabilities in a regular education class for the purpose of educating them in a least restrictive learning environment. Often involves individual adaptation of activities and assignments according to the specific needs of the student.

Materials Manager (Cooperative Learning)
Cooperative learning student role responsible for obtaining and returning equipment, materials, and supplies necessary for the activity.

Media Center
An updated term for the school library, as it now offers access to information in a variety of ways including video tapes and computers in addition to traditional books and magazines.

Medication
Any substance, either over-the-counter or prescription, used to treat disease, injury or pain.

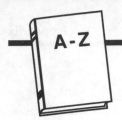

Monitor
To supervise or keep watch over student actions and behaviors.

Motivators
Consequences which inspire and encourage students to accomplish tasks or behave in an established manner. Motivators can either be tangible objects such as stickers, candy and certificates; special privileges such as being first in line, talk time, and fun activities; or recognition and acknowledgment of efforts through either verbal or nonverbal communication. (See also Rewards.)

Negative Consequences
Undesirable actions or circumstances that are designated as a punishment when established standards for student behavior are not met. Example: A student brings a weapon to school, the weapon is confiscated and the student is expelled.

Negative Interactions
Any teacher/student interaction, either verbal or nonverbal, which is critical, derogatory, unfavorable, or accusatory in nature.

Neglect
A failure to provide a child under one's care with proper food, clothing, shelter, supervision, medical care, or emotional stability.

Noncoercive
Practices and methods that do not utilize force, pressure, criticism, fear, or other negative motivators to achieve desired student behavior.

Nonverbal (Interactions)
Communication which does not involve speaking (i.e., smile of encouragement, written praise, disapproving look, etc.).

Normal Voice
The tone and volume of voice one would use in everyday conversations with friends or family members.

Note Cards
A set of index cards (3x5 or 5x7) with one card designated for each school where you might be assigned to teach. On the card is listed the name of the school, school address, school telephone number, school start time, name of the principal and secretary, driving and parking directions, and approximate travel time.

Off-task
Not engaged in an assigned learning activity. Example: Student is writing a note when they are supposed to be completing a crossword puzzle.

On-task
To be actively and appropriately engaged in an assigned learning activity.

Operational (Expectations)
Expectations or rules for student behavior which define a student operation or action. Examples: keep your feet on the floor, follow directions the first time they are given, set your pencil on the desk, raise your hand for permission to speak, etc. (See also Instructive Language.)

Pacing
The speed at which students are expected to complete an assignment or the rate at which a teacher moves from one activity to the next, in order to complete a designated number of activities in a specified amount of time.

Permission Slips
Document signed by the parent and/or legal guardian of a student authorizing permission for the student to participate in a specific activity, i.e. field trip. A signed permission slip must be received before a student can legally leave school property in conjunction with a learning experience. (See also Field Trip and Supervision.)

Physical (Force)
The inappropriate use of one's body to compel a student to behave appropriately or in administering punishment for inappropriate behavior. Examples: hitting, shoving, lifting, spanking, slapping, kicking, etc.

Physical and Verbal Force Trap
Classroom management trap in which the teacher resorts to physical force or verbal threats and abuse to achieve desired student behavior. Not only are such actions inappropriate but in most situations they are also against the law. (See also Traps.)

Positive Interactions
A favorable action or communication between teacher and student which recognizes student effort or appropriate behavior. Example: A teacher makes a positive comment about how well a group of students is working together.

Positive Reinforcement
A positive interaction used to acknowledge and compliment appropriate student behavior for the

purpose of encouraging the continuation of such behavior in the future. Example: A teacher verbally praises the class for working diligently and quietly on a writing assignment.

Praise
Positive teacher-to-student interactions that acknowledge and compliment students regarding their behavior or accomplishments. Example: Teacher, "It looks like you've put a lot of time and effort into this project, keep up the good work."

Preventative Measures
Actions or steps taken to avert the occurrence of inappropriate behavior, i.e. establishing expectations and engaging students in constructive learning experiences.

Proactive (Instruction)
Instructing students regarding their behavior using language which describes the specific actions or activities they should be engaged in. (See also Instructive Language.)

Procedure Director (Cooperative Learning)
Cooperative learning student role responsible for reading instructions, explaining procedures, and making sure that the activity is completed correctly.

Professional Dress
Clean, neat, and appropriate clothing attire for the teaching situation. As a general rule, jeans, t-shirts, sandals, and other casual clothing are not considered professional or appropriate for the classroom setting. You should always dress at least as professionally as your permanent teacher counterparts.

Prohibitive Language
Words or phrases that detail actions or activities which students are forbidden to participate in. Using prohibitive language in the classroom may actually increase the occurrence of inappropriate student actions because it draws attention to these types of behaviors. Examples: don't run in the hall, quit tapping your pencil, stop being rude. (See also Instructive Language.)

Proximity
The physical distance between student and teacher. Often used in classroom management, where close proximity or nearness to students encourages appropriate behavior and often stops inappropriate behaviors that are occurring.

Questioning (Teaching Strategy)
An instruction strategy that involves asking topic related questions, and eliciting student responses.

Successful and effective questioning involves the utilization of higher level questions, directing questions to a specific student, and allowing appropriate wait-time for student responses.

Questioning Trap
Classroom management trap in which the teacher wastes time and is drawn off-task by asking a student questions whose answers provide information unnecessary for stopping inappropriate behavior or getting the student on-task. (See also Traps.)

Racial Diversity
Similarities and differences of groups of individuals with certain physical or genetic features. These features may include skin color, body type, and facial features. (See also Cultural Diversity and Ethnic Diversity.)

Recorder (Cooperative Learning)
Cooperative learning student role responsible for recording information regarding the assignment including writing down activity results and other information provided by group members.

Reevaluate the Situation
To take an objective second look at classroom circumstances in an effort to determine if there are underlying reasons why students are unable to complete assignments or meet expectations.

Reinforce
To encourage a specific student behavior by providing rewards or attention when the behavior is exhibited.

Reinforce Expected Behaviors
To encourage students to continue to behave in an appropriate or expected manner by providing ongoing praise, rewards, or positive attention when they behave in accordance with expectations.

Removal, Identify, and Redirect
Strategy for dealing with inappropriate student behavior which involves removing the student from the immediate learning environment, acknowledging disapproval of the inappropriate behavior, and providing specific instructions and expectations for future behavior.

Restate (Expectations)
To repeat or explain again student behavior expectations or assignment completion instructions.

Review Technique
A strategy used to recap important events and items students need to remember from the instructional day. Examples: listing homework assignments on the

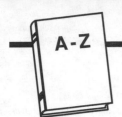
board, brainstorming things learned during the class, having students construct a concept map of what they learned from a lesson, asking students to name the things they need to remember and bring to class the following day, etc.

Rewards
Praise, tokens, or tangible items given to recognize student achievement, accomplishments, or attitudes. (See also Motivations.)

Risk-free Classroom Environment
A classroom environment where students feel comfortable sharing appropriate ideas and opinions without fear of being ridiculed or criticized for incorrect or original responses.

Safe Schools (Policies)
Policies and/or practices adopted by a school district for the purpose of fostering a school environment that is safe, conducive to learning, and free from unnecessary disruptions.

Sarcasm Trap
Classroom management trap that involves making contemptuous or ironic remarks aimed at belittling students. Usually results in a negative classroom atmosphere and bad feelings between students and the teacher. (See also Traps.)

Seating Chart
A chart or diagram depicting the arrangement of desks in the classroom and listing the name of each student in reference to where they sit. A seating chart can be easily made using a file folder and small Post-it Notes®. Have each student write their name on a Post-it Note® then arrange the notes on the folder to reflect where students sit.

Self-starter Activity
A simple project or assignment typically used at the beginning of the day or class period, which students can complete on their own without instructions or help from the teacher.

Sexual Harassment
Behavior that is unwanted or unwelcome, is sexual in nature or gender-based, is severe, pervasive and/or repeated, has an adverse impact on the workplace or academic environment, and often occurs in the context of a relationship where one person has more formal power than the other (i.e. supervisor/employee, or faculty/student).

Short Activity
Teacher-directed lessons or activities that require 20 minutes to an hour to complete. Often implemented when the lesson plans left by the permanent teacher are unable to be carried out or there is a significant amount of extra class time.

Special Duties
Extra teacher responsibilities or assignments in addition to usual classroom teaching activities. Examples: bus duty, hall monitor, cafeteria supervisor, playground duty.

State the Facts
A direct and to-the-point classroom management technique that involves clearly and concisely stating student behavior expectations and consequences if the expectations are not met, then immediately instructing students to engage in an assigned task. Appropriate for situations when students are testing the limits, willfully being off-task or making excuses for inappropriate behavior.

Step-by-step Process (Transitions)
Providing a clear course of action for students to make the transition from one activity to the next. The process involves instruction regarding what to do about the activity they are currently engaged in, what to do with the materials they are using, what new materials they will need, what to do with these new materials, and how much time they have to make the transition. Example: "You have one minute to finish your science crossword, put it in your desk, take out your silent reading book, and start reading. Please begin." (See also Transitioning.)

Stop and Redirect
A classroom management strategy for dealing with inappropriate student behavior. It involves instructing the student to stop the behavior they are currently engaged in and redirecting their actions through further instructions as to what they should be doing. Example: "Jason, please stop wandering around the room. Sit down at your desk and spend the rest of the class period working on your homework assignment."

Substitute Teacher Report
A report written by a substitute teacher and left for the permanent teacher. It outlines the activities of the day, explains any deviation from the lesson plans, and notes student behavior (including inappropriate behavior the permanent teacher needs to be aware of and information about students who were particularly helpful).

SubPack
A box, bag, briefcase, or backpack filled with teaching

resource materials including personal and professional items, classroom supplies, student rewards and motivators, and activity materials, which a substitute teacher assembles and brings to teaching assignments.

Supervision (of Students)
To oversee all of the activities and actions of students in one's charge at all times and in all settings and circumstances (i.e., field trips, field trip transportation, recess, assemblies, evacuations). (See also Field Trip and Permission Slips.)

Threat Trap
A classroom management trap that involves the teacher verbalizing drastic, highly undesirable, and often unrealistic consequences if students do not behave appropriately. The premise of making threats is that students will fear the consequences so much that they don't dare behave inappropriately. Most threats are issued out of frustration and the teacher often loses credibility when students do behave inappropriately because the teacher does not really want to, or can not, enforce the threatening consequences they have established. (See also Traps.)

Transitioning
The act or process of changing from one activity, topic of study, or assignment to another. (See also Step-by-step Process.)

Traps
Classroom management scenarios (7) in which the teacher becomes "trapped" due to poor or improper choices in dealing with student behaviors. Once in a trap the teacher loses some of their ability and authority to direct student actions. (See also Criticism Trap, Common Sense Trap, Questioning Trap, Despair and Pleading Trap, Threat Trap, Physical and Verbal Force Trap.)

Verbal Interactions
Communication or other interactions involving speaking.

Verbal Force
The inappropriate use of language, threats, tone or intensity of voice to compel a student to behave appropriately.

Verbal Recognition
The use of spoken word to praise and/or acknowledge student effort, progress or accomplishments.

Wait Time
The elapsed time or pause between when a question is asked and a response is expected. A recommended wait time is 5-10 seconds. This allows students time to formulate an answer and verbalize a response.

Warm-up/Starter Activity
An introductory activity used at the beginning of a lesson or assignment to engage students, channel their thoughts, or prepare students to achieve the lesson objective.

Whisper
Classroom management strategy in which the teacher uses a very quiet voice to communicate instructions and get the attention of the entire class, rather than speaking loudly or shouting to be heard over the classroom noise level.

Work Together
Students working together to accomplish a task or complete an assignment. (See also Cooperative Learning.)

To learn more about Substitute Teaching:

visit us on the Internet at http://subed.usu.edu

or call us at

1-800-922-4693

Substitute Teaching Institute
Utah State University
6516 Old Main Hill
Logan, UT 84322-6516

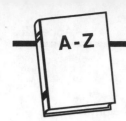

Substitute Professional
Reference Guide

Substitute Teacher Handbook: Elementary for Grades K-8, ISBN 1890563110, Substitute Teaching Institute, Utah State University, 2001.

Substitute Teacher Handbook: Secondary for Grades 9-12, ISBN 1890563129, Substitute Teaching Institute, Utah State University, 2001.

SubInstructor, Interactive computer CD for use with the Substitute Teacher Handbooks. Substitute Teaching Institute, Utah State University, 2000.

SubOrientation Video, An introduction to the world of substitute teaching. Substitute Teaching Institute, Utah State University, 1999.

The Guest Teacher: A Fresh Approach to Substitute Teaching, Barbara L. Goldenhersh, Ph.D., 2001. ISBN 1890563250, Substitute Teaching Institute, Utah State University.

Mastering the Art of Substitute Teaching, S. Harold Collins, 1995. ISBN 0931993024, Garlic Press.

Classroom Management for Substitute Teachers, S. Harold Collins, 1982. ISBN 0931993032, Garlic Press.

Instant Success for Classroom Teachers, New and Substitute Teachers, Barbara Cawthorne, 1981. ISBN 0960666605, Greenfield Publications.

The First Days of School, How to be an Effective Teacher, Harry K. Wong & Rosemary Tripi Wong, 1998. ISBN 0962936006, Harry K. Wong Publications.

Substitute Teaching: A Handbook for Hassle-Free Subbing, Barbara Pronin, 1983. ISBN 0312774842, St. Martin's Press.

Super Sub: A Must-Have Handbook for Substitute Teachers, Cary Seeman & Shannon Hofstrand, 1998. ISBN 0673363805, Goodyear Pub Co.

A Handbook for Substitute Teachers, Anne Wescott Dodd, 1989. ISBN 0398060975, Charles C Thomas Pub Ltd.

Substitute Teaching: Planning for Success, Elizabeth Manera, Marji Gold-Vukson & Jennifer Kapp, 1996. ISBN 0912099062, Kappa Delta Pi Publications.

Available From The Substitute Teaching Institute, Utah State University, 6516 Old Main Hill, Logan, UT 84322-6516, 1-800-922-4693, http://subed.usu.edu.

Classroom and Behavior Management Books

The Acting-Out Child, Coping with Classroom Disruption, Hill M. Walker, 1995, 420 pages. Sopris West, 1140 Boston Avenue, Longmont, CO 80501, ISBN 1570350477

Antisocial Behavior in School: Strategies and Best Practices, Hill M. Walker, Geoff Colvin, Elizabeth Ramsey, 1994. Brooks/Cole Publishing Company, A division of International Thomson Publishing Inc., ISBN 0534256449

Bringing Out the Best in People, How to Apply the Astonishing Power of Positive Reinforcement, Aubrey C. Daniels, 2000. McGraw-Hill, Inc., ISBN 0071364099

Coercion and its Fallout, Murray Sidman, 1989. Authors Cooperative, Inc., Publishers, P.O. Box 53, Boston, MA 02199, ISBN 0962331112

Discipline with Dignity, Richard L. Curwin and Allen N. Mendler, 1988. Association for Supervision and Curriculum Development, Alexandria, VA, ISBN 0871201542

The First Days of School, How to be an Effective Teacher, Harry K. Wong and Rosemary Tripi Wong, 1991. Harry K. Wong Publications, 1030 W. Maude Ave., Ste 501, Sunnyvale, CA 94086, ISBN 0962936006

Talented But Troubled, Reclaiming Children and Youth, Journal of Emotional and Behavioral Problems, Vol. 6, No. 4 Winter 1998, Pro-Ed Journals, 8700 Shoal Creek Blvd., Austin, TX 78757-6897

The Teacher's Encyclopedia of Behavior Management, 100 Problems/500 Plans, for Grades K-9, Randall S. Sprick and Lisa M. Howard, 1995. Sopris West, 1140 Boston Avenue, Longmont, CO 80501, ISBN 1570350310

"You Know the Fair Rule" and much more, Bill Rogers, 1998. The Australian Council for Educational Research Ltd, 19 Prospect Hill Road, Camberwell, Melbourne, Victoria 3124, ISBM 0864312547

School Supply Companies

ATCO School Supply	1-888-246-ATCO to request a catalog. Providing quality and value in Home Schooler's Education Products. www.atco1.com
Canter	1-800-262-4347 to request a current catalog. Professional development programs for today's teachers. www.canter.net
Cuisenaire	1-800-445-5985 to request a current catalog. K-9 materials for Mathematics and Science. www.etacuisenaire.com
Delta Education	1-800-442-5444 to request a current catalog. Hands-On Math activity books and supplies; Hands-On Science activity books and supplies. www.delta-education.com
Glenco	1-800-334-7344. 6-12 Science materials. www.glencoe.com
Nasco	1-800-558-9595 to request a current catalog. Health, Arts & Crafts, Math, Science, Language Arts, Social Studies, and Music Materials. www.enasco.com
Schoolmasters	1-800-521-2832 to request a current catalog. Science materials. www.schoolmasters.com
Stenhouse Publishers	1-800-988-9812 to request a current catalog. Professional resources for teachers. www.stenhouse.com
Summit Learning	1-800-777-8817 to request a current catalog. K-9 Math, Language Arts, Science; Early Childhood. www.summitlearning.com

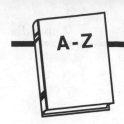

Education Activity Books

Read It With Bookmarks, Barbara L. Goldenhersh, 1992. ISBN 1882429079, Substitute Teaching Institute, Utah State University.

Substitute Ingredients, Grades 3-8, S. Harold Collins, 1974. ISBN 0931993016, Garlic Press.

Substitute Teacher's Reference Manual, Carol A. Jones, 1998. ISBN 088280135X, Etc Publications.

Substitute Teacher's Handbook Activities and Projects, Mary F. Redwine, 1970. ISBN 822466007, Lake Pub Co.

Teacher (Substitute) Survival Activities Kit Vol. 1, Thomas J. Randquist, 1998. ISBN 1884239218, Nova Media Incorporated.

At Your Local Bookstore

Monster Mad Libs, Roger Price & Leonard Stern, ISBN 0843100583. Commercial version of the *Silly Stories* found in this handbook.

I SPY, Walter Wick & Jean Marzollo, ISBN 0590450875. A picture book of riddles.

The Mammoth Book of Fun and Games, Richard B. Manchester, ISBN 0884860442. Over 400 games, jokes, and puzzles.

The Giant Book of Games, Will Shortz, ISBN 081291951. Games and puzzles compiled from <u>Games</u> magazine.

Kids' Giant Book of Games, Karen C. Anderson, ISBN 0-12921992. Games and puzzles compiled from <u>Games</u> magazine.

Word Games For Kids, Robert Allen. ISBN 1559585935. Word puzzles for kids divided into four levels of difficulty.

Brain Bafflers, Robert Steinwachs, ISBN 0806987871.

Puzzles Perplexities & Obfuscations, George Hardy, ISBN 0806982101.

More Two Minute Mysteries, Donald J. Sobol, ISBN 0590447882. Over 60 mysteries to read and solve in two minutes or less.

More 5 Minute Mysteries, Ken Weber, ISBN 156138058X. Mysteries to read and solve in five minutes or less.

1000 Crazy Jokes For Kids, Ballantine Books, ISBN 0345346947. Jokes for children of all ages.

Smart Alec's Knock Knock Jokes For Kids, Ballantine Books, ISBN 0-345-35196-7. Knock Knock jokes kids love.

Recommended Children's Books

*	*Adventures of a Taxi Dog*	Debra Barracca
	Alexander and the Terrible, Horrible, No Good, Very Bad Day	Judith Viorst
	Amelia Bedelia	Peggy Parrish
	Anansi and the Moss-Covered Rock	Eric Kimmel
	Animals Should Definitely Not Wear Clothing	Ron Barrett
	Brown Bear, Brown Bear, What Do You See?	Bill Martin Jr.
*	*The Butter Battle Book*	Dr. Suess
*	*Charlie Parker Played Be Bop*	Chris Raschka
	Cloudy With a Chance of Meat Balls	Judi Barrett
*	*Cremation of Sam McGee*	Robert Service
	The Day Jimmy's Boa Ate the Wash	Trinka H. Noble
*	*Eleventh Hour*	Grahame Base
*	*Faithful Elephants*	Yukio Tsuchiya
*	*The Frog Prince Continued*	Jon Scieszka
	George and Martha	James Marshall
	Giraffe and a Half	Shel Silverstein
*	*The Giving Tree*	Shel Silverstein
	Grandfather Tang's Story	Lee Tompert
	Harold and the Purple Crayon	Crockett Johnson
	Henny Penny	Paul Galdone
	Horton Hatches the Egg	Dr. Seuss
	If You Give a Mouse a Cookie	Laura J. Numeroff
	It Could Always Be Worse	retold by Margot Zemoch
	Koala Lou	Mem Fox
	Lily's Purple Plastic Purse	Kevin Henkes
	Lyle, Lyle, Crocodile	Bernard Waber
	Mike Mulligan and His Steam Shovel	Virginia L. Burton
	Miss Nelson is Missing	Harry Allard & James Marshall
*	*The Most Important Book*	Margaret Wise Brown
	The Napping House	Audrey Wood
	Not in the House, Newton!	Judith Gilliland
	Pinkerton, Behave!	Steven Kellogg
	The Principal's New Clothes	Stephanie Calmenson
*	*Rose Blanche*	Roberto Innocenti
*	*Round Trip*	Ann Jonas
*	*Sir Gawain and the Loathly Lady*	Selina Hastings
	Slugs	David Greenburg
*	*Smoky Night*	Eve Bunting
*	*Squids Will Be Squids: Fresh Morals, Beastly Fables*	Jon Scieszka
*	*The Stinky Cheese Man*	Jon Scieszka
	Stone Soup	retold by Marcia Brown
*	*The Stranger*	Chris Van Allsburg
	Swamp Angel	Anne Isaacs
*	*Sylvester and the Magic Pebble*	William Steig
	There's a Nightmare in My Closet	Mercer Mayer
*	*Things That Are Most in the World*	Judi Barrett
*	*The True Story of the Three Little Pigs*	John Scieszka
	The Very Hungry Caterpillar	Eric Carle
*	*The Wall*	Eve Bunting
*	*Where the Sidewalk Ends*	Shel Silverstein
	Where the Wild Things Are	Maurice Sendak
*	*Z Was Zapped*	Chris Van Allsburg

*   This book would also work well to teach a moral in the secondary classroom.

Substitute Teacher Report

Substitute: _____   Date: _____

Phone Number: _____   Grade: _____

Substituted for: _____   School: _____

Notes regarding lesson plans:

I also taught:

Notes regarding behavior:

Terrific helpers:

Students who were absent:

Messages for the permanent teacher:

Please let me know of any areas you feel I can improve to be a better substitute for you.

Substitute Teacher Report

Substitute: _____   Date: _____

Phone Number: _____   Class: _____

Substituted for: _____   School: _____

Period	Notes about lessons (see back)	Notes about students (see back)
1		
2		
3		
4		
5		
6		
7		
8		

Messages for the permanent teacher:

Please let me know any areas you feel I can improve to be a better substitute for you.

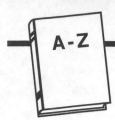
Teaching Journal

Date	School	Grade	Who's Class	Notes

Journal of Lessons Taught

Date	School	Permanent Teacher	Subject Taught

Teaching Notes

Teaching Notes

Teaching Notes

Teaching Notes

Teaching Notes

Visit STI on the Web
http://subed.usu.edu

Substitute Teachers and SubManagers
have access to the dynamic SubFriendly information
right at your fingertips!

- Lesson Plan and Activity Ideas
- SubSuccess Stories
- Handbook Supplements
- SubManager Spotlights
- SubPolls
- Trivia
- Listserv
- Quick Links
- Tips for SubManagers
- National SubHeadlines and News
- Bookstore
- Online Training

Substitute
Teaching
Institute

UNIVERSITY

6516 Old Main Hill • Logan, UT 84322-6516
1-800-922-4693 • Fax: 435-797-0944
http://subed.usu.edu